Faith

CHUCK SMITH

THE WORD
FOR TODAY

P.O. Box 8000, Costa Mesa, CA 92628 • (800) 272-9673 • www.twft.com • info@twft.com

Faith
By Chuck Smith

Edited by Steve Halliday and Shannon Woodward

Published by The Word For Today
P.O. Box 8000, Costa Mesa, CA 92628
(800) 272-WORD (9673)
Web site: www.twft.com
E-mail: info@twft.com

ISBN: 978-1-59751-088-2

Unless otherwise indicated, Scripture quotations in this book are taken from the New King James Version of the Bible. Copyright © 1979, 1980, 1982 by Thomas Nelson, Inc., Publishers. Used by permission. Translational emendations, amplifications, and paraphrases are by the author.

Scripture quotations identified KJV are taken from the King James Version of the Bible. Translational emendations, amplifications, and paraphrases are by the author.

Printed in the United States of America

Faith

A NOTE FROM PASTOR CHUCK

Just after Christmas 2009, I encountered a minor bump in the road—a slight stroke according to my doctors. A great many people prayed for my full recovery, and I want to thank all of you for those prayers. I'm happy to report that because of your faith and God's goodness, those prayers were answered. I'm feeling stronger every day, and to date, I've been able to resume my full responsibilities in pastoring the flock God has entrusted to my care. He has blessed me tremendously. And I've been able to see, yet again, that He is true to His promise as stated in Deuteronomy 33:25: "As thy days, so shall thy strength be."

God has strengthened me day by day and I have faith that He will continue strengthening me. I purpose to continue in my full schedule of service to Him for as long as He gives me the strength and ability to do so.

Pastor Chuck

CONTENTS

INTRODUCTION

WHEN I WAS GROWING UP, my dad was a salesman who worked on commission. That was great when he had a huge real estate deal in the works worth thousands of dollars in commission, such as the time he was involved in the sale of the Anaheim property to Disneyland. That was a "feast" time for our family. But we had our share of "famines" too.

I remember as a kid how quickly a change in circumstance could alter my mood. My father would have some big deal percolating and I'd get pretty excited. I'd think, *Oh, boy. Dad's deal is in escrow, and when it goes through we can buy this and that, and we can go here and there* ... and then the deal would fall through, and so would my hopes.

My dad's faith was always stronger than his circumstances. He had this little motto—just two words—framed and positioned on his desk. "All things," it said. And whenever disappointments came along, my dad would look at those two words and he'd remember the rest of the verse, and the promise God gave within it:

> All things work together for good to those who love God,
> to those who are the called according to His purpose
> (Romans 8:28).

A motto like that takes real faith to believe because it's not our natural reaction to difficulty. When we go through some hardship or crisis, we do not just automatically say, "Hey, it's no big deal. Everything will work out in the end. It's nothing to worry about." We're more likely to cry, "Oh *no*! There goes our future!" But my dad's faith was real. He truly believed in the promise of "All things," and his life showed it.

Faith is the key to a successful Christian life. It enables you to reach out and accept the gift of salvation. And it is faith that takes you by the hand and walks you from one level of spiritual maturity to another. That is why the Word of God says, "Without faith it is impossible to please God" (Hebrews 11:6).

But what is faith? Where does it come from and how does it work? What does it accomplish? Why does it please God?

Those are a few of the questions I want to explore in this book. If faith is so crucial to a joyful walk with God—and it is—then we had better learn how to begin exercising the faith we've been given. Without a vibrant faith, the Christian life soon becomes tedious, burdensome and discouraging instead of being marked by joy, peace, hope and power as God means it to be (Romans 15:13).

Faith means believing in God's sovereignty. It means trusting He is on the throne, in command of all things, and working through every circumstance that comes our way. When we have that kind of faith, we have peace in the midst of trials. But when we forget God's sovereignty, troubling circumstances cause us to despair. We survey the landscape with our eyes instead of with our faith.

Jacob did this. When his sons came home with the news that Pharaoh's right-hand man was holding Simeon and wanted Benjamin brought to him as well, Jacob was filled despair. He had already lost his beloved son, Joseph, and now this! "Everything is against me," he moaned (Genesis 42:36).

And as far as his eyes could see, it was true. All things really did appear against him. But Jacob didn't know the full plan of

God. He didn't yet know that the rough lord in Egypt whom he thought was causing so much trouble for his family was, in fact, none other than Joseph, the long-lost son whom he loved. He didn't realize that before long he would be embracing Joseph and weeping joyfully with him. He didn't know of the wonderful things God had in store for him.

We all have a choice to make when trouble comes. We can respond with Jacob's "All things"— believing wrongly as he did that "All things are against me," or we can respond with my dad's "All things"—believing correctly that "All things work together for good to those who love God, to those who are the called according to His purpose." One choice will arm us with peace and hope. The other will fill us with turmoil and despair.

Faith waits for the next chapter, trusting that despite all we see, God is working out His plan in our lives. And what a perfect plan it is. How could it not be? It has the infinite thoughts of God backing it up.

The Bible tells us that God is thinking of us constantly. King David once wrote,

> How precious also are Your thoughts to me, O God! How great is the sum of them! If I should count them, they would be more in number than the sand (Psalm 139:17-18).

The next time you get discouraged, take an hour or so and go sit on the beach. Pick up a handful of sand and let it trickle through your fingers. Throw it in the air. Try to count the grains as they come down. Look along the shoreline and try to guess how many grains of sand it contains.

If you could number God's thoughts toward you, you would find they exceed the sands of the sea—and not just the sand on that one beach, but every grain of sand on every beach in the world, and every grain of sand lining the floor of every ocean. That's a lot of sand, which should give you an idea of the number of God's thoughts toward you. God is thinking about you constantly. And what kind of thoughts are they? God has said,

> I know the thoughts that I think toward you, thoughts of peace and not of evil, to give you a future and a hope (Jeremiah 29:11).

God isn't thinking, *Well now, how can I teach him a lesson that he'll never forget? What kind of miserable thing can I put him through?* No. God is thinking of ways to demonstrate to you that He really cares, that He is in control, and that He loves you. And He thinks those thoughts about you continually, every second of every day. Oh, how glorious to be a child of God, to be under the Father's care and concern.

But in order for such a truth to impact your soul, you must take it in and believe it. You have to trust that God speaks the truth when He describes in His Word all the magnificent things He wants to do for you.

The temptation always before us is to trust in our own abilities instead of trusting in the Lord. The flesh says, "I can handle it. I can do it." In my own life, I have found that when the Lord wants to give me victory over some area that my flesh dominates, I tend to say, "Well, Lord, I understand that's got to go. That thing is not like Your character at all. I haven't realized that before now, but thank You for revealing it to me. I'll take care of it, Lord. I'll have it whipped by next Saturday."

I wrestle and I struggle, and I try my hardest to bring that area of the flesh under control. But eventually, after a long battle and an utter defeat, then at last I cry, "Lord, help me! I can't do it. I need Your help." Finally through faith I access His divine power … and the Lord takes over.

At this point, however, I sometimes make another mistake. As the Lord begins to take over and starts to free me, I often say, "I knew I could do it!" So He lets me wrestle and struggle again for a while until I return to the place where I say, "Lord, I just can't do it. It's not in me. Lord, please help me." And once more, I tap into His power by exercising my faith in Him.

The apostle Paul went through this experience in his own walk of faith. In Romans 7, he spoke of a perverse law at work within him that caused him to do the very opposite of what he really wanted to do. He wrote that whenever he wanted to do what was good, he found evil present inside him. So the good he wanted to do, he did not do; and the evil that he wanted to avoid, he kept doing. He went through this frustrating struggle until he finally cried, "O wretched man that I am! Who will deliver me from this body of death?" (Romans 7:24). In his cry for deliverance he found the answer. Through faith, the Lord delivered him by the power of the Spirit.

You might think that this would be a once-in-a-lifetime experience. The very first time you struggled to do the work that only God can do, and then saw His victory when you handed that struggle over to Him, you'd say, "I've learned my lesson. I can't do it, but the Lord is able. Blessed be the name of the Lord!" But that's not the case. Once we relinquish control of one area of our life to God and watch Him conquer it for us, He then reveals another area of the flesh. And what do we say?

"Oh, Lord, I really learned the last time. I can handle this one now." And again we struggle and suffer defeat and face our own weakness.

You and I need to come to the same realization that hit Paul: "I know that in me (that is, in my flesh), nothing good dwells" (Romans 7:18). God has one edict for the flesh, and that's the cross. We have been crucified with Christ. Through faith and by the power of the Spirit, we are to crucify the deeds of the flesh so we might live.

When I see that God did it and I had no ability to do it, I don't go around bragging about what I accomplished. All I can do is give glory to God for what He has done through faith. That eliminates all boasting.

Also, I cannot judge someone else who has the same problem I do. I can't turn up my nose and say, "I don't know *how* he can continue doing that." I *do* know how he can continue doing that because I continued to do the same thing until the Lord delivered me. I tried, I cried, I struggled, I vowed, I promised— but all to no avail until, through faith, the Spirit of God moved in me and gave me His strength and His victory. Faith keeps me from getting judgmental about the weaknesses of others, because I know that apart from God's help, I'm just as helpless as they are. Only through faith in God can I make any progress in my Christian walk.

Sometimes people come up to me and say, "Chuck, I have the hardest time trusting God." Do you know what they are really saying? "Chuck, I don't know God very well."

Those who know God well have no problem trusting Him. That's why the Bible tells us, "Faith comes by hearing, and hearing by the Word of God" (Romans 10:17). The Word of God reveals the faithfulness of God. It declares the fact that the Lord will always keep His word. When we learn to know God through the Scriptures and experience the faithfulness of the Lord to keep His word, then faith is easy. We have no trouble at all believing in God's goodness and His sovereignty.

If this book can help you to get on that glorious road, then I shall be very happy indeed. To God be the glory, great things He has done!

Faith

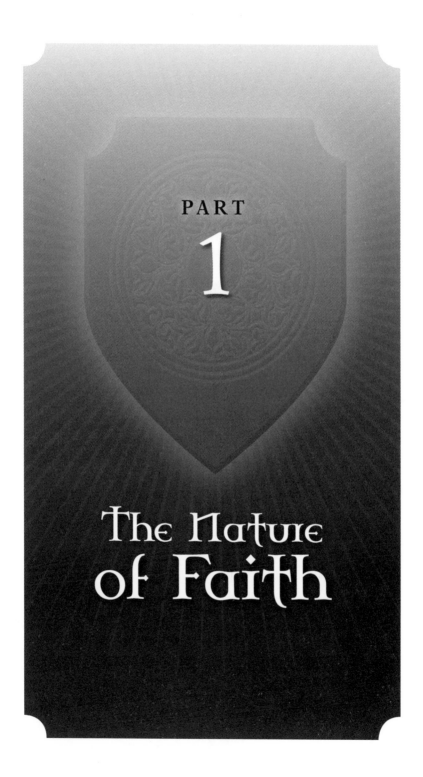

PART

1

The Nature
of Faith

Faith

What Is Faith?

*Now faith is the substance of things hoped for,
the evidence of things not seen.*

Hebrews 11:1

WHEN MY BOYS WERE GROWING UP, they wanted to grow beards so badly that they used to check the mirror daily to see if any whiskers had developed overnight. For a long time, it was a thing of faith—"The substance of things hoped for, the evidence of things not seen." But they trusted that one day their faith would come to fruition and they would have beards like the hippies they saw all around them.

Faith is "the evidence of things not seen." It is believing God to keep His word, though there may not exist any evidence of it at the moment. All I have is the promise of God—but that is sufficient. I can rest on that.

When the Old Testament prophet Elijah prayed that it would not rain, no water fell from the sky for many years. Nothing at all—not a single raindrop, not even a sprinkle. At the proper time he went up to the top of Mount Carmel and began to pray that God would send rain. After he prayed, Elijah sent his servant to look out toward the sea. The servant returned and said, "I don't see anything but blue sky."

Elijah prayed again and then sent the servant back for another look. When the man returned, he reported once again, "I don't see anything but blue sky."

Elijah continued to pray until the servant came back and said, "I see a small cloud about the size of a man's hand."

Elijah responded, "Let's get out of here—it's going to start pouring any second."

Genuine faith expects God to act simply because God said He would act, and faith continues to believe even when it can't yet see any evidence of His work.

CONSIDER THE EVIDENCE

When the Bible says, "Now faith is the substance of things hoped for, the evidence of things not seen," it is not so much defining faith as it is declaring what faith does.

Some versions translate the word "evidence" in this verse as "conviction." We are convicted of certain truths despite the fact that we may not have seen them. Take the wind, for example. We can't see it, but we still believe in it because we've seen its effects. We see mighty trees bowing in its force. We see little columns of leaves swirling into the air. Not only do we see the evidence, we can also *feel* it. We say, "Brrrr, that's a cold, biting wind," or "That's one of those warm Santa Anas."

I believe in the magnetic force, though I've never seen it. I see opposite poles together and watch them attract. I see its force as I bring like poles together and watch them repel one another. This clear evidence for the magnetic force causes me to believe, although I have never seen it.

In the same way, I see abundant evidence for the existence of God. I feel His presence. I sense His power. I experience His love. I do not doubt His existence because I see the evidence of Him all around me. Faith blossoms in my heart.

Since I believe in God, I also believe the Word of God. I accept the promises He has made to His children and that He has caused to be written down in the Bible. Some of them I have not yet experienced, but I know I shall, because I know God is faithful. And while I wait for God to fulfill His promises, it is faith that sustains me, faith that encourages me, and faith that keeps me going.

THE WONDER OF DIVINE FIAT

The writer of Hebrews gives us an interesting take on the nature of faith:

> For through faith we understand that the worlds were framed by the word of God (Hebrews 11:3).

In the very beginning God said, "Let there be light," and there was light. God said, "Let the waters above the firmament be divided from the waters beneath the firmament," and it was so. God said, "Let the earth bring forth herb-yielding seed after its kind," and everything happened just as He said. God simply spoke His word and the universe was born.

God created everything we see (as well as everything we don't see) by what we call the divine fiat. That is, God simply spoke it all into existence. He gave the word of command and what had never existed before immediately sprang into being. We believe all of this through faith. We understand that "the worlds were framed by the word of God."

The writer then makes an even more interesting statement:

> ... so that things which are seen [the material universe] were not made of things which are visible (Hebrews 11:3).

At the time this Scripture was written, no one knew anything about electrons, protons and neutrons, much less about smaller subatomic particles such as quarks or leptons. Yet by faith, the writer proclaimed that everything you see was made of things that were invisible. God used unseen things and out of them He made the material, visible universe in which we live.

Far-flung worlds, distant galaxies, and stars of varied sizes and colors are made up of atoms that the human eye can't see. These atoms exist but they remain invisible. *All* of the material things that we see are made up of things unseen—as the writer to the Hebrews declared almost 2,000 years ago by faith.

FAITH IN WHO, EXACTLY?

People are often quick to say, "I believe in God," and they think that the declaration of that belief is enough to get them to heaven. But what is that person's definition of God? He might be referring to some unintelligible force in the universe. She might be talking about some ethereal essence of love. Or that person might even be talking about one's self.

Heaven doesn't open to you just because you believe that God is. James said, "You say you believe in God. That's fine. But don't you realize that even the devils believe—and tremble?" (James 2:19). Heaven opens to those who understand and accept *who* God is. There is only one true God, the eternal Creator of the universe. When the disciples of Jesus prayed, they said, "O Lord, You are God. You've created the heavens and the earth and everything that is in them" (Acts 4:24). So when a believer in Christ says, "I believe in God," he or she is talking about the eternal God, the Creator of all things, the God of Abraham, Isaac, and Jacob.

When the apostle Paul visited Athens, the local philosophers invited him to come up to the Areopagus to expound this novel teaching of his. He began to address the Athenians and said,

> I perceive that you are a very religious people. As I've walked through your marketplace, I've observed the many altars you have erected for your various gods. And I noticed you had one altar inscribed to, "THE UNKNOWN GOD." I'd like to tell you about this God, because He's the One who created the universe. In Him we live and we move and we have our being. You see, there's only one true God and the rest are false gods (Acts 17:22-28).

Before anything else of importance can happen in your spiritual life, you must know that the one true God does indeed exist. So the writer of Hebrews says,

> Without faith it is impossible to please Him [God], for he who comes to God must believe that He is (Hebrews 11:6).

Many of us recite the Apostles' Creed:

> I believe in God the Father, Almighty, Creator of heaven and earth, and in Jesus Christ, His only Son, who was conceived by the Holy Spirit, born of the Virgin Mary, suffered under Pontius Pilate, was crucified, died and was buried and descended into hell. The third day He rose again from the dead. He ascended into heaven. He sits at the right hand of God the Father, Almighty, from thence He shall come to judge the living and the dead.

It's important that we believe those things. But do we *truly* believe them, or do we merely recite the words by rote? Are we just mouthing familiar phrases, but in our heart of hearts do not truly believe in such a God?

The Creator sent His Son to this earth to die for our sins. On the third day Jesus Christ rose again from the grave and today is in heaven, making intercession for us. Do we really believe this? Do we believe it more than we believe in our bank accounts, in our investments, or in our plans for tomorrow? Temporal things come and go, they change and wither and fall into decay. But Jesus Christ, the One in whom we place our faith, "is the same yesterday, today, and forever" (Hebrews 13:8).

WHO WILL YOU BELIEVE?

Despite the many ironclad promises we have received from God in Christ, we always face the same question: Will I believe the Bible or not? God says one thing, but sooner or later Satan comes along and says the opposite, trying to put us under condemnation.

"You are a rotten sinner," he'll say. "You have no right to come to God and ask for His help. Look at how many times you've failed Him! You might as well forget it. God's not going to forgive you."

Will you believe Satan? Or will you believe God who said that if you'll confess that Jesus Christ is Lord and believe in your heart that God raised Him from the dead, you'll be saved? Will you believe God when He says if you confess your sins, He is faithful and just to forgive your sins? Will you believe God when He says that although your heart may condemn you, He is greater than your heart and knows all things? Will you believe that God will impute Jesus' righteousness to you, apart from your failings? Will you believe that God justifies the ungodly by faith?

God said to Adam, "In the day that you eat of that fruit, you will surely die." Adam told his wife about God's warning—but Satan soon whispered to her, "No, you won't die." Eve was now faced with a choice: Would she believe God's word, or Satan's word? You know the answer—and you also know the catastrophic consequences that resulted.

Satan *always* contradicts what God has said. So when God promises something, the Devil comes right back with, "Oh, you can't believe that. Be serious. Be practical." So it becomes a matter of choice: Will we believe what God has said? Or will we listen to Satan and doubt the promises of God—and so remain in condemnation, feeling worthless and under an unbearable sense of guilt?

A PROMISE SECURED WITH AN OATH

When you base your faith on the promises of God, you tie your future to the most solid foundation possible. God always stands by His promises.

> For when God made a promise to Abraham, because He could swear by no one greater, He swore by Himself, saying, "Surely blessing I will bless you, and multiplying I will multiply you" (Hebrews 6:13-14).

To highlight the complete reliability of God's pledges to us, the writer points out that God gave Abraham a promise—which is solid gold by itself—and then confirmed that promise by taking an oath *on His own name* that the promise would surely come to pass.

> God, determining to show more abundantly to the heirs of promise the immutability of His counsel, confirmed it by an oath, that by two immutable things, in which it is impossible for God to lie, we might have strong consolation, who have fled for refuge to lay hold of the hope set before us (Hebrews 6:17-18).

God, who cannot lie, made a promise to Abraham and then *confirmed* that promise by taking an oath that He would surely keep His promise. He wanted to affirm to Abraham— and to us—that what He promised would certainly take place. Throughout the Scriptures we find the Lord swearing this or that would happen. And then we learn that whatever He said would happen, would happen—always.

God confirmed His promise with an oath as an invitation to you and to me—that when difficulty rises, or when confronted with uncertainty, doubt or fear, we can run to Him and find shelter from the storm. His name is sure and faithful. His Word is true. And He is a refuge to His children in their time of trouble.

How do you access those promises confirmed by God's divine oath? You do it by faith. Everything God promises us is available by faith … including the biggest promise of all.

SALVATION THROUGH FAITH

The Old Testament prophet Habakkuk saw the rapidly deteriorating spiritual condition of his nation, yet God didn't seem interested in doing anything about it. That frustrated Habakkuk and he let God know.

"God," he said, "things are horrible around here and getting worse. You can't trust the leadership. They're lying to the people. Things are really bad, Lord, and You're not lifting a hand to stop any of it."

God responded, "Habakkuk, if I told you what I was doing, your ears would tingle." Then the Lord began to tell the prophet how He intended to bring the Babylonians as His instrument of judgment against the nation of Judah.

Habakkuk never expected to hear that and cried out, "Lord, wait a minute—that's not fair! We're bad, yes; but they are much worse than we are. Why would You use a nation more wicked than Judah to punish Your own people?" Habakkuk concluded, "I don't understand this at all. I'll just go into my tower and wait to see what You do." As he sat in the tower, watching to see how God would act, the word of the Lord came to Habakkuk:

The just shall live by his faith (Habakkuk 2:4).

"Habakkuk, you are going to have to trust Me. You're not going to understand. You're going to see things that will shake you— but the just shall live by faith."

This great declaration of God—"The just shall live by faith"—is the very statement that set Martin Luther free when he read Romans 1:17. As a monk, he had been trying his best to mortify the flesh. He struggled to rid his life of sin, yet the more he struggled, the more guilt-ridden he felt. He tried to observe all of the works that the church had said would enable him to be perfected in the flesh. And he felt miserable. "The just shall live by faith" set him free.

As the apostle Paul put it:

> For by grace you have been saved through faith, and that not of yourselves; it is the gift of God, not of works, lest anyone should boast (Ephesians 2:8-9).

Grace is unearned, undeserved favor. It is the blessing of God poured out upon people who could never earn it. You cannot possibly work hard enough or try hard enough or keep enough rules to earn yourself a spot in heaven. Salvation is a gift—pure and simple. It's a gift that none of us deserves. And since it is a gift given by God, it is a gift we can receive only through faith.

The rich young ruler who came to Jesus seeking the way to eternal life went away sorrowful because he valued his earthly riches more than the riches of heaven. Jesus turned to His disciples and said, "How hard it is for those who trust in riches to enter the kingdom of God! It's easier for a camel to go through an eye of a needle than for a rich man to enter the kingdom of heaven."

The disciples looked at one another in astonishment and asked, "If it's so difficult, Lord, who then can be saved?"

"With men, it's impossible," Jesus replied. "But with God, all things are possible" (Matthew 19:24-26).

Aren't you glad God has provided eternal life for you by grace, through faith in Jesus Christ? You can't earn it. You can't work for it. You can only accept it by faith.

Just think what it would be like if God had set forth a list of do's and don'ts and then said, "Now, if you do this—if you will read so many chapters of the Bible a day, if you will spend so many hours in prayer, if you will witness to so many people a week, if you will give so much of your tithes to the church and spend so much time with widows and orphans and prisoners—then you will be saved." If you could earn your salvation—if you got a gold star every time you witnessed to someone and another gold star every time you prayed or gave or served—then, when you got to heaven, you'd run around showing off your card. "Look at how many stars I got!"

You know what would happen, don't you? Heaven would become one big bragging session—and that would be miserable. As you boasted about everything you did, the next person would surely say, "Would you *please* shut up? I want to tell you about all the wonderful things *I did*."

Salvation is not of works, lest any man should boast. For what does the Scripture say? "Abraham believed God, and it was accounted to him for righteousness" (Romans 4:3).

Salvation by grace through faith in Jesus Christ eliminates boasting. You and I can boast of nothing. All we can do is give glory to Jesus Christ and say, "Praise the Lord! I was a lost sinner. I was living after the lust of my flesh and of my mind. I was, by nature, a child of wrath—but Jesus reached down and lifted me out of the miry clay. He washed me off. He set my feet upon the solid rock and now I stand in Him in heavenly places. Glory to God! *He* did it all!"

Have you placed your faith in Jesus? The Bible insists that God sees believers as complete in Christ. We are wrapped in the righteousness of our Savior, which God has imputed to us through our faith and trust in Jesus. It doesn't change with our changing or waver with our wavering.

When you put your faith in Jesus Christ, your relationship with God becomes certain. It's established because it isn't predicated on something as weak as you and your works. Rather, it's predicated upon the work that Jesus Christ has accomplished for you. If God accepts the finished work of Jesus Christ, then you also need to rest in His completion.

> But to him who does not work but believes on Him who justifies the ungodly, his faith is accounted for righteousness (Romans 4:5).

> For all the promises of God in Him [Jesus] are Yes, and in Him Amen, to the glory of God through us (2 Corinthians 1:20).

> God has given us exceeding rich and precious promises by which we become partakers of the divine nature (2 Peter 1:4).

And we lay hold of them all by faith.

LESSONS IN THE DARK

From this point in my life I can look back and begin to see how, from the very beginning, God was preparing me for my assigned task. I can see now that God had His hand on my life all the way along, though I didn't realize it at the time. Through the most difficult periods of my life, God was teaching me vital lessons to equip me for the work He has ordained for me to accomplish for the kingdom.

It's wonderful from this vantage point to look back and say,

"Oh, God *was* in that trial! I remember how miserable I was. I thought that God had forsaken me. I complained to God in the midst of that. But look—that was just the thing that God used for His glory and for my benefit. I see and understand how He has put the pieces together now."

You can start saying things like that when you reach eight decades of life. By then, you have gained a bit of perspective that you don't have when you're twenty. When you were going through those hard, miserable times, you couldn't see any sense in them. It didn't feel as though God cared. You wondered if He even saw.

The only way you can make it through those tough times is by walking by faith in the goodness of God and in His sure promises. Later, you may see. Right now, you can't. But you can still move forward confidently, knowing that God will always honor His promises.

> If we could see beyond today
> As God can see
> If all the clouds should roll away
> The shadows flee;
> O'er present griefs we would not fret
> Each sorrow we would soon forget
> For many joys are waiting yet
> For you and me.
> If we could know beyond today
> As God doth know
> Why dearest treasures pass away
> And tears must flow;
> And why the darkness leads to light
> Why dreary days will soon grow bright,

Some day life's wrong will be made right,
Faith tells us so.
If we could see, if we could know
We often say,
But God in love a veil doth throw
Across our way.
We cannot see what lies before,
And so we cling to Him the more,
He leads us till this life is o'er,
Trust and obey. [1]

Many times that is all we can do. We can't see. We don't know.
But we can cling to the Lord, trusting and obeying Him.

---

[1] "If We Could See Beyond Today," words and music by Norman Clayton, © 1943.

How Does
Faith Operate?

*Abraham believed God,
and it was accounted to him for righteousness.*

GALATIANS 3:6

MANY YEARS AGO OUR CHURCH met in a little chapel. We had built the church on the grounds of an old school using material we salvaged from the school building itself. While planning the layout of the new church, we were certain it would accommodate the needs of our fellowship. And it did—for about five minutes. But then it began bursting at the seams with people sitting in the aisles and leaning against the walls. We opened the windows to the patio and set up as many chairs as we could. But even so, people crowded around the back of the patio and stood for the entire service. We had to expand. We needed another building and we needed it quickly.

One day the property we now own came on the market after a foreclosure. Someone suggested we purchase all ten acres.

With my tremendous faith, I felt that ten acres would be far too much. I thought we only needed five.

"Well, then," someone encouraged, "why not buy the ten and sell off five?"

Again, exhibiting enormous faith, I thought, *But where are we going to get the money?*

Out of the blue, a man from Fresno came to me with a proposition. He said, "I invested some money a few years ago and put it in a portfolio. This is God's money, and it has increased so much I'm afraid of it. Now I want to give it away." Without hesitating he said, "I have over a million dollars and I want to give it to you."

"Whoa," I said. "That's a lot of money. I'd better pray about that." And that's what I did. I went home and prayed. And as I did God revealed, "I am going to do a work that will cause people to marvel. If you will trust in Me, I will take care of the finances completely. If you take this man's money, it will always be said that this work was due to his gift. People will say, 'Anybody with that much money could build something big.'"

"I want the glory for what I do," God told me. "You go tell that man to give his money to someone else."

I obeyed but it was the hardest thing I ever did. We needed this property and we needed it fast. So for me to tell him, "I'm sorry, I can't take your money," nearly killed me. But when I told him the reason why, he understood.

Fast forward to today. God has blessed! The Lord has built this church and He did it His own way. Everything we have is the provision of the Lord. All the glory is His. And I learned once more that God loves to work through us and for us—by faith—so that He gets the credit and the glory for what He has done.

FOUR KEYS TO FAITH

Scripture always points to Abraham to remind us of a classic example of a person who believed God's promise. How did Abraham's faith actually work? Paul gives us some great insight into Abraham's faith in Romans 4:19-21. Note carefully the four keys to Abraham's faith.

ONE: ABRAHAM DID NOT CONSIDER THE HUMAN DIFFICULTY

> And not being weak in faith, he did not consider his own body, already dead (since he was about a hundred years old), and the deadness of Sarah's womb (Romans 4:19).

Abraham did not consider the frailty of his own body, by now practically dead, nor did he take into consideration Sarah's barren womb. The utter difficulty seen from a human standpoint simply did not stand in the way of his faith.

In contrast when we are faced with a problem or a situation, the first thing we do is try to measure that problem: Is it simple, difficult, or impossible? Once we determine this, we know how to pray.

Simple problems take only a simple prayer. "God, take care of that. Thank You, Lord." We feel that we don't have to pray too deeply when the problem is simple.

Difficult problems require that we pray a little harder. "Oh, Lord, I thank You that You are my God and You're the Creator of the universe. Now, Lord, would You ..." Our prayers get a bit more involved for difficult problems.

And when we get into those impossible situations—well, that takes some real heavy-duty praying.

We so often make the mistake of carrying over our limitations to God. We think, *If it's difficult for me, it must be difficult for God too. If it's impossible for me, while I certainly hope God could somehow work this out, I'm not too sure.*

That's wrong. We should never do that.

When King Asa came to the throne, a huge number of Ethiopians invaded the land. But Asa had only a small army. So he went to God and said, "LORD, it is nothing for You to help, whether with many or those with no power; help us, O LORD our God" (2 Chronicles 14:11). Asa realized that it didn't make any difference with God if he had a big or a small army, a strong army or a weak one. The only question was whether or not God would help them.

In exactly the same way, God's help is all you need. Your own strength isn't in question because the human factor is no factor at all. When God gets involved, you have to eliminate the human factor altogether. That's just what Abraham did. He eliminated the human factor—He did not consider it, because he trusted the promise of God for his need. That's the first key to genuine faith.

TWO: ABRAHAM DID NOT STAGGER AT GOD'S PROMISES

He did not waver at the promise of God through unbelief (Romans 4:20).

Whatever situation you might be facing, God's Word is so rich and so full that you can go into it and find a promise totally appropriate to your present need. God covers all the bases. Nothing has happened or will happen to you that will prevent you from finding a promise in God's Word that will apply directly to your situation. You'll always find something you can hang on to.

While we like to sing the old hymn, "Standing on the Promises," in many cases I think we should sing, "Staggering on the Promises." So often we find ourselves stumbling over the promises of God instead of standing on them.

"Well now, Lord, I know that You said You would help, but I don't know if that applies to me. You can help others, but I'm not sure about me, Lord." That's staggering at the promises of God.

In the Old Testament we find many examples of those who staggered at the promises of God. Usually they staggered from trying to figure out how God could work something out. Although God promised it to happen, they couldn't ascertain *how* He might do it. But the "how" isn't our problem.

King Joram of Israel did evil in the sight of the Lord and encouraged his people to worship Baal and other false gods. During his wicked reign, idols and pagan worship sprang up all over Samaria. So God allowed the Syrian king Ben-Hadad to invade the land. The Syrians surrounded the city of Samaria, choking off all supplies so that the people within the city walls slowly starved to death. The famine got so bad that they began selling the head of a donkey for eighty pieces of silver. Consider that Judas betrayed Jesus for thirty pieces of silver—and at this time in Samaria, the head of a donkey sold for three times that amount. What can you eat off of the head of a donkey? I'm sure

I don't know—maybe you can boil it for soup. But the desperate people were willing to hand over eighty pieces of silver just for the head of a donkey. Things became so drastic they began cannibalistic practices.

When this disaster came along, Joram blamed God for the problem. He also blamed God's prophet, Elisha. "God help me if I don't kill that Elisha," he threatened. So he marched down to Elisha's house with the intention of murdering the prophet. "Ah," he said, "I've finally caught up with you—you who have been troubling Israel."

"You've got things wrong," Elisha answered. "*You're* the one who's troubled Israel by encouraging the worship of false gods. But don't worry; by this time tomorrow they'll be selling a bushel of fine flour for sixty-five cents in the gate of Samaria."

When the king's counselor heard this prediction, he mocked Elisha. "Even if God would open the windows of heaven," he scorned, "could such a thing be?" (2 Kings 7:2).

Understand that Elisha had just announced an amazing promise. People were starving to death in the city, but by the next day God said they would be selling a bushel of fine flour for sixty-five cents—not eighty pieces of silver for a donkey's head. This wicked official's mind simply couldn't comprehend how such a thing could be. How could God do something that big? So Joram mocked the prophecy of Elisha. He staggered at the promise of God.

Elisha didn't take kindly to the man's skepticism. He said, "Watch your mouth. You'll see it, but you won't eat it. You'll see it happen, but you won't get to enjoy any of it." Sure enough, the next day when the people discovered that the Syrians had completely vacated their camp, they stormed out of the city and ransacked everything their enemies had left behind. As this cynical royal counselor stood in the gate watching the people exult in their unexpected bounty, he saw them selling a bushel of fine flour for sixty-five cents. In their zeal to take advantage of the prophesied windfall, however, the people trampled the king's counselor to death as he stood in the gate. Just as Elisha had predicted, he saw God's provision—but he didn't get a single bite. He staggered at the promises of God.

Abraham did not stagger at the promise of God. He accepted the Lord's promise when God told him that his elderly wife, Sarah, would conceive and bear a son. He didn't stagger at the promise because he never considered the human impossibility of its fulfillment.

THREE: ABRAHAM'S FAITH PROMPTED HIM TO GLORIFY GOD

[Abraham] was strengthened in faith, giving glory to God (Romans 4:20).

As soon as he received the promise, Abraham thanked the Lord for his promised son. "Lord! What a blessing to have a boy ... my own son! How happy Sarah will be! Oh, thank You, Father!"

If you had happened to stop by Abraham's tent that day, you would have seen an elderly man sitting inside, beaming and happy, almost bubbling over. You might even have heard him whistling and shouting, "Lord, You're so good to me!"

"Hey, old man," you might have said, "why are you so happy?"

"My wife and I are going to have a son."

"Really? How old are you?"

"Oh, I'm about a hundred years old."

"Well, how many children will this make for you?"

"It will be our first."

"Your first? How long have you been married?"

"About eighty years or so."

"That's … interesting. Is your wife pregnant?"

"Oh no, not yet."

At this point you'd be prone to walk away and say, "Poor fellow. Senile, you know. But he's not hurting anybody. Let's just let him be." Here Abraham is giving glory to God before there is any evidence at all that God will keep His promise. All Abraham has is God's word. But on the basis of that word alone, he gives glory to God.

We find it very easy to praise God when we begin to see evidence of His answer. We think, *All right! Looks like God's going to work.* We find it especially easy to praise Him when we see the thing come to pass. "Thank You, Lord. You're so good!" We rejoice at that point—and that's good. But that isn't faith. Faith is rejoicing *before* there is any evidence of the fulfillment.

Years ago when our first three children were still very small, we were living in Corona and pastoring a very small church. It wasn't able to support the family, so I had taken a job with Alpha Beta Markets. One day we received a call that my mother-in-law had died in Phoenix. We made arrangements with Alpha Beta for a short leave of absence and went down to Arizona. It took us about two weeks to get all of the affairs in order after her death.

By the time we got back to Corona, I went in to Alpha Beta to check the schedule to see when I was to work. The manager saw me and said, "Chuck, before I can put you back to work, you have to check with the union. You're late on your dues."

I went over to the union house to pay my back dues and they stated, "You've been assessed a fifty-dollar fine for being late."

"But I don't have the fifty dollars," I replied.

"Well, you can't go back to work until you pay the fine and catch up on the dues," they said.

"I can't pay the fine unless I'm working," I answered.

"That's your problem," they retorted. They had absolutely no sympathy for my situation. I told them my mother-in-law had died and that I had been out of state. But they had only one reply: "You have to come up with the money."

I couldn't work for some time because of that, and as a result we found ourselves slipping deeper into debt as the days went by. The situation discouraged me considerably.

About this time, the Alpha Beta Markets made me an offer. They proposed I go into management, which meant I wouldn't have to belong to the union. The company laid out a very attractive salary and some excellent opportunities to go into marketing, with only one requirement: I had to leave the ministry and make marketing my career.

I was very tempted. One morning, feeling frustrated and confused, I woke up early and thought, *Maybe I should forget the ministry. I'm just not making it and the church isn't growing. We're in debt and going deeper every day.*

About ten o'clock that morning the phone rang. The person on the other end of the line was an old friend of the family. After exchanging hellos, she said, "We called to let you know that we're sending you a check for $425. We sent it special delivery airmail so you should get it tomorrow."

I had totaled up my bills that morning—$416. Overjoyed, I began praising God and rejoicing in His provision. "All right, I'm out of debt! Lord, You're so good. Oh, thank You, Jesus!"

I went to the kitchen and grabbed my wife and swung her around. "We're out of debt. Praise the Lord! Hallelujah!" About a half-hour later, when I began to settle down, the Lord spoke to my heart. "Why are you so happy?"

"Oh, Lord," I said, "You're too much. I thank You, Jesus. You're just so good to me."

Once more He spoke to my heart. "How do you know they're going to send that money?"

Come on, Lord, You've got to be kidding, I thought. *What do You mean, how do I know they're going to send the money? They told me it's already in the mail. It's coming by special delivery airmail. Lord, these are good people. I've known them for a long time. I would trust their word any day, Lord.*

"This morning," He said, "when you woke up feeling so discouraged, complaining and griping to Me as you were totaling up your bills, and I had to listen to all your guff, you already had My promise that I was going to supply all Your needs. But I didn't see you rejoicing or waltzing your wife around the kitchen then. Now that you have the word of a man that a check is on the way, you're ecstatic. Whose word is greater?"

I had to apologize to the Lord and repent for my attitude. I had staggered at the promises of God. Because my faith wasn't strong, I failed to give Him glory. Only when I had evidence of His provision did I start up with the hallelujahs.

Just knowing Philippians 4:19 should have been enough to cause me to praise Him. There the Word promises, "My God shall supply all of your needs according to His riches in glory." I should have said, "All right, hallelujah! Thank You, Lord. It's all taken care of." But I wasn't strong in the faith. The Lord was teaching me to become stronger—but He still met my need before I grew new faith muscles.

How many times have you staggered at Philippians 4:19? "My God shall supply all of your needs according to His riches in glory." Instead of stumbling and staggering, go to the Word of God and find a promise that relates to your situation. Read that promise, meditate on it, and then begin standing on it. Thank the Lord and praise Him for what He's shown you through His Word.

FOUR: ABRAHAM HAD CONFIDENCE IN GOD'S PROMISES

> And being fully convinced that what He had promised He was also able to perform (Romans 4:21).

Here's the bottom line: Is God able to do it? The answer depends upon how you view God. If your concept of Him is based upon your own experience and your own logic, then I can assure you that your concept of God is limited—because you are limited. The things that are hard for you will be hard for the god you create in your own image. We do this by thinking, *If I were God, this is what I would do and this is how I would do it.* That's a pointless way to think because God's ways are beyond our understanding.

> For My thoughts are not your thoughts, nor are your ways My ways, says the LORD. For as the heavens are higher than the earth, so are My ways higher than your ways, and My thoughts than your thoughts (Isaiah 55:8-9).

If, however, you believe in the God who has revealed Himself in the Bible, then any talk of difficulty is absurd, because He is the God who created the universe, the heavens, the earth, and everything that is in them.

> Ah, Lord GOD! Behold, You have made the heavens and the earth by Your great power and outstretched arm. There is nothing too hard for You (Jeremiah 32:17).

What could be too hard for the God who created every galaxy, every star, every planet, every asteroid and every piece of dust in this vast universe?

God doesn't measure things in categories of simple, hard, or difficult. He is all-powerful. That's why it is just as easy for God to help in a major crisis as it is in a minor crisis. It's just as easy for God to supply a million dollars as it is for Him to deliver five cents.

We don't see it that way, of course. If I need a quarter, then I'll go flip open the change boxes in telephone booths (back when we still had such things) and candy machines, hoping to find a coin or two. "I know God can supply. There's a telephone booth—let's go see if God supplied." That works sometimes for small change. But what if you need a million dollars?

"Oh, God! That's tough." But that's carrying my limitations over to God who is unlimited. God has never promised anything that He lacks the ability to fulfill.

Nebuchadnezzar, the Babylonian king, made a decree that at the sound of certain music, everyone had to bow before the great golden image he had erected in the plain of Dura. He scheduled the day for this new decree to begin, and when the music sounded everyone bowed—all except Shadrach, Meshach and Abednego. These three Hebrew boys were brought as captives from Judah and made governors by Nebuchadnezzar over the provinces of Babylon. Soon, someone reported their disobedience to the Babylonian king. He called them in and said, "I hear you didn't bow when the music sounded. I'll give you one more chance, and if you don't bow, you're going to be thrown into the furnace. And what god is there who can deliver you from my hand?"

"O King," they answered, "we're not even careful how we answer you in this matter. For the God we serve is able to deliver us from your burning, fiery furnace" (Daniel 3:17). And, of course, we know that He did.

You must never measure any problem by your ability to handle it. You must measure it by God's ability to handle it, for He is the One in whom you trust. God is able to do whatever He has promised to do.

EVEN IF IT TAKES A MIRACLE

One day Abraham found himself cradling his little boy in his arms. Holding the child of God's promise, he looked down and said, "I'm going to call you Laughter (Isaac means laughter), because it makes me laugh to think that you should have ever been born to Sarah and me." God kept His word to Abraham, even though it took a miracle.

What situations are you facing today? What are your worries? Are there difficulties in your path? Whatever it is, search the Word of God and find a promise suitable to your situation and appropriate it. Then immediately start praising the Lord: "All right, Lord. I have Your word here. Thank You." Begin to give glory to God, because surely He is able to do exceedingly abundantly above anything you could ask or think.

This very week, may you find great victory in your life as through His ability you begin to stand where you've always stumbled. May you watch your needs supplied through His provision. As you exercise your faith and grow in faith, you will begin to benefit from the fruit of that faith—all through the grace and mercy of Jesus Christ.

What Does Faith Accomplish?

If you have faith as a mustard seed, you will say to this mountain, "Move from here to there," and it will move; and nothing will be impossible for you.

MATTHEW 17:20

YEARS AGO MY WIFE AND I rented a house on South Bell Street in Corona, California. Kay is very inventive and artistic, and with a little bit of cheap fabric she can make a house look great. And I, of course, had the capacity to paint and complete some general repairs. So we made a good team.

When the landlady came to collect the rent, she saw how much nicer the house looked. So she decided to move back in and gave us an eviction notice. Kay was expecting our third child at the time, and since we couldn't afford more than fifty dollars a month, we knew it would be tough to find another house.

Two weeks before we were to vacate the house, our landlady called to ask how our plans were going for the move.

"They're going fine," I answered.

"Do you have a house yet?" she asked.

"No."

"Well, I've given you notice and you're going to have to get out of there because I'm moving in."

"Don't worry. We'll be out on the date that you wanted."

"But why don't you have a house yet?"

"We look every night," I told her. "We're checking all the ads in the paper and following every lead. I promise you, we're looking."

A week before we were to move, she called again. "Do you have a house yet?"

"No, we don't." The woman had a fit. Honestly, I didn't know how the Lord would work out everything, but I assured her again we would be out on time.

Every day that week she called to see if we had found a place. "Ma'am," I said, "I've already ordered the moving van. It's coming Saturday."

"But where are you going to move?"

"I don't know yet."

Of course, our landlady assumed that we would take her to court. I think she pictured us walking in with Kay, great with child, and our two little ones, laying our sob story before the judge who would say, "My! Cruel woman, give these kids more time." She seemed fearful of that possibility and was very upset with us even though we kept reassuring her, "We're going to move out, don't worry."

Saturday came and we still didn't have a place, but we had rented a moving van. Some people from our church said, "We have a garage. You can move your stuff in there until you find a house."

My parents lived in Santa Ana, so we figured we'd just move in with them. That Saturday morning we moved everything into the garage and then took off for my parents' home. No sooner had we sat down to eat dinner, when the phone rang—it was the people who had so graciously allowed us to store our furniture in their garage.

"This afternoon," they said, "a moving van came to the little house next door. We asked the people moving out if the place was rented yet; it hasn't been. We told them we knew some people who would rent it. When we asked how much it would be, they answered, 'Fifty-five dollars.'"

"We'll take it," Kay and I told our friends. That very evening, we moved everything out of the garage and into the house next door—and we didn't even have to rent another moving van.

To top it off, this house was cuter than the other one. I didn't have nearly as much work to do on it—only minor things, such as installing a new tile floor in the bathroom. After we fixed it up, it was ideal for us.

"Lord, we rest in Thee." That had been our motto. "I'm not sure what God is going to do. He's going to do *something,* that I know. And what He does will be right, so why worry about it?" We knew the Lord would take care of the situation and He did. It's wonderful to be able to rest in the Lord even when we don't know how God will work out the circumstances.

I have found that God seems fond of showing up at the eleventh hour. Often He doesn't come through until you're right at the deadline—and in some cases, beyond the deadline. But when God answers past the cut-off, you can be sure He's doing a greater work than you had anticipated.

A CORRECT PERSPECTIVE

Whenever the subject of faith comes up, someone will invariably quote the words of Jesus:

> If you have faith as of a grain of mustard seed, you will say to the mountain, "Move from here to there" and it will move; and nothing would be impossible for you (Matthew 17:20).

It's important that we put those promises in perspective, remembering whom Jesus was addressing. He revealed the potential of faith to His closest associates—His disciples.

So what constitutes discipleship? Jesus had said earlier, "If any man would come after Me (be My disciple), let him deny himself, take up his cross, and follow Me" (Matthew 16:24).

When Jesus talks about the great potential of faith, He is talking to men who have denied themselves, who have taken up the cross and submitted themselves fully to the will of God. These men and women no longer seek after things only for themselves—they follow Jesus.

A lot of teaching today suggests that if you could only develop and learn the keys of faith, you could use this faith to produce all kinds of wealth, luxurious living, and wonderful things for yourself. But Jesus is talking here to those who have denied themselves. Faith is not a medium through which I can amass diamonds, homes and other extravagant merchandise for myself. Consider a few of the things the Bible says have been accomplished through faith:

> By faith Enoch was translated into heaven without dying (Hebrews 11:5).

> By faith Noah escaped the judgment of God upon the earth (Hebrews 11:7).

> By faith the walls of Jericho fell (Hebrews 11:30).

> By faith kingdoms were subdued (Hebrews 11:33).

> By faith the mouths of lions were stopped (Hebrews 11:33).

> By faith the three Hebrew children survived the fiery furnace (Hebrews 11:34).

> By faith the weak were made strong (Hebrews 11:34).

> By faith foreign armies were put to flight (Hebrews 11:34).

> By faith women received their dead back to life (Hebrews 11:35).

What great potential faith has to change our difficult circumstances!

FAITHFUL, BUT SUFFERING

Faith has enormous potential to turn negative situations into triumphs, but true men of faith have also been tortured. They've endured cruel mocking. They've been scourged. They've been imprisoned. They've wandered about in sheepskins—destitute, hungry, afflicted and tormented. And they've been stoned, or sawn in two, or slain with the sword—though they were men of genuine faith (Hebrews 11:35-37).

What does this tell you concerning faith? It tells us that it does not always deliver us from adverse circumstances. Faith didn't deliver Daniel from getting thrown into the lion's den. It preserved him there, but it did not keep him from it.

When things go badly for us, we tend to say, "Everything is against me." No, no, no. You don't know all things. You know only part of the story and you're making judgments without complete knowledge. Wait until you get all the facts and then you'll see it is quite different from what you suspect.

I have apologized to God many times for believing and complaining that all things were against me. When He finished the picture, I could clearly see how wrong I had been. God was working His plan of love in my life the whole time. When my faith wavered, God used even that to accomplish His purposes in my life. And He'll do exactly the same thing for you.

Your faith may not necessarily keep you out of difficult straits, just as faith did not keep Daniel's friends from the fiery furnace. I walk in faith but that will not keep me from walking through the valley of the shadow of death. On that day, however, He will sustain me. The Lord said,

> When you pass through the waters, I will be with you; and through the rivers, they shall not overflow you. When you walk through the fire, you shall not be burned, nor shall the flame scorch you (Isaiah 43:2).

He didn't promise that floodwaters wouldn't engulf us or promise escape from the fires, but He promises that His presence will remain with us no matter what situations we face.

Faith brings you confidence that God is in control and that nothing happens to you but what He has allowed to happen. Because He has allowed it, He has a good purpose in and through it. As you commit your way to the Lord, the fretting, the struggling and the anxiety starts to melt away. In their place you begin to say with confidence, "The Lord is in control. The Lord will take care of it. I don't know how, but I know He will."

Faith is never intended as a means by which you might get your will done. It is a means by which God can accomplish His purposes through your life—and it may be God's will that you suffer. It was surely His will that His only begotten Son should suffer. Peter speaks about suffering according to the will of God:

> Therefore let those who suffer according to the will of God commit their souls [to Him] in doing good, as to a faithful Creator (1 Peter 4:19).

The greatest faith is not manifested in a complete escape from all suffering, but in trusting God to keep you in the midst of suffering. We make a great mistake when we think that if we just had enough faith, we wouldn't have any problems. Not true! Nevertheless, God will be with us and will give us the strength to face every problem victoriously. That's the true potential of faith.

HECKLING THE HEATHEN

We used to sing the chorus, "I have the joy, joy, joy, joy down in my heart." Over the years all kinds of verses got added to it. One said, "I have the happy hope that heckles heathens down in my heart."

This kind of faith simply trusts God. You don't get upset when trouble comes—you don't wring your hands or mope around saying, "I don't know what we're going to do." Instead, you smile and wait.

"Have things changed for you yet?" people ask.

"No, they're still pretty desperate."

"Then how can you be so happy?"

"Because God is in control."

It heckles unbelievers that you aren't disturbed. "But what are you doing about it?"

"I'm just trusting the Lord, just resting in Him."

"Oh, come on now! God helps those who help themselves. You've got to do something. You can't just sit there."

When you rest in the Lord, it flusters the heathens. They don't understand why you're not in a frenzy. Faith is knowing that God is in control of every issue of your life.

Unfortunately, sometimes we lay the problem before God … and then we go to bed and wrestle with it all night. We wake up at three o'clock in the morning thinking, *What's going to happen? What if I do this? What if I do that? Maybe I should do this.* We can't rest because we aren't trusting in God's ability to take care of the situation. So we continue to carry the burden—and that wears us out.

After you call upon God for His help, you need to take the second step and rest in God. "I've placed it in the hands of God and I'm trusting Him to take care of it." Then see what He wants to accomplish in your life through faith.

TWO DESPERATE PEOPLE

In Mark 5 we meet two desperate people who discovered the huge potential of faith in God. One came requesting the touch of Jesus; the other came touching Jesus.

Soon after Jesus began His ministry it became common knowledge that many people were healed of their diseases simply by touching Him. So when the Lord arrived in Capernaum, the people crowded around Him reaching out to touch Him. One man named Jairus, a ruler in the synagogue, bulled his way through the crowd. He moved out of desperation to seek healing for his dying twelve-year-old daughter.

Now, remember not too long before, Jesus had healed a man on the Sabbath in the Capernaum synagogue, which prompted its leaders to plot to put Him to death. And now Jairus, one of those leaders, has come in desperation to Jesus because his own precious daughter lies at death's door. Prejudice is a difficult obstacle to overcome, but Jairus believes that Jesus has the power to heal.

He falls at the feet of Jesus, begging Him to come and touch his child. At that moment, Jairus could not have cared less what the other rulers of the synagogue thought of him. "If You will just touch her," he says to Jesus, "I know she will be healed."

Jesus goes with him willingly. He doesn't chide him for that day in the synagogue. He doesn't say, "So now that you're in trouble you come to Me, huh?" He doesn't bring up the past—and I love Jesus for that. When you come to Jesus, He won't lay a guilt trip on you about all your misdeeds. No one who came to Jesus for help ever received a rebuke. He's willing and eager to help when you come to Him in faith.

The second person in this story also felt desperate to get to Jesus. For twelve years, this woman had suffered an issue of blood—a physical condition that made her a social outcast. Leviticus 15 taught that a woman with this particular condition was to be ostracized from the community. This woman had spent all of her money on physicians and her condition only worsened. Twelve years seems a short time when filled with joy and happiness, but when your life overflows with tragedy and suffering, it can seem like an eternity.

This poor woman also had faith in the power of Jesus. Like Jairus, she believed, correctly, that just one touch from Jesus could heal her. She was certain that if only she could make it through the crowd and touch the hem of His garment, she would be healed. Several obstacles stood in her way—mainly, the crowd thronging Him. But her desperation and determination drove her to push through that crowd until she got close enough to grab the hem of Jesus' garment.

I can see Jairus trying to clear the crowd yelling, "Stand back! Let Him through!" He has to get Jesus to his house at once. But when this woman touches the hem of Jesus' garment, suddenly Jesus stops and asks, "Who touched Me?" (Mark 5:30).

His question amazes the disciples. "What are You talking about, Lord?" they ask. "We're being shoved all over the place and You say, 'Who touched Me?' Are You kidding?" The Greek word translated "touch" here should be translated "grasp" or "grab hold." Jesus used this word in the garden when Mary first saw Him after His resurrection from the dead and He said, "Touch Me not," or more literally, "Don't hang on to Me" or "Don't clutch unto Me." It is a firm grasping. Thus, Jesus wants to know who grabbed hold of His garment.

Many were grabbing at Him, so why does Jesus stop now? I believe Jesus stops to talk to this woman in order to increase the faith of Jairus, the father who in just moments would receive news that his daughter has died. As the woman describes her story of affliction and her healing, Jesus tells her, "Daughter, your faith has made you well. Go in peace, and be healed of your affliction" (Mark 5:34).

Even as Jesus spoke, messengers arrive and tell Jairus, "Your daughter is dead. Why trouble the Teacher any further?" (Mark 5:35). At that point Jesus turns His whole attention to the distraught father and says, "Do not be afraid, only believe" (Mark 5:36). Jesus takes Peter, James, and John with Him, and along with Jairus they continue to the house. As they approach, they hear people weeping and wailing. Entering the house, Jesus asks the mourners, "Why all of this fuss? She's not dead, she's just sleeping." Instantly, their wailing turns to scornful laughter.

Jesus then takes the girl's mother and father, along with His three disciples into the room containing the dead body of this little girl. Jesus touches her, takes her by the hand and says, "*Talitha, cumi,*" an Aramaic phrase which means, "My little lamb, arise." Immediately she stands up and walks, amazing them all. The Lord instructs them, "Don't tell anyone about this; don't let it be known." He did not want any premature attempts at making Him the Messiah. Then He adds, "Just give her something to eat" (Mark 5:41-43).

The touch of Jesus is a touch of love and healing. It is a touch of life, deliverance and power. Jesus wants to touch you today to bring you those things. He wants you to feel His love and experience His healing. He wants to give you eternal life to deliver you from the power of darkness that has been destroying you. He wants to give you His power this day.

Oh, how we need that touch of Jesus. Get in touch with Jesus today by reaching out in faith. There's healing for you. There's deliverance for you. There's help for you the moment you touch Jesus.

I do not know what your particular need may be. I do not know how long you may have been in that condition—but I do know that a touch from Jesus is all you need to be made perfectly whole.

PERFECT IN HIM

Because God is both omniscient and eternal, He can speak of things that have not yet happened as though they already existed. In His Word He often speaks of the future as though it already had come to pass.

When you place your faith in Jesus, God sees you in that future state when He completes His work in your life. When Jesus presents you to His Father and says, "Here's My bride," He will present you without spot or wrinkle. His bride will have no blemishes at all. Jesus "is able to keep you from stumbling, and to present you faultless before the presence of His glory with exceeding joy" (Jude 1:24).

When Jesus presents you to the Father, it will be in that perfected state—but even now, He sees you in that perfected state. He doesn't see you with your failures and your weaknesses and your faults. Instead He sees you perfected in Him, because He knows that "He who has begun a good work in you will complete it" (Philippians 1:6). The Lord won't give up on you.

He didn't choose you and call you to be His bride and then cross His fingers, hoping He will be able to complete His work in your life. No, God always finishes what He starts.

You don't have to worry that one of these days, when you've had a particularly bad day and you've blown it again, He's going to say, "Ah, forget it. She'll never make it. I quit. I give up." He knows all things—and on the basis of what He knows, He's going to do for you what you cannot do. He's chosen you and called you and He will perfect those things concerning you. What miracles He can accomplish in you and me when we place our faith in Him!

The Scripture says, "Love will cover a multitude of sins" (1 Peter 4:8). As a grandfather, I realize more and more the truth of that statement. Others might consider some of my great grandkids brats, but I surely don't see them that way. I'd be ready to fight anybody who called one of them a brat. They're cute and they're just expressing themselves.

I love how the Lord sees past my flaws and my failures. I love that He sees me as complete in Him. Speaking of the church Christ says, "You are all fair, you're completely fair, my love. There's no spot in you" (Song of Solomon 4:7). As He looks at you, He sees only your beauty—no flaws, spots or blemishes.

We tend to say, "But, Lord, look at this and that." How foolish to call attention to every flaw you have. Just accept by faith that He loves you and sees you as perfect in Him. Enjoy it!

GOD WATCHES YOU

One Sunday, when my grandson Will was a small boy, he asked his dad a question on the way home from church. "Dad," he said, "is it true that God is always watching us?"

Before answering, Chuck asked, "Why do you want to know, Will?"

"Because our Sunday school teacher said God is always watching us and I wanted to know if it's true."

"Why do you suppose your Sunday school teacher told you that?"

"Well, we were goofing off when we were supposed to be listening to our Bible lesson. But is it true? Is God really watching me all the time?"

Wise father that he is, Chuck replied, "Yes, William, it is true. God is always watching you because He loves you so much He can't take His eyes off of you."

Have you ever been so in love that you can't stop thinking about that person? That's the same way God feels about you. He adores you. He can't get you out of His mind. He thinks of you constantly.

So how hard should it be to place your faith in a God so overflowing with love for you? He really does love you. And because of that great love, He wants to accomplish amazing things in your life as you live by faith in Him—no matter what circumstances you may face.

What Most Pleases God?

Without faith it is impossible to please Him.

Hebrews 11:6

IT DOESN'T TAKE MUCH to please God. Just a little bit of faith blesses God's heart.

It's a biblical fact—profoundly simple, but glorious in the extreme. From cover to cover, the Bible exhorts us to trust in the Lord with all of our hearts and not to lean on our own understanding (Proverbs 3:5).

Oh, how God smiles when we put our trust and our faith in Him. In the same way, the Word of God urges us to put our faith and confidence in the promises of God. "Trust in the Lord," we hear repeatedly, "and He will deliver you." That's His promise.

WHY DON'T WE BELIEVE HIM?

If it's true that faith pleases God, as the Bible insists, don't you think it would naturally follow that the converse would also be true—that God is *dis*pleased when we don't trust Him? When we doubt His promises, when we live in constant fear and anxiety, our conduct cannot please Him. I've often wondered how God looks upon a prayer like this: "Oh God, help me to believe You. Lord, please help me to believe Your promises."

Suppose I were to say to my grandson, "Son, on your sixteenth birthday, Grandpa is going to give you a car." If he knew that I had bought cars for all the rest of our grandkids on their sixteenth birthdays, how do you think he'd respond? I'm pretty sure he'd expect the same thing would probably happen for him too.

So what would you think if, after I gave him this promise, he replied, "Oh Grandpa, help me to believe you. Help me to believe in your promise, Grandpa!" I would think, *Son, why can't you believe me? Have I given you false promises before? Have I promised wild things and failed to come though?*

God has given us a Bible full of amazing promises—and yet so often we say, "Oh God, please help me to believe You. Lord, please help me to believe You'll do as You promise."

Why don't we believe Him? What is it about His promises that we find so difficult to trust? The Old Testament saint, Enoch, did not have nearly the number of divine promises we do in the Scriptures, yet His faith delighted God's heart:

> By faith Enoch was taken away so that he did not see death, and was not found, because God had taken him; for

before he was taken he had this testimony, that he pleased God (Hebrews 11:5).

The world had grown dark with sin, but despite the vile culture, this godly man walked with God. We learn that Enoch was also a prophet, as Jude quotes one of his prophecies:

Enoch, the seventh from Adam, prophesied about these men also, saying, "Behold, the Lord comes with ten thousands of His saints, to execute judgment on all" (Jude 1:14-15).

Enoch fathered a son whom he named Methuselah, which more or less means, "In the year of his death, it shall come." Could this have been a prophecy concerning the great flood of Noah's day? If you add up the years in the genealogies of Genesis, you discover that the flood came in the year that Methuselah died. Enoch was a prophet who walked with God.

According to one old legend, Enoch took a daily walk with God. The Lord would meet him every morning and Enoch would fellowship with God. One morning God said to Enoch, "Let's walk a little farther today. Bring your lunch along." So Enoch brought his lunch. They walked a bit, had lunch together, and then kept walking ... and walking ... until finally Enoch said, "It's getting late, Lord. We had better head for home." But the Lord said, "We're closer to My house than to yours. How about if you just come on home with Me?"

I love that story. I don't know how true it might be, but Enoch's faith pleased God so much that He took him home so that he should not see death. Pleasing God is the very purpose of our existence—and the Bible says we delight His heart through faith. It's a basic fact of our existence: you and I were created for God's pleasure.

In a vision the apostle John saw cherubim around the throne of God, worshiping the Lord and declaring His holiness and eternally pure character. The twenty-four elders fell on their faces before the throne and cast their crowns upon the glassy sea and said,

> Thou art worthy, O Lord, to receive glory and honor and power: for thou hast created all things, and for thy pleasure they are and were created (Revelation 4:11 KJV).

A man who lives for his own pleasure is living out of sync with God, constantly trying to find something new, something different, some new sensation. A person will never be satisfied until he fulfills the purpose for which he was born: to please God by faith. Without faith, remember, it is impossible to please God. It simply cannot be done. That's why Paul says that anything not of faith is sin (Romans 14:23).

GOD, THE REWARDER

To please God, you have to believe that He is good and that He delights in rewarding those who diligently seek Him. And what a reward He offers. It's completely out of proportion to the faith we express. A reward is not a paycheck. We can't "earn" God's rewards by our faith. Rather, faith so pleases God that He rewards us for it in ways immeasurably above and beyond the expression of our faith itself.

The Bible speaks of many "crowns" which God will reward to victorious believers. As Paul awaited his execution, he wrote,

> For I am already being poured out as a drink offering, and the time of my departure is at hand. I have fought the good fight, I have finished the race, I have kept the faith.

> Finally, there is laid up for me the crown of righteousness, which the Lord, the righteous Judge, will give to me on that Day, and not to me only but also to all who have loved His appearing (2 Timothy 4:6-8).

I think it's pretty clear that Paul was a sports fan. You can't help but reach that conclusion when you note how often Paul used sports to illustrate an idea. He probably had the ancient Olympics in mind as he jotted down,

> Do you not know that those who run in a race all run, but one receives the prize? Run in such a way that you may obtain it (1 Corinthians 9:24).

In other words, put everything you have into it. Run to win.

> And everyone who competes for the prize is temperate in all things. Now they do it to obtain a perishable crown, but we for an imperishable crown (1 Corinthians 9:25).

That is, they are very disciplined to finish in first place. If you're going to enter the Olympics, you have to be very disciplined—you watch what you eat, you watch your weight, you work out regularly. In ancient Greece, winning Olympic athletes received a wreath of laurel leaves woven into a crown. They endured all of their rigorous training—months of discipline, months of passing up a slice of pie, constantly denying themselves—all for a laurel wreath placed upon their head.

Paul is saying, "If a person is willing to live a disciplined life just to have a wreath placed on his head, then how much more should we work for the incorruptible crown that God wants to give us? That laurel wreath is going to turn brown, its leaves will die and disintegrate; but we work for an incorruptible crown that will never tarnish or crumble."

James spoke of yet another crown, the crown of life:

> Blessed is the man who endures temptation; for when he has been approved, he will receive the crown of life, which the Lord has promised to those who love Him (James 1:12).

Jesus mentioned this same crown of life. As He comforted the church of Smyrna, which was to suffer horrible persecution under Roman rule, He said,

> Do not fear any of those things which you are about to suffer. Indeed, the Devil is about to throw some of you into prison, that you may be tested, and you will have tribulation ten days. Be faithful until death, and I will give to you the crown of life (Revelation 2:10).

For the believers in Smyrna, faith could mean martyrdom; but God promised to reward each martyr with the crown of everlasting life.

When Peter wrote to the church elders to encourage them in their ministry, he said, "And when the Chief Shepherd appears, you will receive the crown of glory that does not fade away" (1 Peter 5:4). This crown lasts forever, remaining brilliant throughout eternity. And Jesus has promised to give this crown to every faithful church leader.

A SHINING EXAMPLE

One day Abram heard that his nephew, Lot, had been taken hostage by a powerful confederation of kings. Abram put together a posse and pursued the kings until he came upon them at night and defeated them in a surprise attack. He freed the hostages and seized the spoil the kings had grabbed in their conquest of some ten cities.

When Abram returned home, the king of Sodom met him. Thrilled to have his people back, he presented Abram all of the spoil he had recovered. But Abram refused to take any of it. "I've raised my hand before God that I am not going to take even as much as a sandal strap," Abram said, "lest you might say you made Abram rich" (Genesis 14:22-23). Then something truly amazing happened:

> After these things the LORD came to Abram in a vision, saying, "Do not be afraid: I am your shield, your exceedingly great reward" (Genesis 15:1).

"Do not be afraid," God said. But Abram had reason to fear. He had just defeated several powerful kings in a surprise attack, seized their spoil and brought back the hostages—with only 318 trained servants (Genesis 14:14). These kings controlled forces far superior to those of Abram. No doubt he soon thought, *What will I do if they regroup and come down here? I'm not capable of defeating them without the element of surprise.* But knowing his thoughts, God told Abram, "I Myself will be your shield."

It is also possible that Abram had "seller's remorse." It could be that as Abram saw the king of Sodom taking away all of the loot on donkeys—spoil that Abram had refused to accept—he may have thought, *Man, that was a foolish thing to do. That's a lot of wealth. Maybe I should have kept at least some of that.* Perhaps he had second thoughts about giving away all of those riches. And so the Lord said to Abram, "I am your exceedingly great reward. You don't need any of that loot that's being carted away. I Myself am your exceedingly great reward."

I think Abram would have appreciated a long-haired young man named Bruce who used to sing a song around our church. Today Bruce is a well-groomed accountant, but in his hippie days he used to sing, "I've got Jesus, and that's enough." How true that is. If you have Jesus, that's enough—you're rich.

My great grandchildren often say to me, "Grandpa, are you rich?" They ask because I take them to the toy store and say, "Pick out whatever toy you want." They rummage through the whole store and select one toy of their choice. It's always fun to watch as they pick up one, hold it for a while, put it down and pick up another. They go through the entire store like that. They have a hard time with that "only one toy" rule. But eventually they settle on "the one" and then Grandpa shells out the money to buy it. So they ask me, "Grandpa, you're rich, aren't you?"

"Yes," I say, "I'm the richest man in Orange County."

"Grandpa," they ask, "do you have lots of money?"

"No," I say, "I don't have lots of money, but I'm rich."

What do I mean? I'm rich in the things that really count. I'm rich in the beautiful family I have. I'm rich in the love I experience. I'm rich in my love for the Lord. I've got Jesus! I've got God's love. He is my exceedingly great reward.

In the same way, God says to you, "I am your exceedingly great reward. Your faith pleases me, and I intend to reward you far beyond your wildest imaginations."

A REWARD ABOVE ALL

Abram rejoiced in the Lord's words about being his shield and reward, and he believed Him. But he also said, "Lord, I already have more than I could possibly spend in my lifetime—but I don't have a child to inherit it."

When you're both wealthy and old, your thoughts tend to center on your estate. To whom are you going to leave your assets and how are you going to apportion them? The joy is in giving it all away. Therefore Abram says, "Lord, You have been amazingly good to me. You have blessed me—but I don't have a child to inherit it. The only heir I have is my head servant, born in my house: Eliezer of Damascus."

Believe me, the Lord understands how to reward someone in the best way possible. So God said to Abram, "This one shall not be your heir, but one who will come from your own body shall be your heir" (Genesis 15:4).

To drive His point home, the Lord then said, "Come on outside, Abram." Abram stepped outside of his tent and God said to him, "Look up into the sky." Abram craned his neck and saw an impossible number of bright pinpricks of light staring down at him. Imagine this in the days before smog or city lights, when a man could clearly see the vast canopy of stars in the heavens above. As Abram stood looking up at that glorious sky and the countless stars in the heavens, God said, "Abram, if you can number the stars, so shall your descendants be" (Genesis 15:5). How did Abram respond?

> And he believed in the LORD, and He accounted it to him
> for righteousness (Genesis 15:6).

How is it that God accounted Abram righteous? It certainly was not because of anything Abram had done. To be sure, Abram had done many good works. He had ventured out in faith from Babylon, without the slightest idea of where he was going. The writer of Hebrews records he was searching for a city that had foundations, whose maker and builder was God. Abram was looking for the kingdom of God and so he walked by faith in obedience to God.

When Abram came into the land God had promised him, he built an altar and offered a sacrifice to God. Later, he graciously separated himself from his nephew, Lot, giving him the choice of land. And we just read how Abram defeated a potent confederacy of kings, refusing to take the spoils himself. These are all good works—but Scripture doesn't give a single hint that God declared him righteous because of any of them.

Nor did the Lord declare Abram righteous because he had fulfilled some ceremony or had gone through some spiritual ritual. The apostle Paul takes special care to point out that God declared Abram righteous long before He ever gave him the ritual of circumcision. Paul taught that the Lord had declared Abraham righteous as the result of his faith, not as the result of some ceremony (Romans 4:2-3).

This should speak to our dear brethren in Christ who seem so concerned about the ritual of water baptism. They appear to look to that ritual for salvation, but the ritual does not save you, nor can it save you. It is when you come to Jesus in faith that God declares you righteous.

The same is true of the ritual of infant baptism. That ritual does not save a child, nor does the ritual of "confirmation" save a person. Those are just rituals of the church, much like partaking of the Lord's Supper or the "last rites" administered just before you die in order to have all your sins absolved. These man-made rituals have nothing to do with God declaring you to be a righteous person.

In Romans 4, Paul carefully points out that Abraham was justified by faith and not by works. Had works justified him, he would have been able to boast. Because he was justified by faith apart from works, all he could do was boast in the God who justified him—the Lord who rewarded him out of all proportion.

Abram simply looked up into the heavens, saw the countless stars, and believed the promise of God. And for that, God smiled upon Abram with great pleasure and rewarded him out of all expectation or hope.

HOW MUCH FAITH?

Who can argue against the idea that salvation is the greatest reward of all? Jesus said, "For what will it profit a man if he gains the whole world, and loses his own soul?" (Mark 8:36).

So then—how much faith does it take to be saved and receive the greatest reward possible? Jesus said that if you have faith like a grain of mustard seed or if you have the faith of a child, that's enough for God to account you as righteous.

Faith itself, of course, cannot save you. Many people who believe in God are not saved, tragically, because many people make a work out of faith and look to their faith itself for their salvation.

If you say, "I believe in God," that declaration in itself won't save you. The devils believe in God—and they fear and tremble (James 2:19).

If you say, "I believe that Jesus Christ is the Son of God," that will not save you. The demons also believe in Jesus and said to

Him, "I know who You are—the Holy One of God!" (Luke 4:34). Yet demons are not saved.

Everyone believes in something. The question isn't *whether* you believe in something, but *what* do you believe?

God promised Abram that one day He would bring from him a seed, a child, and that through this child He would bring salvation. In fact, this child would make possible the salvation of the whole world. "In your seed all the nations of the earth shall be blessed" (Genesis 22:18).

So in what did Abraham have faith? He believed that God would one day bring to earth the Savior of the world through his offspring. It was his faith in the coming of the Messiah that prompted God to say, "This is a righteous man."

Do you want to be declared righteous by God? If so, you need to believe more than the fact that there is a God or that Jesus came to earth. You must believe in the promise of God that if you place your faith in Jesus Christ, you will not perish, but will have everlasting life. Salvation becomes yours when you trust that He came to die in your place, bearing your sins and the guilt and the penalty of your sin, and by so doing purchased your salvation. When you believe in the promise of God, which is salvation through faith in Jesus Christ, God looks at you and says, "You're righteous."

JUST AS YOU ARE

Our church helps to support a missionary who grew up on the Bolivian mission field. His father had a tremendous burden for the Saranoy Indians, a nomadic, tribal group that lived in the wet forest—what was known as the green-hell country of

Bolivia. These people had no permanent home, but would hunt out an area, get food, and then move on.

When this missionary died, his son carried on the ministry. Of course, since he grew up among the Saranoy, he knew all about them. They considered him something of a curiosity—how did this white kid know their dances, their culture, and their language? For years he remained with them under difficult circumstances, faithfully sharing the gospel.

Eventually he and other missionaries built a village for the Saranoy. They taught them how to farm. They taught them certain practices of hygiene, thereby cutting down the incidence of tuberculosis, which had become a tremendous problem. These missionaries did a lot of social good for the Saranoy— but this one man's heart beat to bring them to Jesus Christ. For seven long years he witnessed and labored among them, without a single convert. Yet he had the writer of Hebrews to encourage him:

> Do not become sluggish, but imitate those who through faith and patience inherit the promises (Hebrews 6:12).

Finally, after seven years, this missionary had a breakthrough as God began to touch the hearts of the Saranoy Indians in a marvelous way. Today a vast majority of the Saranoy are Christians—but it took years of seed planting, years of patience and prayer before these faithful missionaries saw the fruit of their ministry.

God loves the kind of faith that works patiently without growing sluggish. He loves it so much that He causes such believers to "inherit the promises." Paul said it like this:

And let us not grow weary while doing good, for in due season we shall reap if we do not lose heart (Galatians 6:9).

Faith pleases God, and it especially pleases Him to reward it beyond all measure.

Many years ago in London, a fine young preacher named Caesar Milan received an invitation to enjoy a musicale at a large, prominent home, where a young lady thrilled the audience with her singing. When she finished, this young preacher made his way through the crowd, gained her attention and said, "Young lady, when you were singing, I sat there and thought how tremendously the cause of Christ would be benefited if you would dedicate your talents to the Lord." He then added, "You're as much a sinner as the worst drunkard on the street or any harlot on Scarlet Street. But I'm glad to tell you that the blood of Jesus Christ, God's Son, can cleanse you from all sin, if you will just come to Him."

In a very haughty manner, she turned her head aside and replied, "You are very insulting, sir." She started to walk away, but he called out, "Miss, I didn't mean any offense and I pray that the Spirit of God will convict you."

That night the young woman couldn't sleep. Finally, at two o'clock in the morning, she knelt beside her bed and received Christ as her Savior. And then she, Charlotte Elliott, sat down to write these words, made famous through the crusades of Billy Graham:

> Just as I am, without one plea,
> But that Thy blood was shed for me,
> And that Thou bidst me come to Thee,
> O Lamb of God, I come, I come.

Just as I am, and waiting not
To rid my soul of one dark blot,
To Thee whose blood can cleanse each spot,
O Lamb of God, I come, I come.

Just as I am, Thou wilt receive,
Wilt welcome, pardon, cleanse, relieve;
Because Thy promise I believe,
O Lamb of God, I come, I come. [2]

Faith pleases God. When we believe His promises and so declare His faithfulness, His heart rejoices. God loves to reward our faith, starting with salvation and then spilling over into all other areas of our lives.

And do you know the best thing of all? It's that He'll take you just as you are. When you come to Jesus Christ, believing His promise, He welcomes, pardons, cleanses, and relieves. He removes each dark spot of sin in your life. When you come to Him "without one plea," trusting in the sufficiency of Jesus' shed blood, God opens the gates of heaven for you.

---

[2] "Just As I Am Without One Plea," words by Charlotte Elliott, 1835.

A Faith That Works

Remembering without ceasing your work of faith.

1 THESSALONIANS 1:3

IF I WERE TO STAND BEFORE YOU on a Sunday morning and say, "I have credible information that terrorists have planted a bomb in this church. In fact, it's going off in thirty seconds," but then I continue to give my message in a calm voice, how would you react? You'd probably say, "He's just teasing us."

But if I were to say, "Terrorists have planted a bomb in this church! IT'S EXPLODING IN THIRTY SECONDS!" and I sprint toward the door, I'll bet you'd say, "Let's get out of here!"

In the second scenario, my actions lined up with my words. My actions followed my professed belief. It is exactly the same with a life of faith. If I tell you that Jesus Christ is my Lord and I continue to walk and live after the flesh, you would have reason to doubt my faith, for true faith will always reveal itself in a life of obedience to God. This is why John wrote in his first epistle,

> Now by this we know that we know Him, if we keep His commandments. He who says, "I know Him," and does not keep His commandments, is a liar, and the truth is not in him (1 John 2:3-4).

To profess one thing and then do the opposite is to lie. If you say, "I know Jesus Christ," and you don't obey His commandments, you do not have a saving faith. The only faith that will save is a faith that responds and reacts in obedience to God. Glad obedience proves your faith.

THE WORK OF FAITH

Many people have the idea that work and faith are mutually exclusive. They consider this pair of words to be something of an oxymoron—if you have faith, then you don't work; and if you work, then you don't have faith.

Wrong.

It is true that Paul places great emphasis on the fact that our works can never obtain a righteous standing before God, no matter how good those works might be. He states repeatedly that it is not by the works of the law, but by faith, that we are saved.

> By grace you have been saved through faith; and that not of yourselves; it is a gift of God, not of works, lest anyone should boast (Ephesians 2:8-9).

A man is justified by faith without the deeds of the law—this is Paul's theme throughout his writings. And yet in 1 Thessalonians

1:3, this same apostle Paul commends his believing friends for their "work of faith."

What does Paul mean? If we have true faith in Jesus Christ, our faith will manifest itself in our works. We respond to the blessings and grace of God by the works we do for Him freely, out of a heart overflowing with love. We do not look at our works as gaining any special favors with God. We don't think, *I'm righteous because I pray so much and I read the Bible so much and I study so much and I minister so much.* We do these things because we have received a glorious position of righteousness in Christ through faith. Good works come out of a believer's life as a natural response to the grace of God.

FIGHTING EPISTLES?

Some people say that the apostles Paul and James are at variance with each other, contradicting one another in their epistles, but that's simply not so. Paul speaks of the kind of faith that produces works; James speaks of the kinds of works produced by faith. The two apostles are talking about the same thing. True faith always manifests itself in the works of a life of faith. James asks,

> What does it profit, my brothers, though a man says he has faith if he doesn't have works? Can faith save him? (James 2:14).

If your faith does not prompt a positive change in your life, then you're no different from anyone else.

You might say, "But I believe in Jesus!" If nothing godly follows your belief—if it doesn't result in obedience or in serving the Lord—then can that kind of faith save you? James answers bluntly: "Faith without works is dead." He writes, "Someone will say, 'You have faith, and I have works.' Show me your faith without your works and I will show you my faith by my works" (James 2:17-18).

True faith is more than just a verbal affirmation that you believe in Jesus Christ. True faith demonstrates its reality in the work you do for Jesus. Paul said,

> By the grace of God I am what I am, and His grace which was bestowed upon me was not in vain; but I labored more abundantly than they all (1 Corinthians 15:10).

The apostle insisted that the grace of God in his life provoked him to greater labor—more labor than all of the other apostles. Paul did not labor for the Lord in order to develop a righteous standing before God or to boast that he outworked his fellow apostles. His works grew out of the abundance of blessings that God had bestowed upon him, by grace through faith.

And so it must be with us. When I declare Jesus is my Lord, this means I am His servant. Whatever He says, I am to do without question. Since Jesus commands us to deny ourselves, to take up our cross, follow Him, and to be a witness of Him in the world, He can rightfully say, "When you have done all those things which you are commanded, say, 'We are unprofitable servants. We have done what was our duty to do'" (Luke 17:10).

You and I therefore need to ask ourselves a question: What works of faith are being manifested in my life?

A FUTURE RECKONING

When the Lord comes again, He will require of His servants an accounting of what they have done with all He has entrusted to them. That's the thrust of the parable in Matthew 25:14-30. Whatever the Lord has given you, you are to use for His purposes and for His glory.

In the parable, Jesus says that a master gave to each servant according to their unique ability. The "talents" He speaks of are actually units of money. The talent was a certain weight, and its worth depended upon the metal it was made of, whether gold, silver or brass. The master entrusted five talents to one servant, two to another, and one to a third servant, each according to their ability. Then the master left on an extended trip.

In a similar way, the Bible says God has given to each man a measure of faith (Romans 12:3). God has invested in us a certain amount of faith from which He expects to receive some kind of return. Jesus' parable asks, "What are we to do with whatever God entrusts to us?" One day we will stand before God and give an account. Jesus says that some are given more than others. God will not require of you more than you can produce—God invests in you according to your ability.

I recommend you do a personal inventory. Ask yourself, "What has God entrusted to me? What has God put in my keeping for which He will require an accounting upon His return?"

The servant who had received five talents traded them and gained another five. The one given two talents doubled them. But the man given a single talent put it in a napkin and buried it. He hid his master's money in the ground. "After a long time," Jesus said, "the lord of those servants came and reckoned with them."

I wonder if in this instance Jesus was trying to suggest that He would not return immediately? The disciples expected the Lord to return right away, yet He never said He would. Jesus said He would return unexpectedly. "For the Son of Man is coming at an hour you do not expect" (Matthew 24:44).

I personally believe that the coming of the Lord is near at hand. It could be further down the road than I expect. Still, I live in the expectancy of the soon return of Jesus Christ. When the Lord comes—and our Lord is coming—I should be watchful and ready for Him. I must be doing something profitable with whatever He has entrusted to me, that I might give back to Him more than He gave to me.

While the coming of the Lord will be a day of judgment for the world, His coming will be a day of reckoning for His church. We shall give to the Master an account of what we have done with what He has given us.

> For we must all appear before the judgment seat of Christ, that each one may receive the things done in the body, according to what he has done, whether good or bad (2 Corinthians 5:10).

> For the Son of Man will come in the glory of His Father with His angels; and then He will reward each according to his works (Matthew 16:27).

> Why do you judge your brother? Or why do you show contempt for your brother? For we shall all stand before the judgment seat of Christ. For it is written: "As I live," says the LORD, "every knee shall bow to Me, and every tongue shall confess to God." So then each of us shall give account of himself to God (Romans 14:10-12).

Jesus said that the servant who had been given the five talents brought another five. The Lord said to him, "Well done, good and faithful servant. You've been faithful over a few things. I will make you ruler over many. Enter into the joy of the Lord." The same thing happened to the man who had been given two talents and he received the same words of commendation. What matters is not how much you were given, but how faithfully you've used whatever God entrusted to you.

The servant who had received just one talent immediately began offering excuses for returning only that which he had been given. In so doing he also expressed his misconceptions of the Lord.

"You are a hard man," he said. That's not true, for Jesus said, "My yoke is easy, and My burden is light" (Matthew 11:30). God does not require unreasonable things of us. I have found that it is much easier to please the Lord than it is to please people. Next, the man accused the Lord of reaping where He did not sow. The Lord does not do that. That would be dishonest. Lastly the man said, "I was afraid," which is an excuse. Ben Franklin once said, "A man who is good at making excuses is seldom good for anything else."

This servant tried to excuse himself, but his master accused him of being wicked and lazy. What was wicked was his false conception of his master. But his basic problem was slothfulness. He was lazy and careless with the things that God had entrusted to him.

"If you really thought that I reaped where I did not sow," the master said, "then at least you should have put the money in the bank so when I returned I would have interest on my investment." Because of the man's slothfulness, the talent given to him was taken back and given to the one who had faithfully doubled the five.

If you're faithful in using what God has placed in your hands, then God will give you more. The issue is, what are you doing with whatever God has entrusted to you?

> Therefore let a man examine himself. For if we will judge ourselves, then we will not come under the judgment of God (1 Corinthians 11:28, 31).

One day, I'm going to stand before Jesus Christ, my Lord. What will I be able to present to Him? Have I used what He has entrusted to me for His glory? Will I be able to say, "Lord, You gave me five and I've gained another five"? Or will I be able to say, "Lord, You gave me two, and I've gained another two"?

You too are going to stand before the Lord. You too are going to give an account of yourself. That's serious business. Our Lord is coming, and when He does, it will be a day of judgment for the world and a day of reckoning for believers. Let us never be lazy about serving God, but may we be diligent in using the things He has entrusted to us for His purpose and His glory, for the expanding of His kingdom.

All that you have done and are doing for the Lord should be for the purpose of one day hearing these remarkable words of approbation from our Lord: "Well done, good and faithful servant. You have been faithful in a few things; I will make you ruler over many. Enter into the joy of your Lord!"

A FAITH LIKE RAHAB'S

One of the most surprising people listed in the great "hall of faith" in Hebrews 11 is Rahab, a prostitute from Jericho at the time of the conquest of the Promised Land. As far as we know, she never gave any great sermons. She never addressed a crowd of thousands, imploring them to come to faith. But she did take action that revealed her faith:

> By faith the harlot Rahab did not perish with those who did not believe, when she had received the spies with peace (Hebrews 11:31).

The book of Joshua tells the story of Rahab, and how, despite great danger to herself, this pagan prostitute hid two Hebrew spies sent out from the Israelite camp. To the spies, she said,

> I know that the LORD has given you the land, that the terror of you has fallen on us, and that all the inhabitants of the land are fainthearted because of you. For we have heard how the LORD dried up the water of the Red Sea for you when you came out of Egypt, and what you did to the two kings of the Amorites who were on the other side of the Jordan, Sihon and Og, whom you utterly destroyed. And as soon as we heard these things, our hearts melted; neither did there remain any more courage in anyone because of you. For the LORD your God, He is God in heaven above and on earth beneath (Joshua 2:9-11).

That is a statement of faith.

Rahab had genuine faith, manifested in specific works—she received and hid the spies, then helped them escape. Rahab did this because she knew that God was going to give the land to Israel. At the risk of her own life, she expressed her genuine faith in God through her hazardous works. So James says,

> Likewise, was not Rahab the harlot justified by works when she received the messengers and sent them out another way? (James 2:25).

James draws upon Rahab as a prime illustration to show that this prostitute's faith—as undeveloped and immature as it must have been—led her to perform certain works, even placing her life in grave jeopardy. She could have sold out the spies when her own people came looking for them, but instead she hid them on her rooftop and sent their pursuers off on a wild goose chase. James considers her story and makes a bold application based on this little history lesson:

> For as the body without the spirit is dead, so faith without works is dead also (James 2:26).

No one will ever be moved to Spirit-led action without faith. One's faith is not genuine unless it moves him or her to action. Faith and works are necessary companions. The faith produces the works, while the works demonstrate the genuineness of the faith.

So James declares, "Be doers of the word, and not hearers only, deceiving yourselves" (James 1:22). Those who merely hear about faith and who only profess their faith, without ever putting it into action, deceive themselves. They don't have real faith at all. Genuine faith cannot help but reveal itself in works of faith. If you have faith, it will be demonstrated—it will bring forth the fruit of righteousness. As Jesus said: "You will know them by their fruits" (Matthew 7:16).

So what kind of fruit is your life producing? Is it the fruit that demonstrates the flesh is in control? Or is it the fruit of the Spirit that demonstrates the Spirit is in control? Paul said, "But when we are judged, we are chastened by the Lord, that we may not be condemned with the world" (1 Corinthians 11:31-32).

Remember that Jesus clearly warned us, "Not everyone who says to Me, 'Lord, Lord,' shall enter the kingdom of heaven, but he who does the will of My Father in heaven" (Matthew 7:21).

At the final judgment many will say to Jesus, "Lord, Lord," but He will answer, "Why do you call Me, 'Lord, Lord,' and not do the things which I say?" (Luke 6:46). It is an empty declaration when someone calls Jesus "Lord" and yet has no desire or intention to obey His commands.

Faith produces works—if it doesn't, then it's not true faith.

A BOAT WITH TWO OARS

As I mentioned earlier, I worked at a market many years ago in order to provide for my family while I pastored a small church. One Friday I went to the bank to get some cash for the market. A lot of customers came to the market on the weekends to cash their checks, so we needed to have plenty of cash on hand to satisfy the demand.

As the teller counted out the cash to me, I noticed that she had made a mistake. She had given me $500 more than she should have. So when she finished giving me the money, I said, "Maybe you should count the money again."

"Well …" she began.

"No," I insisted, "I think you should count it again." So for a second time she counted out the money—and made the same mistake again.

Now, I'm not quite like Jesus. My immediate thought was, *Whoa, that could help us out a whole lot.* But I said to the woman, "Okay, do it once more."

When she saw her $500 mistake, she almost fainted.

Now, what would faith without works say in a situation like that? It would probably say, "Whoa, that could help us out a whole lot—hey, it's not my mistake. I'm under no obligation to do this teller's job for her. If she wants to give me the money, I'll take it."

Faith and works go together, like sun and summer, like apples and pie, like fish and water. Faith and works are like two oars on a rowboat. You have to use both if you want to make it across the lake. If you try using a single oar, you're going to spin in circles. If you focus on faith only, then you're going to revolve around and around and get nowhere. On the other hand, if you focus only on works apart from faith, you'll merely rotate in the other direction.

Do you want to get somewhere in your life of faith? Most importantly, do you want to stand before the Lord one day and hear, "Well done, good and faithful servant! Enter into the joy of your Lord"? If so, don't neglect either oar. Faith empowers the works, and works prove the faith.

The Marvel of Unbelief

And He marveled because of their unbelief.

MARK 6:6

SOME TIME AGO ONE OF OUR Calvary Chapel pastors, Gary, traveled to Rwanda with relief supplies. His group visited an orphanage there and ministered to its children.

On the return flight home, Gary chose the fish plate for his meal. He didn't know that the sauce contained shrimp—and he had a severe allergy to it. No sooner had he taken a bite than he suffered an immediate attack. It was so severe he needed medical attention quickly. So the plane landed in Iceland, where they rushed him straight to a hospital.

Can you imagine? Out of his great love for Jesus, he had left the comforts of his own home to do God's work among the poor children of Rwanda. On the final leg of his trip, he was no doubt looking forward to his nice bed back home, his own comfortable pillow, and a chance to relax—instead he ends up suffering a horrific allergic reaction and gets sidelined in Iceland, of all places.

I'm certain Gary wondered, *Lord—Iceland? I want to get home. What is going on? I've been serving You, Lord, and now look at what's happening to me.* We all know the kind of thoughts that flood our minds when our plans go badly awry.

After a time in the hospital, the airline flew Gary back to London. On his flight home, he was bumped up to first class where he met a couple in charge of a large, charitable foundation. When they heard of his ministry, they pledged thousands of dollars to its work. God had taken Gary on a difficult, roundabout trip so he could meet those very people. He could have spent his time in Iceland complaining in unbelief: "God, why? Why would You allow this? Do You really love me?" But God had a plan the whole time.

Many times unbelief causes us to complain, murmur, weep, and despair—if we only knew what God was doing, we would rejoice instead.

A SECOND TRIP TO NAZARETH

Once Jesus began His public ministry, He began fulfilling Old Testament prophecies of the Messiah. He healed the broken-hearted, opened the eyes of the blind, and preached the gospel to the poor. Soon great crowds followed Him everywhere.

One day Jesus decided to visit Nazareth again. The first time He traveled by Himself, but this time multitudes accompanied Him. Just like His first visit, Jesus attended synagogue services on the Sabbath day. He read the Scriptures and began to preach. Mark tells us that the people were astonished at His teaching and wondered how He had gained such knowledge. "Where did this Man get these things? And what wisdom is this that such mighty works are performed by His hands!" (Mark 6:2).

Astonished, the people marveled at His teaching and His works. They recognized something extraordinary about Him—and yet they did not believe.

THEY DIDN'T REALLY KNOW HIM

When the Nazarenes heard Jesus and observed what He did, they said, "Is this not the carpenter, the Son of Mary, and the brother of James, Joses, Judas, and Simon?" (Mark 6:3). They remembered him as a boy. Perhaps years before, they had brought Him their yokes or plows for repair or purchased tables and chairs from Him. They knew Him in His earlier years—so all His adult wisdom and miracle-working troubled them. They rejected what they saw with their own eyes.

What do you suppose accounted for their unbelief? It may be that they thought they knew Him—but they were mistaken. They did not know Him at all. Oh, they possessed a certain amount of head knowledge about Jesus. They knew He had grown up in Nazareth as a carpenter. They knew His brothers and His sisters and His mother. Although they thought they knew Him completely, they knew Him only partially. Their unbelief stemmed from their insufficient knowledge.

How many people today have opinions of Jesus based upon insufficient knowledge? Christianity's greatest opponents are those who don't know Him. Their prejudice and unbelieving stance emerge from the disparaging remarks others have made concerning Him. Some people have never endeavored to understand Jesus for themselves.

The claims of Jesus are so radical and the consequences of unbelief so great that it would be wise to examine all of the evidence personally. Jesus said that whoever believed in Him would be saved, but whoever did not believe in Him would be condemned (John 3:18). With the stakes so high, you should make more than a cursory examination of the facts. You should study diligently to determine whether Jesus is indeed the Savior of the world. Or is He a fraud and a liar, whereby justifying your unbelief?

Before he became Paul the apostle, Saul thought he knew Jesus. He considered Jesus to be the leader of a dangerous, anti-Jewish sect that needed to be stamped out. Where did Saul develop this concept? No doubt from his sessions with the Pharisees, as he heard them express their negative opinions and their doubts. But then one day Saul had a personal encounter with Jesus and came to know Him firsthand. That supernatural meeting transformed his life completely.

What do you know about Jesus? Where did you get your information about Him? Have you read the gospel of John prayerfully, saying; "Lord, if this is a true record, if You are really the Son of God, then reveal Yourself to me"? Have you read it with an open heart, or is your mind prejudiced against Him?

In our time and culture, hundreds of thousands of lives have been radically transformed by the power of Jesus Christ. Through faith in Him, people who once were hopeless alcoholics, written off by the world, are now whole, healed, and living productive lives. Others, strung out on drugs, met Jesus and had the same radical transformation as Paul. Today they're joyfully serving the Lord. Many felt so miserable they thought of suicide, but now their lives are full and rich as they walk with Jesus in newness of life. With the testimony of so many transformed lives—not to mention the hundreds of thousands who have gone before us and left their own stories to prove the power of Jesus—how is it that so many refuse to believe?

Many men and women think they know Jesus, however their information is based upon false witnesses, lies, and gossip. They've never looked at the evidence for themselves. Yet they've formed opinions that keep them from all the good things Jesus wants to do for them and in them. They miss out on all of this richness simply because of the folly of unbelief.

THE RESULT OF UNBELIEF

Mark tells us what happened when the people of Nazareth refused to believe in Jesus: "He could do no mighty works there, except that He laid His hands on a few sick people and healed them" (Mark 6:5).

What does Mark mean that Jesus could do no mighty works there? Does he imply that their unbelief actually restricted Jesus' power to do miracles? I hardly think so.

The unbelief of the Nazarenes did not hinder the power of Jesus; it simply kept them from it. Because of their unbelief, they didn't bring the lame, the blind, and the sick to Jesus. Thus, He did no mighty work there because they did not offer Him any such opportunity.

Jesus was not reluctant to heal nor did He lack the power to reach out. I don't think He withheld the miracles by saying, "Okay, I'll just teach you a lesson." Their unbelief kept them from coming to Jesus and receiving all that He desired to do.

How many people in Nazareth could have been helped if they had only exercised the faith to come to Jesus? They could have seen and participated in some marvelous works—but their unbelief robbed them.

Throngs of people had met Jesus throughout Galilee. They brought their sick from all over the region in order to be healed. So great was their desire to be near Him and to be healed that they crowded close to Jesus. But here in Nazareth was a totally different story. These people remained standoffish. They didn't bring multitudes of their sick; they hindered their blind and their lame. From a distance, they merely wondered, *Where did this man get this wisdom? And where did He get this power?*

The amazing thing to me is that although God announced Himself to Abraham as *El Shaddai*, the almighty God, yet the omnipotent God permits Himself to be limited by man. For example, the Bible tells us, that God is "not willing that any should perish" (2 Peter 3:9). That's the direct will of God. But in the permissive will of God, men do perish, men do walk in their own evil ways.

The Bible says concerning the people of ancient Israel, "Again and again they tempted God, and limited the Holy One of Israel" (Psalm 78:41). God would have done much more for them, but their unbelief kept them from all of the good things God wanted to do. This was no limitation of God's power. The limitation came from the people's refusal to receive God's love and power.

Not long before Jesus entered Jerusalem for the last time, Jesus cried out,

> O Jerusalem, Jerusalem, the one who kills the prophets and stones those who are sent to her! How often I wanted to gather your children together, as a hen gathers her chicks under her wings, but you were not willing! (Matthew 23:37).

Jesus would have done so much for them—He *desired* to do so much for them—but they refused.

God desires to bless and care for you and use you in a mighty way—but you can limit His work in your life through unbelief. Unbelief will keep you from the love of Jesus Christ and from salvation. Unbelief will keep you from His peace. It will cause you to go on in darkness, to continue in sin, to feel frustrated and to suffer with all the dreadful anxieties, worries and miseries that accompany a life of unbelief.

Or … you could believe—and be blessed.

SOMETHING TO MARVEL AT

Only twice does the Bible say that Jesus "marveled" at something, and in both cases it was a matter of faith. He marveled at the faith of a Roman centurion who recognized His absolute authority to heal—and He marveled when the people of Nazareth refused to believe in Him. Mark says simply, "And He marveled because of their unbelief" (Mark 6:6).

Some people have a hard time believing in the supernatural. Unless it can be reduced to a mathematical formula or a reasonable explanation, they just do not believe. You've heard the phrase, "Seeing is believing," and many people have that attitude: "If I can't see it, I won't believe it." But do you realize how often people have been deceived by what they see?

Magicians create illusions in which you think you've seen something, but in fact you've been tricked. "How in the world did he push that spit wad right through that solid table?" You think you saw it, but it was an illusion. You were deceived by what you saw.

Jesus more or less said the opposite, "Believing is seeing." If you will believe, then you can see the power of God.

The sin of not believing the Word of God is probably one of the worst sins a person can commit. It is something to marvel, since disbelieving the Word of God can hold you back from a life of rich abundance. Unbelief causes many Christians to wander in the wilderness. They continue to struggle with the flesh and they don't go anywhere. They mark time. They don't gain ground. They can't move forward and they don't conquer the things God wants them to conquer. Instead of living a victorious life, they feel totally defeated.

How often we come to some crossroads of faith and moan, "Oh, but this is a weakness of mine," or "This is a problem that I'm facing," and we say we can't do it. We don't trust God to do the things He has promised to do, tempting God by our unbelief.

Peter said, "Unto us are given exceeding great and precious promises, that through these you may be partakers of the divine nature" (2 Peter 1:4). God has given us glorious promises of victory—promises of deliverance from the powers of darkness—but unbelief will keep us from pressing in. God has provided all we need. All we have to do is step up and take it.

As the people of ancient Israel prepared to enter the Promised Land—after wandering around the desert for forty years—God said to Joshua, "Every place where you put your foot, I have given it to you for your possession" (Joshua 1:3). It's all there! Every place where you put your foot down, it's yours.

You'd think they would have run around the whole country and just kept on running. Even with Joshua leading the way, the Israelites didn't take all the land God had promised them. They stopped short. They were living in the Land of Promise, but when they looked at the power of the enemy rather than at the power of God, fear gripped their hearts.

God could be saying to you, "You've been in the wilderness long enough. It's time to move into the Promised Land. It's time to go in, conquer, and take the victories I have for you. Experience the richness and fullness of a life of faith in Jesus Christ." Don't let unbelief keep you from all the great things God wants to do in your life. Don't choke off God's blessings. By fixing your eyes on Jesus, the door remains wide open. He is merciful, gracious, kind, loving, and He delights in doing good things for His children.

Let Jesus marvel at you for following the Roman centurion's example, not for following the Nazarenes' unbelief.

TOO GOOD TO BE TRUE?

I'm always leery of an offer for a free lunch. I just know they want to sell me something or they're going to push some fund-raising program. There's always some sort of hitch to the thing. And TV offers usually seem too good to be true—and that's because they really *are* too good to be true. Most of the time they're selling junk.

When the Bible says God made the sinless Jesus to be sin for me, that I might be made the righteousness of God through Him—that sounds too good to be true. Why would Jesus take all of my sin upon Himself and give me His righteous standing before the Father? And to believe that though He was rich, yet for my sake He became poor—that through His poverty, I might obtain the promises of eternal life in the kingdom of God—this all seems too good to be true. This challenges our intellect.

But when we come to Jesus, we're no longer talking about free lunches or TV gizmos. We're talking about Someone who made all kinds of outrageous promises—*and then kept them all.*

The disciples of Jesus mourned and wept after the crucifixion because they thought the man they had considered to be the Messiah had perished forever. Even when Mary came to them with news that He had risen, they didn't believe her. It was too good to be true—men don't just rise from the dead.

But remember the disciples had accompanied Jesus to the little town of Nain. As they approached, they heard people wailing in a funeral procession. The grief of one pitiful woman seemed unbearable, because in the coffin lay her only son. Stopping the procession, Jesus commanded the corpse to rise. Incredibly, the young man's eyes flittered opened, he sat up, and Jesus presented him to his mother—alive.

You'd think they would have remembered Lazarus. After all, that event had taken place only a few days earlier. They all saw Lazarus come out of the tomb, still wrapped in his grave clothes. But again, it seemed to have slipped their minds.

Jesus had told them repeatedly, "They're going to crucify Me, but on the third day I will rise again." Now here it was, the third day after His crucifixion. You'd think they'd be all excited, waiting with anticipation and joyful expectancy. But no. They've given up. They're weeping and they're wailing ... all because of their unbelief.

Jesus had asked them to believe something clearly supernatural. But He had also claimed to be more than a mere man—and then He proved it by His works. Still, they didn't believe. At the very moment when they should have had tremendous rejoicing and unutterable happiness and joy, they had grief, wailing and hopelessness. Why? Because of unbelief.

Do you see what unbelief does? It robs you of the joy you should have. It puts you in the slough of despondency and despair. The day Jesus rose from the dead should have been the happiest moment of the disciples' lives. The tomb was empty; the stone was rolled away. Jesus had triumphed over death, hell and the grave. He had risen from the dead to live forevermore. That should have been the most exhilarating day they had ever known. But instead, it was a day of sorrow and gloom.

A POINT OF NO RETURN

A man can come to a place where he has said no to God's grace so many times that finally God just confirms it. Some have refused the gospel so regularly that the invitation to eternal life is no longer extended to them. It isn't because they will not believe; it's that they cannot believe.

> But although He had done so many signs before them, they did not believe in Him, that the word of Isaiah the prophet might be fulfilled, which he spoke: "Lord, who has believed our report? And to whom has the arm of the LORD been revealed?" Therefore they could not believe,

because Isaiah said again: "He has blinded their eyes and hardened their hearts, lest they should see with their eyes, lest they should understand with their hearts and turn, so that I should heal them" (John 12:37-40).

It is tragic when a person has gone so far in his rebellion against God that God allows him the blindness of his own folly. He shuts the man's eyes so that he cannot see. It is possible for a person to reject the Lord so much that he'll come to a place where he *cannot* believe. This is a tragic place—the point of no return.

> There is a time, we know not when,
> A place we know not where,
> That marks the destiny of men
> To glory or despair.
> There is a line by us unseen,
> That crosses every path;
> The hidden boundary between
> God's patience and His wrath. [3]

WHAT WILL YOU CHOOSE?

To believe or not to believe—that is the question. Will you believe in Jesus Christ as the Son of God who died to save you from your sin so that you might enter a life of confidence, joy, blessing and peace? Or will you continue to battle the tides, doing your best to keep your head above the water, living from day to day in fear and anxiety because of what's happening in the world around you?

It's your choice. What you choose makes all the difference in this world and in the world to come.

---

[3] "Life's Boundary Line" (The Doomed Man), words by Dr. J.A. Alexander, 1860.

The Triumph of Faith

For I know that my Redeemer lives.

JOB 19:25

MY MOTHER LIVED WITH US during her final days as she lay dying with cancer. I would sit at her bedside and talk and pray with her. She was a gift of God to me and I loved her deeply.

Cancer is a terrifying diagnosis and its power is unfathomable. As I watched it take the healthy, vibrant life of my mother and reduce her to a shell, I felt both awed and overwhelmed by its ability to destroy.

One morning I sat at the end of her bed, weeping inside. I knew she was suffering. "I'm no hero," I prayed to God, "but I'm willing to take her suffering for a day. Would You just take her pain and put it on me, Lord? Let me bear it for today, that she would have one day of relief from this pain."

Immediately, I felt the presence of Jesus beside me. "Chuck," He said, "that is a foolish request, because I bore the suffering for her."

"Oh, Lord," I said, "how true. Forgive me."

In that moment I witnessed the power of Jesus Christ. What are a few malignant cells compared to the supremacy of Jesus, the Creator of the universe? My focus shifted from the power of cancer to the authority of Jesus—and I realized cancer had no power against Him at all.

At that very instant, my mother suddenly said, "Oh, the pain is gone." God had touched her. And from that time on she never suffered any more pain.

"Lord," I said, "she is Yours. I thank You that I have been blessed by her life. But I'm not going to hang on to her. Though it's going to hurt like everything, Lord, she belongs to You and if You want to take her, that's fine. But, Lord, not with pain—not with suffering." The Lord took her home shortly thereafter. We willingly released her because she had always belonged to Him anyhow. She was just on loan to us.

This incident is one of the most remarkable spiritual experiences of my life. I've never felt closer to Jesus. I knew He was standing right beside me as He spoke to me that day. The experience came at an extremity, where I knew I had come to my own limitations. I reached out because I felt desperate, and the Lord was there to help and to give me victory.

Whatever we face, we need to remember to focus on Him and on His power, not upon the problem. That's how we lay hold of the triumph of faith.

THIS I KNOW

Outside of Jesus, who suffered more than we can ever comprehend, perhaps Job had the roughest time. He had lost nearly everything he had—his possessions, his children, his health, his reputation—and he couldn't figure out why it all happened.

His friends gave him no help. They insisted that Job must have sinned to deserve such pain. No man would suffer as Job had, they said, unless he had done some violent thing against God, either in his heart or overtly. The fact that Job protested his innocence only increased his guilt in their eyes. Nevertheless, Job continued to maintain his innocence, and then he began to describe his misery. No one stood with him. First his friends forsook him, then his own family.

Still, in the midst of his deep despair, Job made a tremendous declaration of faith. "Oh, that my words were written!" he began. "Oh, that they were inscribed in a book! That they were engraved on a rock with an iron pen and lead, forever!" (Job 19:23-24). Ultimately, of course, his words were written and printed in a book, so that we might learn from his extraordinary experience.

What did Job mean? I think he was saying, "I don't know everything. In fact, there are a lot of things that I don't understand at all. But listen to me: I do know one thing. And what I'm about to say is so trustworthy that I wish it could be placed somewhere permanently." What words did Job want engraved in stone for all time? Listen to his amazing confession:

> For I know that my Redeemer lives, and He shall stand
> at last on the earth; and after my skin is destroyed, this I

know, that in my flesh I shall see God, whom I shall see for myself, and my eyes shall behold, and not another (Job 19:25-27).

Job did not know why he had been stripped of everything, suffering miserably and enduring excruciating pain. All this troubled him profoundly: *Why has God allowed me to lose all of my possessions, my children, and my reputation? Why has God allowed me to lose my own health and to go through all of these miseries?*

In the middle of describing his misery, however, he stops and says, "But this is what I do know: My Redeemer lives."

A lot of things in life happen that we cannot and will not understand. Why the problems? Why the suffering? We seek to find answers, but many times we simply cannot know. When I try to comfort someone in pain, I don't say, "Well, maybe it's because of this or that." I often just confess, "We don't know why these things happen. But we do know what is important."

And what is most important? *Never let go of what you do know because of something you don't know.* Or as some say, "Don't doubt in the dark what you know in the light."

Job held tightly to what he did know: "I know that my Redeemer lives." And in that great statement of faith he came to experience the triumph of faith.

GOEL, THE REDEEMER

The word "redeemer" in Hebrew is an interesting term. It's the word *goel*. The word describes that person who would be for you in the day of calamity or trouble, the one who would stand by your side to support and defend you, no matter what.

In those days, if you could not pay a debt and your creditor took you to court, you would be sold as a slave to repay the debt. But if you had a *goel*, he would pay your debt so that you could be freed from slavery. If you bought a house and couldn't make the payments and your house landed in foreclosure, your *goel* would come and pay off the mortgage in order that you might preserve your possession. The *goel* settled the obligations you could not meet. He was your redeemer.

By this point in his story, Job stood alone. His brothers, his family, his friends, his acquaintances, his servants had all turned against him. Even his wife had turned on him. Every earthly support was taken from him, leaving him totally alone … but not quite.

"I know that my Redeemer—the One who stands with me and who stands for me—I know He lives. And He shall stand in the latter day upon the earth." Job believed that his *Goel* lived, and that even though his body would return to the dust, yet in his flesh he would see God.

What makes this so amazing is that Job believed all of these things without the benefit of the New Testament revelation. We have the advantage of the New Testament, which tells us that Jesus lives forever to make intercession for us and that He will never condemn us (Hebrews 7:25; Romans 8:34). Job had no such thing. Yet this despondent man could say, "I still have One who stands with me. All may have forsaken me and turned on me, but I know that my Redeemer lives, my *Goel*, the One who stands for me and is with me. He lives!"

Job had a glorious hope of one day seeing his Lord establish the righteous kingdom of God upon the earth. In the midst of his agony, he focused on his Redeemer, his *Goel*, and so Job began to experience the triumph of faith.

THE PATIENCE OF JOB

Years ago when my Sunday school teacher would ask, "Who is the most patient man who ever lived?" hands would shoot up all over the classroom.

"I know! I know!"

"Yes, Sally?"

"Job."

"That's right."

Job's patience is always highlighted. Since he endured such terrible afflictions, he must have been a very patient man. But the secret of patience is faith, for patience is merely an outgrowth of faith. Though he did not understand the calamities that had befallen him, Job's beliefs about God enabled him to endure his intense sufferings with patience. And what did Job believe that caused him to have such great patience?

Job believed that God was in control of all the circumstances of his life. When he received word of the loss of his cattle, his possessions and all ten of his children, he fell on his face and worshiped God.

> Naked I came from my mother's womb, and naked shall I return there. The LORD gave, and the LORD has taken away; blessed be the name of the LORD (Job 1:21).

Job remained confident that God was in control of every circumstance of his life. God is in control of your circumstances, whether they seem to be of benefit or of pain. Nothing happens to you except what God has allowed to happen.

When Job's wife saw his miserable condition, she couldn't take it. "Job," she said, "why don't you curse God and die? Just get it over with." But Job replied, "Shall we indeed accept good from God, and shall we not accept adversity?" (Job 2:9-10).

Job knew there was One who stood for him in heaven. "Surely even now my witness is in heaven," he declared (Job 16:19). In Hebrew, the word translated "witness" is more literally, "the one who vouches for me." Even if everyone else had turned against him, he knew that One remained who stood for him, who took up his cause and vouched for him.

Paul asked, "If God is for us, who can be against us?" (Romans 8:31). Somehow, despite his awful circumstances, Job knew that God was for him. "My *Goel*—my Redeemer—lives." This conviction allowed Job to triumph over his trial. His utterances of faith were flashes of light in the darkness of his grim circumstances.

When everything shakes and the earth around us crumbles, we must stand upon certain foundational truths:

> God loves us.
>
> God watches over us.
>
> God keeps us and He will neither slumber nor sleep.
>
> God will preserve us.
>
> God will cause us to come forth triumphant.

We need to know our God.

As Paul wrote in 2 Timothy 1:12, "I know whom I have believed and am persuaded that He is able to keep what I have committed to Him until that day." This is coming from Paul, who endured stonings, beatings, and shipwrecks. He endured all of that suffering because he knew in whom he believed. He had placed his trust in the living God, and therefore he could wait with confidence for God to bring him through triumphantly.

One of the hardest Scriptures for me to obey is, "Wait on the LORD" (Psalm 27:14; 37:34). I don't want to wait on the Lord—I want to see it done now. What I need is more patience. And what creates patience? Faith. Faith in God enables us to wait for the purposes of God to be fulfilled.

Rather than praying for patience, pray for faith. "Lord, increase my faith that I might truly understand that I have One who stands for me in heaven—my Redeemer. You're in control of the circumstances of my life, even though I cannot and do not understand why I'm experiencing this awful pain and suffering. I have faith that You're going to work things out for Your eternal plan and purposes."

That's patience fueled by the triumph of faith.

WHY THE PAIN?

Imagine that you have such sharp and constant pain in your abdomen that you finally go to the doctor. He begins to probe and push and asks, "Does that hurt?"

"Yeah."

He pushes the other side. "How about there?"

"Oh, yeah."

"That looks like appendicitis," he says. "Let's take some tests."

He takes a sample of your blood, sends it to the lab, and gets back the results. "Your blood count's pretty high. It indicates appendicitis. We need to go in and take that thing out."

"Oh, but I don't know," you say. "You're going to have to cut me, aren't you? And there's going to be blood. I don't want to be cut. I'd have to lie in bed for a few days, and that means I'd get weak and I wouldn't be able to play golf tomorrow. I don't know if I really want this."

"Okay," he replies, "then let me describe the alternative. If we leave it in and your appendix bursts, the poison will spread through your system, peritonitis will set in, and that will be it for you."

"You mean, I could die?"

"Oh, yes. You bet you could die."

"Well, if you operate, how soon before I could play golf?"

"A couple of weeks."

So you go through all the pain and the weakness of an operation in order that you might recover and resume your normal activities.

In a similar way, some things in your spiritual life can destroy you—and God sees fit to remove these things. You say, "Oh, Lord, that hurts. Please don't do that. You've got to cut that thing out? No, no, no, Lord."

"If I don't, it can destroy you."

And so God allows these times of weaknesses, these times of pain, as He cuts away from you those things that would destroy you. If you want to experience the triumph of faith, sometimes pain and suffering is the only way to get there.

IT'S ROUGH OUT THERE

We always love to have our great grandkids stay with us. One thing about being a grandparent, you want your house to be fun for the kids. Fortunately, my wife, Kay, knows just how to create that sort of atmosphere. She always has dishes of candy all over the house and all kinds of things for them to play with. You only have them for a few days, so you want them to have fun at Grandma and Grandpa's.

Some time ago when our grandson, William, was still small, he stayed with us for a few days. We had a really wonderful visit, but the time eventually came when William had to leave Grandma and Grandpa's and go home. Seeing that the hour of his departure was at hand, he came to me and sat down for a grandfather-to-grandson talk.

"Grandpa," he said, "I don't want to go home."

"William," I answered, "we've had a great time, but the time has come. You have to go home."

"No, Grandpa," he replied. "I don't want to go home. I want to stay with you and Grandma." Of course, that's what every grandparent wants to hear.

"Grandpa," he continued firmly, "You don't understand. There's not a lot of candy at my house. It's awfully rough living at home."

I find it can be awfully rough living here in this world too. I don't understand why many things happen, but I do know that our present sufferings are not worthy to be compared with the glory that shall be revealed. Our Redeemer lives and one day we will stand with Him in victory.

VICTORY OVER EVERY CIRCUMSTANCE

It is possible, of course, for you to program failure into your life. You can say, "Well, I can never do that." And so you won't. You've already preprogrammed your failure.

However, you can also preprogram victory. "I can do all things through Christ who strengthens me" (Philippians 4:13). If you'll learn to trust in the Lord, you can have victory over every circumstance of life. God will take care of you and enable you to triumph over anything that harasses you.

In high school, I worked one summer as a framer building barracks at El Toro Marine Base. As the guys on my crew sat and ate lunch, I would witness to them about the Lord.

One day while doing some heavy pounding, I hit the nail but the hammer slipped and hit my thumb. I blew up, yelled and hurled my hammer far out into the field. Too bad I wasn't in a hammer throw contest—I would have won. I had to slink all the way out into that field to find the hammer. The whole time I heard snickering, and my conscience worked me over good. *Great witness you are, telling them you're a Christian and blowing up like that.* I went through all kinds of condemnation and spiritual torment because of my foolish action. I had a quick temper and a tendency to respond vehemently.

I felt so bad about the incident that I actually quit the job. *What a miserable witness I am to the Lord,* I thought. What used to upset me worse than anything else was self-inflicted pain. I'd bump my head on a cupboard door, or trip and slam into a chair—and it would always trigger a strong response. So I confessed to the Lord that I just didn't have the ability to control the steam building up inside me, and I asked Him to help.

About five years had passed. I had finished Bible college and was pastoring a church in Tucson, Arizona. One fellow from church, Nells, came to help me remodel the platform to make a couple of extra Sunday school rooms. Together we framed a wall and lifted it up, and I got ready to fasten the floor plate. I had to set a sixteen-penny nail, and I have to confess, I wanted to show off by driving it in with one blow. So I brought down that framing hammer hard—and just like five years before, the hammer hit the nail but slipped off and slammed into my thumb. My thumb split open and excruciating pain shot through my body. To this day, I still have a deformed thumb from that experience. I looked up at Nells, smiled and said, "This is wonderful."

He looked at me as if to say, "What's wrong with you? There's blood all over the place and you say that's *wonderful?*"

"Nells," I said, "there's no boiling inside."

Suddenly I recognized that the Lord had given me victory over my temper, an area that I had tried so hard to control, but couldn't. And then I realized, *I haven't blown up since that day at El Toro.*

Because I am a new creature in Christ, the Lord will work in me to give me victory over the old nature that once controlled my life. I have found that to enjoy this kind of triumph I must acknowledge my inability to do it myself. For a long time I sought to control my temper. I would do well for a while, but then something would come up and it erupted again. I tried different strategies—count to ten and similar methods—until that experience at El Toro when I finally confessed, "Lord, I just can't control it."

Years ago a retired Navy man in our church accepted Christ. He had a beautiful, sound conversion and really began growing in his relationship with the Lord. Of course, as a retired Navy man, his language wasn't always the best.

One day he was mowing his lawn and singing a praise chorus when he accidentally ran into the branch of a tree. It hit him in the forehead, knocked him to the ground and raised a big, red lump on his forehead. He turned off the mower and strode into the house to see his wife.

"What happened to *you?*" she asked.

"Oh, the greatest thing in the world," he replied.

"What do you mean?"

"I ran into the limb of a tree and it knocked me over—but I didn't cuss."

She smiled and said, "Well, Honey, I haven't heard you cuss since you accepted the Lord."

"Really?" he wondered aloud. The Lord had delivered him, and he hadn't noticed. Often, that's the way Jesus works. It's the triumph of faith—something that the Lord wants you to experience and enjoy for yourself.

HE BURIES YOUR FAILURES

When God finally writes the records for you, He's going to write the triumphs of your faith—but all your failures will be buried. God accounts you righteous in and through your faith in Jesus. Even though your faith is not yet perfected, when God makes His final account, He will remain faithful to His promise to completely blot out every record of your sin and your failure.

As Job learned, there is One who paid the price. You owed a debt you could not pay and you stood condemned. You were sold into slavery in order to satisfy your debt—but your Redeemer, Jesus Christ, paid it for you. He set you free from the bondage of sin. Your Redeemer lives and He stands in your stead. He is making intercession for you at this moment, and one day He will stand upon the earth—and you will stand with Him in the glories of His kingdom.

Even though your body will die and be cremated or buried, yet you will see God. You're going to dwell with Him forever, because your Redeemer lives. And so, forever, you will experience the thrill of the triumph of faith.

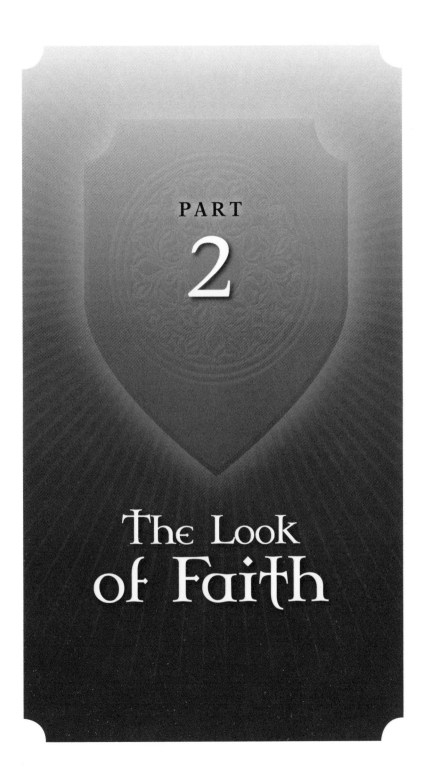

PART

2

The Look
of Faith

Faith

Abraham:
Man of Faith

*Grow in the grace and knowledge of our
Lord and Savior Jesus Christ.*

2 PETER 3:18

WE ARE LIVING IN AN IMPATIENT, instant, get-it-now society. Have you noticed? With the advent of the microwave oven, we've conditioned ourselves to expect hot food to appear within two minutes of discovering we're hungry. And woe if it takes longer than two minutes! Unfortunately, we have those same expectations of faith.

Just as we expect a big bag of microwave popcorn to appear almost instantly out of a flat bag, we want to become spiritual giants quickly—overnight, if possible. We read about the kind of super-faith that can move mountains and we think, *I'd like some of that. And I'd like it now.* I'll confess that I wouldn't mind having the ability to say to a mountain, "Be thou removed and cast into the sea."

We think if only we had the faith of Abraham, we'd have instant spiritual success. What we're forgetting is that Abraham's faith grew through a prolonged fellowship with God. It didn't happen overnight. It was only as he got to know God better, discovering and then rediscovering His faithfulness, Abraham's faith expanded and developed—even as your faith will expand and develop as you walk with God and encounter His faithfulness.

LEAVING HOME

At the time God first called Abram, his father, Terah, was an idolater. Although God had instructed Abram to separate from his relatives and leave Ur of the Chaldeans, Abram ended up traveling only as far as Haran, a town in the northwest corner of Babylon—and he traveled there with his father and his nephew, Lot. Abram did not totally obey the command of God.

The text tells us that Abram and his family acquired many servants and goods while living in Haran, suggesting that they enjoyed a time of prosperity. Perhaps that's why Terah wanted to linger there. The name "Terah" means delay. Abram delayed in Haran until he reached the age of seventy-five. Even though the Lord had clearly told Abram, "Get out of your country, from your family and from your father's house, to a land that I will show you" (Genesis 12:1), Abram didn't finish the journey that God had commanded him until Terah died. Only then did Abram begin searching for a city whose foundation and maker and builder was God (Hebrews 11:10).

It's amazing when you stop to think that Abraham took that first step without knowing his destination. Faith enabled Abraham to begin that journey, and faith sustained him along the way.

Abram traveled about 450 miles until he came to Canaan, the future land of Israel. By faith, he lived in that land—but always in a tent. He never built a home. Abram lived as a stranger and a sojourner in the land that he knew would one day belong to his children and to his descendants. And so he journeyed as a stranger, all the while believing the promise of God: "This is the land that God will give to my descendants."

Of course, the Lord had something much bigger in mind for Abram than just a guarantee of land. He promised, "I will make you a great nation; I will bless you and make your name great; and you shall be a blessing." Today, the three major monotheistic religions of the world—Islam, Judaism, and Christianity—all revere the name of Abraham. And how would God make Abram a "blessing"? He said, "In you all the families of the earth shall be blessed" (Genesis 12:2-3). This blessing was to come upon all the families of the earth—a clear prophecy of the Messiah. It is through Abraham's seed, Jesus Christ, that the blessing of God has come upon us all.

Oh, what glorious promises! And these promises were not given because of Abraham's goodness, but because of the Lord's grace. God certainly didn't bless him because he was a good man. Neither does God bless us because we're good.

God's blessings come to us solely by virtue of His grace. That's why we seldom expect them. For some reason, we've convinced ourselves that God blesses us only when we deserve it, as some sort of reward for our goodness. Not so. The blessings of God come to us because of His grace, and for no other reason. Never expect God to bless you because of what you are. Expect God to bless you because of who He is.

ONE STEP AFTER ANOTHER

The Lord appeared to Abram seven times as recorded in the book of Genesis. Each appearance drew Abraham a little deeper into communion and fellowship with God.

The first appearance occurred in Babylon when God said to Abram, "Get out of this place." God caused Abram to become discontent so that he might search out another place to worship God. The Lord did not appear again to Abram until he entered the land of Canaan. His disobedience stalled the work of God in his life.

God leads us a step at a time. I would appreciate it if God told me exactly what He has in mind for me by the end of the year. If I knew only a little further in advance, I could plan accordingly—but God gives you and me only one step at a time. And He won't give us the next step until we take the current one.

I can stand and say, "Lord, where do we go from here?"

And He will respond, "Well, step out there."

"Okay, where am I going after that? What will You do then?"

And He will remain silent. He will not give me the next step. I can stand there for days saying, "I don't know if I want to go that second step. I don't know what it is. Maybe I don't want to do that. Lord, what should I do?"

"Step out."

"Where do I go after that?"

Silence. God never gives us the next step until we take the first step. A genuine walk of faith always comes one step at a time, a lesson Abram had to learn.

When God gave Abram instructions to move away from Babylon, the Lord did not appear to Abram again until he reached the land to which God had called him. How many months or years had elapsed? We don't know. But in Canaan, Abram had finally reached the place where God could give him the next step.

"To your descendants I will give this land" (Genesis 12:7). Abram hadn't known where God was leading him when he left Babylon. But in time he discovered God's chosen place for him.

Abram happily remained in Canaan until a severe drought hit the region, then his faith wavered and he started weighing his options. Thinking that he could take better care of his family in Egypt, he hightailed it there. This was yet another misstep of faith. Disaster awaited him in Egypt: fear, lies, rebuke and deportation. At the close of this sad affair, Abram returned to Bethel, "where his tent had been at the beginning" (Genesis 13:3). The name Bethel means "the house of God." Abram came back to the place where God had last appeared to him, back to where he had built an altar to the Lord.

Abram's choice, Egypt, had proven to be a time of spiritual barrenness. A lack of faith led Abram to turn to a pagan nation for help, instead of depending upon God to supply his needs in Canaan. His Egyptian adventure caused him not only physical problems, but also spiritual death. So Abram returned to Canaan, the Land of Promise, and called upon the Lord once more at Bethel.

It's always good to return to that place where you first met God. Blessings await us there. Returning to our spiritual roots has a way of getting us back on track with the Lord so we can resume our walk of faith. That's exactly what happened to Abram.

ABRAM AND LOT SEPARATE

Not long after Abram and Lot returned to Canaan, a problem arose between them. They each had large flocks, herds and tents, and it became clear that the land could not support them both. So Abram invited Lot to choose a portion of the land and occupy whatever part he desired. If Lot went to the right, Abram would go to the left. We read, "And Lot lifted up his eyes and saw all the plain of Jordan … then Lot chose for himself all the plain of Jordan" (Genesis 13:10, 11). We learn that while Lot was a man of sight, Abram was a man of faith. Abram could see the invisible, while Lot was fixed on the visible.

The sojourn in Egypt had cost Lot as he acquired a real taste for the fine things available in an advanced, pagan culture. So as a man of sight, not of faith, Lot chose the place in Canaan that most resembled Egypt: the plain of Jordan, the home of Sodom and Gomorrah.

By all rights, Lot should have deferred the choice to Abraham—that would have been the honorable thing to do as the nephew and as the younger man. Yet even so, we have no indication that Abram felt animosity toward Lot. Abram had such a strong commitment to God that the choice didn't matter to him. "I'll take what's left, Lot. You take what you want." It's beautiful to witness a life of commitment that is able to say, "Whatever way the Lord leads, I'll take it."

READY TO OBEY FULLY

With Lot moved to the plain of Jordan, Abram had finally obeyed God's instructions fully. Not only had Abram left Babylon, he had now also separated himself from his family. I like that about God. If we're not willing at first to follow His command, then He'll allow things to happen so we will become willing. Because God loves you, He is going to see His plan executed in your life. You may rebel against it. You may disobey, but God will continue to work in your life until you become willing.

That's just what happened to Abram. After Lot and Abram separated from one another, the Lord again appeared to Abram and said, "Abram, look north." From that point, Abram could see Mount Hermon. "Now look south, down toward the Negev. Look east toward Moab and the plain of Jordan. Look west toward the Mediterranean. You see all of that land? I'm going to give it all to you and your descendants, forever." And then God added,

> And I will make your descendants as the dust of the earth: so that if a man could number the dust of the earth, then your descendants also could be numbered. Arise, walk in the land through its length and width, for I give it to you (Genesis 13:16-17).

God was saying, "Abram, I've given all this land to your descendants, who will outnumber the grains of sand on the seashore. That's how much I'm going to bless you. However, you must step out and appropriate it. Walk through the land, from north to south and from east to west, because I have given it to you." So that's just what Abram did. Through this incident, Abram provides us with yet another example of what it means to walk in faith with God.

Just as Abram needed to step out in faith and walk the land, we need to do the same. When God promises something to us, we must step out in faith and appropriate those promises. We need to lay hold of them in order for God to bless us.

THE GREATEST PROMISE OF ALL

Genesis 15 records Abram and God's next conversation:

> "Look now toward heaven, and count the stars if you are
> able to number them. So shall your descendants be." And
> he believed in the LORD, and He accounted it to him for
> righteousness (Genesis 15:5-6).

This time, Abram gave the very best response one can give when
God issues a promise: he believed God. This is more remarkable
than it appears on the surface, because Abram didn't just believe
that God was going to give him a lot of descendants. Abram
believed that God would, through his descendants, bring the
Messiah into the world.

The word translated "descendants" is actually the Hebrew
term for "seed"—in the singular, not the plural. That's why the
apostle Paul said in Galatians 3:16, "Now to Abraham and his
Seed were the promises made." He does not say, "And to seeds,"
as of many, but as of one, "And to your Seed," who is Christ.

Abraham believed God's promise that his Seed, the Messiah,
would one day come into the world. He looked forward in time
and believed the promise of God. We look back in time at the
fulfillment of the promise in the coming of Jesus Christ. When
we believe that Jesus died for our sins upon the cross, and on the
third day after His crucifixion rose from the dead, God accounts
us righteous, just as He did Abraham, the man of faith.

THIRTEEN YEARS OF SILENCE

Genesis chapter 16 tells the story of one of Abram's greatest
missteps. Though he had the very promise of God that his wife

would bear him a son, Abram went along with Sarai's plan to bring a son into the world through Hagar, her Egyptian servant. But such a son, brought into the world through the flesh, could never be the "son of promise" that God promised to Abram.

When Ishmael was born—the son of Abram and Hagar—Abram was about eighty-six years old. God was silent at Ishmael's birth, and did not speak to Abram again for thirteen long years. When God finally broke His silence, it was to inform Abram that Ishmael was not the child of His promise.

> When Abram was ninety-nine years old, the LORD appeared to Abram and said to him, "I am Almighty God; walk before Me and be blameless [or perfect]" (Genesis 17:1).

The word translated "almighty" is the Hebrew term *El Shaddai*. This term *shad* means "breast" in Hebrew, the place of life and nourishment. God is saying to Abram, "I am the place of your life and your nourishment. It all comes from Me. I am God Almighty. I am *El Shaddai*, and you must look to Me for life." The living promises of God can only be fulfilled by the living God Himself.

"I am the Almighty God; walk before Me and be blameless." Walking before God means walking in His presence, conscious that God is watching you and caring for you. As you walk before Him, you walk in the presence of the Lord Almighty and in the awareness that God places His hand on your life. Exactly *how* are you to walk? God says we are to walk in a blameless or perfect way. God's ideal requirement for humankind is perfection.

I'm not surprised God would require me to be perfect. In fact, I would feel shocked if God said, "Hey, go ahead and be slipshod and cruddy. Be as you want." That would not be in keeping with the holy and perfect nature of God. God could not require anything less than perfection of us. So the apostle Paul could write, "Be perfect" or aim for perfection (2 Corinthians 13:11).

Abram had been far from perfect, and after thirteen long years of silence, God had a lot to say to him.

> "And I will make My covenant between Me and you, and will multiply you exceedingly." Then Abram fell on his face, and God talked with him, saying: "As for Me, behold, My covenant is with you, and you shall be a father of many nations. No longer shall your name be called Abram, but your name shall be Abraham" (Genesis 17:2-5).

When God inserted the Hebrew letter "H" into the name of Abram, you might say He inserted Himself into his name. That letter is made with the sound of breath. The Hebrew word *ruach*, which means "breath," doubles as the word for "Spirit." In a significant way, God transformed Abram to Abraham by inserting the Spirit into his name. In so doing, God also made a new covenant with Abram—the covenant of circumcision (Genesis 17:10). In effect He said, "Abraham, in order to become a spiritual man, I want you to cut off the flesh. I want that "H" to become a new reality for you. From this time forward, I want you to walk after the Spirit and follow the things of the Spirit."

God considered this covenant so important that He declared that if any of Abram's family refused the rite of circumcision, they were to be cut off from being the people of God. No circumcision meant no connection to the Lord's people. Why should God place such stress on circumcision? He did so because He wanted to remind His people that they were to live by faith, not by the flesh.

In time to come, no male baby (or new male convert) was considered a Jew until he was circumcised. He didn't become a Jew by natural birth. He became a Jew the day he was circumcised. That was the rite which all males practiced to indicate that he would walk after the Spirit.

Both then and now, *no one* can be a man or woman of God and walk after the flesh. You can only be a disciple of the Lord as you continually walk after the Spirit by faith.

Remember, circumcision was meant as a symbol. When we get to the New Testament, Paul shows the folly of trusting in a mere ritual. He says it's ridiculous to think that you are a Jew just because you've been circumcised. Circumcision doesn't benefit anyone who does not walk and live after the Spirit through faith. The fleshly rite does nothing; therefore, uncircumcised Gentiles who walk after the Spirit and not the flesh are also considered the people of God. True circumcision is of the heart (Romans 2:29).

At the same time God changed Abram's name to Abraham, He also altered the name of Abram's wife, Sarai. He added the same "H"—the breath, the Spirit, the Hebrew letter pronounced with air. Thus God symbolized the insertion of His Spirit and life into this couple, bringing them into a new dimension of life after the Spirit. God said to Abraham about Sarah,

> I will bless her and also give you a son by her; then I will bless her, and she shall be a mother of nations; kings of peoples shall be from her (Genesis 17:16).

When Paul speaks of this vital incident, he calls Abraham's body "already dead," (since he was about 100 years old), and speaks of "the deadness of Sarah's womb" (Romans 4:19). He therefore implies that Abraham was too old to have children and that Sarah could no longer bear children.

God waited to act until Abraham could do absolutely nothing to fulfill the promise by himself. God didn't want Abraham trying to fulfill His promises in his own strength. For the promise to be fulfilled, it would clearly take a miracle of God. The Lord allowed Abraham to get to the place of absolute human impossibility.

Do you know that God often allows us to come to the end of ourselves, to the end of our resources, to the end of our ideas? He lets us get to a place of hopelessness before He works.

When God works, He wants all the glory for what He has done. God allows you to get into totally impossible situations where you throw your hands up in desperation and say, "That's it. I've had it. There is no way." Then God steps in and works—and when He does, there's no way that you or I can boast.

When Abraham heard that he and Sarah would have a son, what do you think he did? The Bible says he laughed—not the laugh of doubt or unbelief, but a laugh of astonishment (Genesis 17:17). If it were the laugh of unbelief, then God would have rebuked him as He did later with Sarah (Genesis 18:12-15).

Once Abraham recovered from hearing this news, God reiterated His promise that Sarah would bear him a son; and then He instructed Abraham to call the child Isaac, which means "laughter" (Genesis 17:19). To think that at their advanced age they should have a baby, how could they call the little boy anything but Laughter?

When God announced to Abraham that his son would arrive at that time the following year, Sarah overheard the announcement—and that's when she laughed in unbelief. God immediately responded by asking, "Is anything too hard for the LORD?" (Genesis 18:14). How could anything be too hard for the One who created the universe and everything in it? We need to remember this when we pray. Nothing is too hard for God.

A REPEAT OFFENSE

Not long after God made His amazing promise, Abraham and Sarah moved south. And, believe it or not, Abraham made the same mistake he had made twenty-five years earlier. He lied. He tried to pass off Sarah as his sister—this time to King Abimelech.

One thing that makes his action so evil is that Abraham had been walking with the Lord for many years at this point. By now he should have advanced further in his faith. Yet by lying to Abimelech, Abraham put God's plan at risk. God had declared that through Sarah would his seed be called. The promise of God was to come through Isaac, the one born not of the flesh but of the Spirit. If Abimelech had sexual relations with Sarah, God's plan could have been jeopardized. How could Abraham prove that any child born after that incident was his? Perhaps Sarah was already pregnant. Had there been any physical relationship with Abimelech, then the question would always be there: Was this truly the child God had promised? And the questions would continue to surface even concerning Jesus Christ, of the seed of Abraham.

When Abraham did not protect his wife, God moved in a sovereign way to protect His plan. God appeared in a dream to Abimelech and warned him that if he so much as touched Sarah, he would die (Genesis 20:3).

God will always protect His plan. I may fail. You may fail. If we do, God will raise up someone else to stand in our place.

I find it interesting that these times of failure can so often become times of growth. God, in His love and grace, reveals our areas of weakness so that He might make us strong. When God shows me those areas of my flesh that displease Him, He does not show them to me in a condemning way, but in order that He might cause me to understand the next area where I can expect Him to work. I just look at it as God putting up an "Under Construction" sign. That's the place in my life where He will go to work next.

That's what He did with Abraham, and that's what He'll do with you too.

THE CHILD IS BORN

Exactly at the time God had specified, Sarah gave birth to a son. The Bible says simply, "And the LORD visited Sarah as He had said, and the LORD did for Sarah as He had spoken" (Genesis 21:1).

That verse has a marvelous ring to it and resonates within my heart. God did exactly what He said He would do, exactly as He spoke it.

When at last God moved to fulfill His promise to Abraham, He did an amazing job of restoring Sarah physically. For not only did she give birth to Isaac, but she nursed him. The Lord totally rejuvenated Abraham too, because after the death of Sarah—when he was 137 years old—he married a woman by the name of Keturah and had six other children by her (Genesis 25:1-2).

THE DEATH OF ABRAHAM

Abraham lived to the ripe old age of 175. "Then Abraham breathed his last," the Bible says, "and died in a good old age, an old man and full of years, and was gathered to his people" (Genesis 25:8). As we look at Abraham's life, we can feel sure that Psalm 1 applies to him:

> Blessed is the man who walks not in the counsel of the ungodly, nor stands in the path of sinners, nor sits in the seat of the scornful. But his delight is in the law of the LORD, and in His law he meditates day and night. He shall be like a tree planted by the rivers of water, that brings forth its fruit in its season, whose leaf also shall not wither; and whatever he does shall prosper (Psalm 1:1-3).

Abraham's leaf did not wither—God prospered him and he lived to be 175 years old. Abraham made the God of the universe his place of refuge—and as a result, the eternal, living God blessed his faith, right up until the day he died.

GOD USES IMPERFECT PEOPLE

The New Testament repeatedly uses Abraham as the classic example of a man of faith. Yet, as we've seen, the Old Testament records several instances where Abraham's faith wavered. Never does the New Testament mention the failure of Abraham's faith. God overlooks those lapses and tells us only of his triumphs.

It proves that God uses imperfect people. Had Abraham been totally perfect—never wavering in his faith—then I would feel discouraged. I would assume that God couldn't use me, because I'm painfully aware of my imperfections. At times I question the things of God. Sometimes I have lapses of faith. I don't trust

God completely as I should. Difficulties come and I try to figure my way out rather than resting in God to see me through the problem.

The experience of Abraham comforts me. It reassures me to know that God will take me in the state I am and will begin His work in me by His Spirit, transforming me into the image of Christ through faith. He uses me, even though I am not perfect.

Maybe you have been using this very excuse for your failure to commit yourself totally to serve the Lord: "I'm so imperfect, God can't possibly use me." We fixate on our imperfections, flaws and weaknesses rather than on our Creator. God wants to use you, as He did with Abraham.

Remember that God uses yielded vessels, not perfect vessels. God desires, of course, to conform us into the image of Christ by His Spirit. But it's a process. No one can stand up and say, "I am thankful that I have been completely perfected in Jesus Christ. I never get angry or upset. I always have the sweetest, most pleasant disposition. I'm great to be around, all the time." Try saying it sometime, and watch everyone around you erupt in laughter.

> But grow in the grace and knowledge of our Lord and Savior Jesus Christ (2 Peter 3:18).

As Abraham got to know God better, his faith increased—and so will yours, as your knowledge of God grows. The more you get to know the Lord, the more you will trust Him—just like Abraham, the man of faith.

Isaac:
Son of Faith

But My covenant I will establish with Isaac,
whom Sarah shall bear to you at this set time next year.

GENESIS 17:21

IF ABRAHAM HAD BEEN ALLOWED to have his way, there might never have been an Isaac.

When God told Abraham that Sarah would bear him a son in their old age, Abraham said to God, "Oh, that Ishmael might live before You!" (Genesis 17:18).

Ishmael—the child of Abraham and Hagar, Sarah's servant—was thirteen years old at the time and Abraham had become very attached. It's possible Abraham was really saying, "Well, Lord, that's all right. There's no need for Sarah to have a son. Let Ishmael live before You."

But God said no. God promised to establish His covenant with Isaac, "an everlasting covenant, and with his descendants after him" (Genesis 17:19). God intended to bless the son of promise, Isaac, and not the son of the flesh, Ishmael.

The next year at the time the Lord had predicted, Isaac came along—and what joy and laughter he brought to the lives of his elderly parents. Eight days after the boy's birth, Abraham circumcised his infant son, as God had commanded, so that Isaac might become one of the covenant people of God. A few years passed and the time came to wean Isaac, calling for a big community celebration.

Ishmael, who was by then fifteen or sixteen years old, no doubt felt jealousy toward Isaac. For thirteen years he had been his dad's pride and joy, but now everyone was so excited about Isaac. This disgruntled teenager sat in one corner of the feast, sneering at the whole affair. When Sarah saw him mocking, she approached her husband and demanded that he evict Ishmael and his mother. Her request deeply distressed Abraham, but God told him, "Whatever Sarah has said to you, listen to her voice; for in Isaac your seed shall be called" (Genesis 21:12). Reluctantly, Abraham sent away Ishmael and his mother. And from that point on, Isaac remained the center of attention.

LOOKING FOR A WIFE

As Isaac grew into adulthood, Abraham desired to find a wife for him—but he didn't want Isaac to marry a pagan woman in the area. He began to think about how he might find a suitable mate from among his own kin in faraway Mesopotamia.

Abraham's brother, Nahor, had several daughters, but they were much too old for Isaac, since Isaac hadn't arrived until Abraham had reached the century mark. That meant the grandchildren of Nahor would be closer to the right age. So Abraham turned to his chief servant, and gave him the task of finding a bride for his son, Isaac.

Abraham's servant knew this would be no easy job. He had to travel 500 miles and then coax a young girl to hop on a camel and ride 500 miles back across the desert to marry a man she had never met. She'd never see her parents or her home again. So the servant asked, "What if she is not willing? Shall I then take Isaac back to the land?"

"No, definitely not," Abraham replied. "Isaac is not to leave this land." Isaac never did leave the Land of Promise. In faith, Abraham declared that God Himself would send His angel ahead of his servant to give him success (Genesis 24:7).

So the servant made the long trek to Mesopotamia. Once there he prayed silently that the God of Abraham would direct his steps. Before he finished praying, the servant met a friendly young woman—gorgeous, caring, and single. The servant must have wondered, *Could this be the one?*

When he asked her name, she replied, "I am the daughter of Bethuel, Milcah's son, whom she bore to Nahor" (Genesis 24:24). She was the granddaughter of Nahor, Abraham's brother. The servant instantly bowed down and worshiped, for here was proof that the Lord had sent His angel ahead of him.

> Blessed be the LORD God of my master Abraham, who has not forsaken His mercy and His truth toward my master: And as for me, being on the way, the LORD led me to the house of my master's brother (Genesis 24:27).

Notice, "Being on the way, the Lord led me." In order to be led by the Lord, it's important that you get moving. If you say, "I'm just waiting on God to lead me and I'll sit here until He does," then you will probably sit for the rest of your life. Stand up and start walking.

The young woman invited the servant to her home, and he explained his errand to her family. It must have excited them to hear of the glory of his master, of the riches and the wonders of his master's kingdom, and of the master's son, appointed heir of all things.

When Rebekah's relatives recognized the obvious hand of God, they agreed to her departure. In return the servant gave them expensive gifts and asked permission to rejoin his master immediately. They requested a slight delay, but when the servant told them how urgent the matter was to Abraham, they sent her off with their blessing.

And then one evening, Rebekah and Abraham's servant saw in the distance a man walking in a field. Suddenly the man started coming towards them and Rebekah asked, "Who is this man walking in the field to meet us?"

"It is my master," the servant replied. Then Rebekah covered herself with a veil and the Scripture reads,

> Isaac brought her into his mother Sarah's tent; and he took Rebekah and she became his wife, and he loved her. So Isaac was comforted after his mother's death (Genesis 24:67).

Sarah had been dead for three years by the time Isaac, at age forty, married Rebekah. As Abraham's own life neared its end, he gave everything he had to Isaac. And when Abraham died soon afterward, Isaac and Ishmael buried him in the cave of Machpelah, where Sarah had been buried before (Genesis 25:9).

Though earlier a breach had opened between the half-brothers, they came together to give their father a proper burial.

With the funeral over, God made a point of blessing Isaac, who then moved to the Negev, to Beer Lahairoi, where he had first met Rebekah.

ABRAHAM'S MISTAKE REVISITED

About a hundred years after Abraham endured a famine, another one hit during Isaac's time. When Abraham had faced his famine, he fled to Egypt. Isaac may have intended to do the same thing, but God instructed him not to go there.

The Lord directed Isaac to "sojourn" in the land of the Philistines, but to "dwell" in the land God would show him. The Hebrew word translated "dwell" means to settle down and make a home, while "sojourn" implies just a stopover or a temporary stay. God told Isaac, "Don't go down to Egypt, but dwell in the land that I will show you. In the meanwhile, you are to sojourn in this land. Stay here temporarily and I will be with you and bless you."

Unfortunately, Isaac did not obey the Lord. Instead of sojourning in Gerar, he settled there. And then he made a very big mistake.

> And the men of the place asked him about his wife. And he said, "She is my sister"; for he was afraid to say, "She is my wife," because he thought, "lest, the men of the place should kill me for Rebekah; because she is beautiful to behold" (Genesis 26:7).

Isaac disobeyed God by settling in the area—and then we find him lying. There are some places where God's children have no business going. Isaac had no business dwelling in Gerar, and as a result, the men of the area began asking about his wife. And his fear—a sign of a lack of faith—led him to lie.

Abraham had done exactly the same thing a century before, in the same place, under the same conditions, with the same lapse of faith. Both patriarchs feared that the men of the land might kill them in order to get their wives.

Eventually the king of the Philistines saw Isaac caressing his wife and recognized the lie—and he called Isaac on it. The story of how God had plagued the Philistines and almost wiped them out because of Sarah no doubt remained in the memory of the people, and so the king rebuked Isaac. It is tragic when a man of God gets rebuked by the world. The Bible says that those who bear the vessels of the Lord must be clean and holy.

The king immediately made it a capital offense for anyone to touch Isaac or his wife. Isaac settled down, probably leasing some land and planting it. Despite his sin, God gave him a bumper crop. As Isaac's wealth grew, the Philistines became envious of him—and fearful, eventually asking him to move away.

Isaac first pitched his tent in a nearby valley, but a feud with local herdsmen caused him to move a bit farther. Another squabble caused him to move farther still, and finally he came to a place that caused no friction. From there he traveled to Beersheba, "And the LORD appeared to him the same night and said, 'I am the God of your father Abraham" (Genesis 26:24).

After Isaac returned to Beersheba, where God had told him to dwell, the Lord spoke to him once again. In fact, God appeared to him on the very same night Isaac returned, as though He had been waiting for Isaac to get back on track. So long as Isaac remained in disobedience, God remained silent.

Like Isaac, we miss the Lord when we disobey. When we get off track, we can't hear His voice any longer. God seems far from us. We don't feel His presence or His power. But it isn't that God has moved. It's that we have left the place of blessing.

Isaac built an altar in Beersheba and there called on the name of the Lord. "Do not fear," the Lord told Isaac, "for I am with you" (Genesis 26:24). Isaac had finally reached the place where God wanted him all along.

A PLEA FOR CHILDREN

For twenty years, Rebekah had been unable to conceive. In those days barrenness was considered to be a cultural curse, so Isaac pleaded with the Lord to give the couple children, and God heard his prayer.

Rebekah had a difficult pregnancy, since she was carrying twins. From the very beginning, these two little guys went at it. She sensed something was amiss, so she asked the Lord to give her wisdom. God prophesied that her two boys would spawn two nations and that the older would serve the younger.

When she finally gave birth, her first son came out red, with hair all over. They named him Esau, which means "hairy." Soon afterward his brother came out, grasping Esau's heel. Him they named Jacob, which means "heelcatcher." Ultimately, the name of Jacob came to mean "supplanter" or "deceiver," so maybe "Heelcatcher" wasn't so bad after all.

These twins couldn't have been more different from one another. Esau was a hairy, rugged outdoorsman, while Jacob was more of a mama's boy. Jacob lived in sturdy tents and had a mild manner, but Isaac loved Esau because he liked the venison he caught and prepared. Rebekah loved Jacob and did all she could to advance his cause.

As Isaac grew old, he went blind. One day he asked Esau to make him his favorite meal. "I want some delicious food that my soul might bless you before I die," he said. Notice that the Spirit had no part in this transaction. Isaac's flesh directed the whole operation.

Isaac probably chose this time to give his blessing because he had reached the age of 137, the same age at which his older brother, Ishmael, had died. He may have thought he was dying. He wasn't. He went on to live another forty-three years. Not knowing, he called Esau to bestow upon his favorite son what he thought to be a final blessing. By doing so, Isaac deliberately sought to circumvent the clear intent of God, that the older son would serve the younger. He acted after the flesh.

Rebekah, on the other hand, favoring Jacob, devised a plot whereby Isaac would mistake Jacob for Esau and therefore give the younger son the blessing. So she's not guiltless either. And how about Jacob? He not only went along with Rebekah's scheme, he lied to his father about who he was and where he got the meal. "The LORD your God brought it to me," he said. (Genesis 27:20). And Esau? Esau already had sold his birthright to Jacob for a paltry little meal.

Here again we meet people who have faith in God, but who somehow convince themselves that God cannot accomplish His purposes without their help. How often we do the same. We believe God will do what He has said He will do—but we worry that He can't manage it without our help.

When it comes to the will and the purposes of God, we never have to worry. They will stand without our help. What God has determined to be will be. He will get His work accomplished—and He doesn't need our help.

When the real Esau entered Isaac's tent, the deception came to light. Isaac couldn't recant his blessing—and he realized that God would accomplish His purpose, no matter what. So Isaac affirmed that the blessing would remain with Jacob: "Indeed, he [Jacob] shall be blessed" (Genesis 27:33). Esau begged for another blessing, but this was all he got:

> Behold, your dwelling shall be of the fatness of the earth, and of the dew of heaven from above. By your sword you shall live, and you shall serve your brother; and it will come to pass, when you become restless, that you shall break his yoke from your neck (Genesis 27:39-40).

Fearing Esau's anger, Rebekah decided to send Jacob to live with his faraway relatives, and Isaac agreed. Rebekah's deception cost dearly because Jacob did not return for twenty years—and by then, she was already dead. Before Jacob left, however, Isaac—figuring he would not see Jacob again—gave him the blessing that had first been passed from Abraham to Isaac:

> May God Almighty bless you, and make you fruitful, and multiply you, that you may be an assembly of people; and give you the blessing of Abraham, to you and your descendants with you, that you may inherit the land in which you are a stranger, which God gave to Abraham (Genesis 28:3-4).

Isaac lived to be 180 years old. When he died, his sons, Esau and Jacob, finally came together to bury him. Esau eventually moved to Edom and became the father of the Edomites, who submitted to Israel. The last Edomite that we read about was Herod the Great, appointed by Rome to serve as king over Israel at the time of Jesus Christ.

A WEALTH OF TYPES

The story of Isaac is rich with types that foreshadow events and important figures in the New Testament. One of the best known is the illustration in Galatians 4, where Paul points out that Isaac became a type of the Spirit, while Ishmael became a type of the flesh. When God said to Abraham, "Take now your son, your only son, Isaac," the Lord did not mention Ishmael at all. Why not? Ishmael was the work of the flesh, and God recognizes only the work of the Spirit.

Paul also writes, "Now we, brethren, as Isaac was, are the children of promise" (Galatians 4:28). We also are the children of promise, the work of the Holy Spirit. We live by God's promises. God has promised to forgive us our sins, based solely on the work He has done. Our own works of righteousness count for nothing.

I'm so glad for that. If salvation was predicated upon my works, then some days I think I'd make it and other days I wouldn't. I would be praying constantly, "Lord, please come for me on a good day." But because my standing with Him depends on His finished work alone, He can come at any time. In Him I am a son of promise.

The story of Isaac provides us with several intriguing typologies. Abraham can be seen as the type of God the Father most clearly in his willingness to sacrifice his son on Mount Moriah. And we see Sarah as a type of Israel, God's wife, in her submissive relationship to Abraham. But I'd like us to look closely at the types of Isaac, Eliezer, and Rebekah.

ISAAC: TYPE OF CHRIST

During the entire three-day journey to Mount Moriah, Abraham considered his son as good as dead, since he planned to sacrifice him on the mountain. So when the pair strode down the mountain after the angel spared Isaac's life, it seemed to Abraham as though he had received his son back from the dead. That event foreshadowed the Savior's death and His rising from the dead on the third day.

After the tremendous foreshadowing of Calvary on Mount Moriah, the Bible says, "Abraham returned to his young men, and they rose and went together to Beersheba; and Abraham dwelt at Beersheba" (Genesis 22:19).

Now, where was Isaac? It's interesting that the text doesn't mention him coming back with Abraham. But it makes sense when you realize that Isaac was a type of Christ, who after His death was taken up into heaven and will not appear again until the Holy Spirit brings back the bride for the Son. Interesting that Isaac is not mentioned again until his bride is brought to him from Mesopotamia (Genesis 24:62).

ELIEZER: TYPE OF THE HOLY SPIRIT

Bible commentators have concluded from Genesis 15:2, that Abraham's chief servant's name was Eliezer, although he is not named in Genesis 24. As a type of the Holy Spirit, Eliezer's name is significant. Jesus calls the Holy Spirit "the Comforter." In the Greek this is *parakletos*, which literally means "one who comes alongside to help." In Hebrew, the name Eliezer means "God my helper."

Eliezer is not identified by name in chapter 24, which I believe is a deliberate omission by the Holy Spirit. For Jesus said concerning the Holy Spirit, "He will testify of Me" (John 15:26). The witness and work of the Holy Spirit in the world is not to magnify Himself, but to magnify Jesus Christ.

Once Eliezer met Rebekah's family, we see him wooing her to become the wife of Isaac. As he woos the bride for the son, he testifies of the glory of his master, the glory of his master's kingdom, and of all that his master possesses—and he speaks of a son to whom the father has given everything.

The witness of the Holy Spirit testifies to the same things. He points to the beauty, the glory, the riches, and the wealth of the kingdom of God, and to God's Son, whom the Father has appointed heir of all things. The Spirit woos you to be the bride of Christ, that you might be joint heir with Him of all of the wealth and glories of the eternal kingdom of God.

REBEKAH: TYPE OF THE CHURCH

Long before Abraham's servant traveled to Mesopotamia, God had appointed Rebekah to be the bride of Isaac. "The angel of the LORD will direct you," Abraham told the servant. "He'll lead you to the one." And He did. Just so, God already has chosen the bride of Jesus Christ. All who have received Jesus as Lord and Savior are a chosen generation, elected before the foundation of the world to bring glory and praise to God as the bride of His Son, Jesus Christ.

Genesis describes Rebekah as being very beautiful. Psalm 45, a prophecy concerning the bride of Christ, says that the king desires her beauty. The Lord looks upon you and sees you as His beautiful bride. Sometimes we don't feel very beautiful. When we feel ugly in our actions and our attitude, we can begin to dislike ourselves. How wonderful to know that the Lord sees us as beautiful.

Just as Eliezer gave Rebekah precious things, the Holy Spirit gives us "precious things" as we receive His marvelous gifts, including Himself. He becomes the down payment of our inheritance until the redemption of the purchased possession. The gifts of the Spirit are a mere foretaste of the glory that awaits us when we arrive in the heavenly kingdom.

With only the descriptions of the servant to guide her, Rebekah had already fallen in love with Isaac—sight unseen. And it is through the descriptions in the Bible prompted by the Holy Spirit that we learn to love Jesus, "Whom having not seen you love" (1 Peter 1:8).

DON'T DELAY

The story of Isaac provides one final type that cries out for consideration. When Abraham's servant found Rebekah and asked her family for permission to return home immediately, they said, "Let the young woman stay with us a few days, at least ten; after that she may go" (Genesis 24:55).

These folks are a type of the world that tries to delay your making a commitment to Christ. "Sure, that sounds great," they say. "But why don't you wait awhile? There's no hurry." Everybody wants to be saved someday. "When I die, I don't want to die as a heathen. I want to die the death of the righteous—but later. I want to live a little first."

Oh, what a misstatement. Those without Christ are dead in trespasses and sins. What they're really saying is, "I want to stay dead a little longer."

You don't know what living is all about until you live in Christ. Paul said, "For to me, to live is Christ" (Philippians 1:21). John said, "He who has the Son has life; he who does not have the Son of God does not have life" (1 John 5:12).

How did Abraham's servant respond to the request for a delay? "Do not hinder me," he said, "since the LORD has prospered my way" (Genesis 24:56).

Don't delay in answering the call of God's Spirit. Don't let anyone hinder you. God is inviting you to be His bride. Will you commit your life to Jesus Christ? Will you begin the journey toward Him? That journey will one day lead you into His very presence in the glory of His kingdom. Will you go?

Ruth:
Adventure of Faith

Wherever you go, I will go; and wherever you lodge, I will lodge;
your people shall be my people, and your God, my God.

RUTH 1:16

THE TIME OF THE JUDGES was a time of moral decay, religious confusion, and outright anarchy. Since no king reigned over Israel, every man did what was right in his own eyes—with disastrous results. But even in this bleak period, God was at work. He was preparing a most unlikely family through which the Messiah would one day come.

The book of Ruth fits between the time of the judges and Samuel the prophet. It also serves as our first introduction to David, the great king of Israel. Traditionally, Jews read the book of Ruth at the Feast of Pentecost, which is fitting, since this feast celebrates the gathering of the grain harvest and the book of Ruth has much to do with the harvest.

The story begins during a period of famine in Judah. A man from Bethlehem took his wife and two sons to Moab to find food, but there the man died, leaving his wife, Naomi, a widow. Her two surviving sons married Moabites, but after about ten years, both her sons also died. That left a penniless refugee from Bethlehem living in a foreign land with two other widows. With nowhere else to turn for help, she decided to return home and hope for a better life there.

Broken, Naomi pleaded with her two daughters-in-law to remain in Moab, their homeland. "Look, girls, you don't need to feel responsible for me. I'm going to return to Bethlehem, and you girls should each go back to your own mother's home. I pray that God will be gracious to you, even as you've been gracious to me and to my sons, your late husbands."

Both young women wept at Naomi's words and refused to leave her. So Naomi told them again, "Listen, I'm old. There's no sense in returning with me. I don't plan to remarry or have any more children, and even if I did, you wouldn't want to wait for them to grow up. So you go back home, find husbands and be happy."

All three women wept together, and eventually one of the women, Orpah, heeded her mother-in-law's advice and returned to her own people. The other woman, Ruth—a name that means "beauty"—insisted on staying with Naomi. And then we read one of the most touching speeches in all of Scripture:

> Ruth said: "Entreat me not to leave you, or to turn back from following after you; for wherever you go, I will go; and wherever you lodge, I will lodge; your people shall be my people, and your God, my God. Where you die, I will

die, and there will I be buried. The LORD do so to me, and more also, if anything but death parts you and me" (Ruth 1:16-17).

Through this impassioned statement, Ruth—a pagan Moabite by birth—declares her spiritual commitment. Somewhere along the line, no doubt through the witness of her deceased husband, she had come to believe and trust in the Lord. She had no interest in returning to the false gods of her own people. She wanted to be with Naomi.

Ruth's commitment has become a magnificent expression of fidelity and love. One line in particular is recognized immediately as being part of our traditional wedding vows: "Until death do us part." Ruth committed herself to Naomi to stay with her so long as she lived.

A SAD RETURN TO BETHLEHEM

When Naomi and Ruth finally made it back to Bethlehem, the whole village started buzzing about Naomi's return. They asked, "Is this Naomi?"

Naomi had not returned with a glad heart, and she replied, "Do not call me Naomi; call me Mara, for the Almighty has dealt bitterly with me" (Ruth 1:20). The name Naomi means "pleasantness." Mara means "bitter." She didn't yet know, but God had already been at work on behalf of the two women.

The pair returned to Bethlehem near the beginning of the barley harvest. That became God's time to do something so extraordinary it would affect the lineage of the Messiah Himself.

As we read the second chapter of Ruth, it introduces us to a wealthy man named Boaz, who happened to be a relative of Naomi's deceased husband. Ruth apparently knew something of the laws of Israel, for she asked Naomi for permission to go out to the fields and glean heads of grain. The law of Moses explicitly provided for such a practice:

> When you reap your harvest in your field, and forget a sheaf in the field, you shall not go back to get it; it shall be for the stranger, the fatherless, and the widow, that the LORD your God may bless you in all the work of your hands ... and you shall remember that you were a slave in the land of Egypt; therefore I command you to do this thing (Deuteronomy 24:19, 22).

God had created a welfare law. Instead of going back to pick up grain that had fallen on the ground or to retrieve a forgotten sheaf of grain, landowners were to let it remain for the poor to glean. So Ruth told Naomi, "I'm going to go out and glean. Maybe I'll find grace in the eyes of one of the landowners and he'll let me glean in his field."

The text says that she just "happened to come to the part of the field belonging to Boaz" (Ruth 2:3). Mere chance, however, played no part in it. God was guiding and directing Ruth's footsteps—in ways so natural, she didn't even recognize His hand.

Somehow we have the idea that God's guidance should be mysterious and mystical. We think that when we stumble upon His will, we should hear a set of rapidly intensifying beeps to assure us we're still headed in the right direction. Not so. God has never guided me in that way. Rather, God tends to guide us in ways so natural that many times we're not aware of His guidance until afterwards. And then we say, "Wow, look at that!

If I had not been there at that precise time, I would have missed it. God's hand was on me."

That was Ruth's experience. From a human standpoint, she "just happened" to end up in the field of Boaz. But from the divine perspective, God led her to that specific field to continue His plan of redemption.

Years ago my car battery was going dead. So at lunchtime one day—deciding it was smarter to pay six dollars than thirty-five—I decided to run over to a wrecking yard and pick up a used battery. When I got there I asked if they had any batteries for an Oldsmobile.

"Oh, I think we've got a wreck out there," one of the guys said, "but you'll have to get it out yourself. I don't have time to do it."

Borrowing their tools, I found the wreck, took out its battery, and put it in my car—and the thing had no juice. So I had to take it out again. As I removed it, I noticed someone familiar walking by. "Charlie!" I called out.

He stopped, looked at me and said, "Chuck!"

"What are you doing here?" I asked.

"Oh," he replied, "I came over to get a piece for my car. I'm living in Riverside now."

Years before, Charlie had attended my Sunday school class in Tucson. As we stood in that wrecking yard talking, it quickly became clear that he had wandered away from God. I had a chance to talk to him about spiritual things and we prayed together, right there in the yard. Then I took the dead battery back to the clerk.

As I left, I realized that God hadn't sent me there to get a battery after all. Generally I don't buy batteries from car wrecking yards, but that day I just had a crazy idea to save a few bucks. Yet God had something else in mind. Driving back to work, I realized, "Wow! God is leading me!" But He led in such a natural way that I had no clue God's hand was guiding me to that specific place at that specific time for that specific encounter.

In the same way, Ruth had no idea that God was guiding her to this specific field. She was looking around for a good place to glean. "I see some people over there, but they look mean. Over there they look pretty nice, though." It didn't "just happen" that Ruth wound up in the field of Boaz.

Nor did Boaz "just happen" to return to his property in time to catch sight of Ruth. "Whose young woman is this?" he asked his servant in charge of the reapers. What he was really saying was, "Who's that beauty over there?"

His servant replied, "It is the young Moabite woman who came back with Naomi from the country of Moab" (Ruth 2:6). And he told his boss that she had been working in the field since early that morning.

Boaz immediately approached Ruth to ask her to stay in his fields and not to go anywhere else. He also had commanded his young workers that she should be allowed to get a drink of water whenever she needed it.

"Why would you do such a thing for me?" Ruth wondered aloud.

"It has been fully reported to me, all that you have done for your mother-in-law since the death of your husband, and how you have left your family and the land of your birth, and have come to a people whom you did not know before," Boaz replied. Then he made a beautiful statement about Ruth's obvious faith:

> The LORD repay your work, and a full reward be given you by the LORD God of Israel, under whose wings you have come for refuge (Ruth 2:12).

Boaz could see that Ruth, this young woman from pagan Moab, had come to trust in the true and the living God. By her own choice she had fled for refuge under the wings of the God of Israel. He saw a beauty in her that went beyond her lovely face. He saw a living faith in the living God. That's a powerful attraction to any man of faith.

Boaz invited Ruth to eat lunch with the regular workers, and after she left to glean once more in his fields, he instructed his employees,

> Let her glean even among the sheaves [that is, the areas where they hadn't yet harvested], and do not reproach her. Also let grain from the bundles fall purposely for her; leave it that she may glean, and do not rebuke her (Ruth 2:15-16).

By the end of the day, Ruth had gleaned about an ephah of barley, which was about forty-five pounds. Naomi's eyes must have bulged when she saw all that grain. She had to suspect that something unusual had happened, so she asked Ruth where she had worked that day. When Ruth reported that she had worked in the fields of Boaz, Naomi replied with great joy,

> Blessed be he of the LORD, who has not forsaken His kindness to the living and the dead! This man is a relation of ours, one of our close relatives (Ruth 2:20).

Ruth told Naomi that Boaz had invited her to stay in his fields and go nowhere else to glean. All the way through barley harvest and wheat harvest, Ruth remained in the fields of Boaz, and then returned each night to Naomi.

WHO ARE YOU?

As the weeks passed, Naomi thought that perhaps Boaz might have as much interest in giving Ruth security as Naomi herself had. Thus she gave Ruth some instructions that seem pretty odd to us.

She told Ruth to wash herself, put on some perfume and a beautiful dress, and then go down to the threshing floor. "Wait until Boaz has eaten and gone to sleep, and then uncover his feet and lie down." Ruth did exactly as Naomi had instructed her. At midnight Boaz awoke with a start and sensed a woman lying at his feet. "Who are you?" he asked.

"I am Ruth, your maidservant," she replied. "Take your maidservant under your wing, for you are a close relative" (Ruth 3:9). The term translated "close relative" is the Hebrew term *goel*, which we first looked at in chapter 7.

If you go back to the law of Moses concerning the obligation of the *goel* to a dead brother, you will read,

> If brothers dwell together, and one of them dies and has no son, the widow of the dead man shall not be married to a stranger outside the family; her husband's brother shall go in to her, take her as his wife, and perform the duty of a husband's brother to her. And it shall be that the firstborn son which she bears will succeed to the name of his dead brother, that his name may not be blotted out of Israel (Deuteronomy 25:5-6).

The law was designed to keep inheritances within the family to keep the family name alive. This law of the *goel*, the kinsman-redeemer, also applied to land. If you were poor and needed to sell your home, you had to take a mortgage on it. If you sold your house within the walls of a city, you had one year's time in which to redeem it back. If you did not buy it back within that period, it remained with the new owner. If you sold your field, then a family member could redeem it. They would pay the market value of the field and bring it back into the family.

In the fiftieth year, the Year of Jubilee, everything reverted back to the original family ownership. That way, God perpetuated the inheritance of the various families and tribes of Israel. If you were poor and desperate and had to sell a piece of property, your *goel*, your kinsman-redeemer, could redeem the field back for you.

The same is true if you sold yourself as a slave. You could be sold as a slave for only six years; in the seventh year you had to be set free. A person needing money would often sell his services: "I'll just become your slave." The kinsman-redeemer, though, could buy you back from slavery. He could come along and say, "Oh, I can't stand seeing you like that," and purchase you back from your bondage.

Ruth is basically telling Boaz, "Fulfill the obligation for your dead brother (her former father-in-law) and raise up a son to carry on the family name." She's actually proposing marriage—something that greatly excited Boaz, who had already fallen in love with Ruth. As an older, unmarried man, he was amazed that she would have any interest in him.

When Ruth made this proposal, Boaz jumped at the chance to tell her that he would pursue the matter as far as possible. Yet he also told her about another relative, another man who had a closer claim than he. Boaz would have to first approach the man to see if he wanted to fulfill the role of the *goel*. If he did, then Boaz would be out of the picture.

Boaz told Ruth to lie down until morning and then return to Naomi. The next morning he gave Ruth six ephahs of barley. She reported back to Naomi everything that had taken place during the night. Wise old Naomi saw the huge pile of barley and understood what it meant: Boaz had an extreme interest in Ruth. So Naomi said to her, "Sit still, my daughter, until you know how the matter will turn out; for the man will not rest until he has concluded the matter this day" (Ruth 3:18).

Naomi was right. Boaz immediately found the other man and told him that years before, Naomi had sold a parcel of land that could now be redeemed, and that the man stood first in line to do so. The man said he'd be glad to redeem it—until Boaz told him that as part of the deal, he'd have to marry Ruth. The man didn't think his wife would go for that, so he backed out of the transaction. And there on the spot, Boaz redeemed the field and won the right to marry Ruth. The elders of the city who witnessed the transaction responded,

> The LORD make the woman who is coming to your house like Rachel and Leah, the two who built the house of Israel; and may you prosper in Ephrathah and be famous in Bethlehem. May your house be like the house of Perez, whom Tamar bore to Judah, because of the offspring which the LORD will give you from this young woman (Ruth 4:11-12).

Boaz was from the tribe of Judah, and of course Rachel and Leah were the wives of Jacob, the father of the twelve tribes of Israel. The elders also mentioned Tamar, who had a son by Judah when he refused her to marry his younger son after her husband, Judah's older son, had died. So the elders recognized that a similar thing had taken place before with the birth of Perez through Tamar.

Ruth conceived shortly after she married Boaz and gave birth to a son named Obed. On that happy day the women of Bethlehem came to Naomi and sang,

> Blessed be the LORD, who has not left you this day without a close relative; and may his name be famous in Israel! And may he be to you a restorer of life and a nourisher of your old age; for your daughter-in-law, who loves you, who is better to you than seven sons, has borne him (Ruth 4:14-15).

Obed grew up and became the father of Jesse, who became the father of David. So in this way Ruth, the young woman from Moab, joined the blessed lineage of Jesus Christ, the Messiah.

REDEMPTION IN FULL

Ruth's love for Naomi and her genuine trust in the God of Israel thrust her into a position that only a select few women ever attained: She became a direct ancestor of Jesus Christ. Ruth is one of only two non-Israelites to be included among that favored number.

When the Messiah finally arrived, He redeemed the world back to God. "For the Son of Man has come to seek and to save that which was lost" (Luke 19:10). Jesus came to redeem the world back to God by paying the full price, which was His death on the cross. The love story of Boaz and Ruth actually presents us with a beautiful picture of what Jesus did for us on the cross.

Throughout the New Testament, you find the word "redemption" always as it relates to the blood of Jesus Christ, "In whom we have redemption through His blood, the forgiveness of sins" (Ephesians 1:7). Although Jesus paid the full price for our redemption, He has not yet taken full possession of His purchase.

Today, the world rightfully belongs to Jesus, but He has not yet come to claim that which is His. That's why we pray, "Thy kingdom come, Thy will be done on earth, even as it is in heaven." We're praying, "Lord, come and set up Your kingdom in this world. Throw Satan out! We want to see a world filled with righteousness, love and peace."

But that can't happen as long as Satan remains "the god of this age" (2 Corinthians 4:4). One day soon, the Lord will return and take ownership of this world He has purchased with His own blood. Our Kinsman-Redeemer is so in love with His bride, the church, that He purchased the field—the whole world—in order that He might take His bride out of it.

Jesus paid the full price to receive you as His bride, that you might be a part of His kingdom forever. He's in love with you! He loves you so much that He gave His life to redeem you from the corruption of sin and from the hopelessness of a life governed by Satan's power. He set you free that you might love Him and live with Him in His kingdom—a kingdom that shall know no end. "Of the increase of His government and peace there will be no end" (Isaiah 9:7).

Just think of it—righteousness, peace, joy and love, forever and ever and ever, throughout all eternity. Oh, praise God! What a glorious redemption is ours through Jesus Christ.

THE ADVENTURE OF A LIFETIME

Because Jesus has become our Kinsman-Redeemer, we do not need to fear death. For a child of God, death is not some horrible monster; it's a blessing. It's the glory of being with God eternally. Through death, we will one day pass through the veil and come into the very presence of the Lord, whom having not seen, we love. When we arrive in the presence of Jesus, we will enter into the fullness of joy, glory, blessing, and excitement.

Nothing on earth can compare with the glory of one moment with Him in heaven. Standing there in His presence, every grief, every problem, every trial will be forgotten. We'll be so taken in by the beauty and the glory of Jesus that everything else will fade into oblivion.

Yes, we sorrow over death—but not as those who have no hope. We sorrow for our own temporary loss. But in thinking of those who already are with the Lord, we can't really grieve. If we have a proper understanding of what heaven is all about, we can only rejoice for them and say, "Oh, they're so lucky! They're so blessed! They're forever with their Kinsman-Redeemer!"

That's what an adventure of faith can do for you.

Faith

Mary: Obedience of Faith

Whoever does the will of God is
My brother and My sister and mother.

MARK 3:35

BEFORE I ASKED KAY TO MARRY ME, I said, "I am not looking for an assistant pastor. I am looking for a mother. I love children and I want to have children. I am not looking for you to have an active role in the church, but to have an active role as a mother in training and guiding our children."

Today, all of our children are walking with and serving the Lord—and I believe that is a direct result of Kay's godly influence in our home. Never underestimate the importance and the power of a godly mother! God certainly didn't when He chose the woman who would bear and rear His own Son, Jesus Christ.

WHY CHOOSE MARY?

A Protestant backlash to the worship of Mary keeps many of us from fully appreciating this remarkable woman. The Bible never calls her the Mother of God, of course, nor does it declare that she was conceived without sin, nor that she serves as an intermediary between believers and Jesus (since surely He would not deny His mother any favors), nor that she ascended into heaven. Protestants rightly object to elevating Mary to a higher position than the Bible gives her.

It must be noted, however, that God chose Mary and granted her the highest honor of any woman who ever lived, to be the human instrument through whom He brought His Son into the world. Mary was a deeply spiritual, godly young woman. Most scholars think she was fifteen or sixteen at the time she gave birth, because in those days marriage usually took place at a very young age.

Many experts believe that Luke personally interviewed Mary before he wrote his gospel, enabling him to hear the story of Jesus' earliest years directly from her—from His miraculous conception and birth to the temple incident when He was twelve years old. This is why Luke's gospel contains many details of Jesus' story that the other gospels do not.

It began when the angel Gabriel appeared to Mary in Nazareth and said, "Rejoice, highly favored one, the Lord is with you; blessed are you among women!" (Luke 1:28). The unexpected greeting startled and troubled Mary, so Gabriel continued:

> Do not be afraid, Mary, for you have found favor with God. And behold, you will conceive in your womb and bring forth a Son, and shall call His name JESUS. He will be great, and will be called the Son of the Highest; and the Lord God will give Him the throne of His father David. And He will reign over the house of Jacob forever, and of His kingdom there will be no end (Luke 1:30-33).

The name "Jesus" is the Greek form of the Hebrew name *Yeshua*, which means "*Yahweh* is salvation," one of the compound names of God. God gave Jesus a name that is above every name, that at the name of *Yeshua*, every knee should bow, and every tongue should confess that *Yeshua ha'Mashiach* is the *Kurios*—the New Testament name for *Yahweh*, Jesus is God.

Can you imagine how you might react to such news as a sixteen-year-old virgin? Mary replied, "How can this be, since I do not know a man?" The angel explained that the Holy Spirit would come upon her and the power of God would overshadow her so that the Holy One born of her would be the Son of God. That is how God intended to fulfill two of the most famous prophecies of Isaiah:

> Therefore the Lord Himself will give you a sign: Behold the virgin shall conceive and bear a Son, and shall call His name Immanuel [which means "God with us"] (Isaiah 7:14).

> For unto us a Child is born, unto us a Son is given; and the government will be upon His shoulder. And His name will be called Wonderful, Counselor, Mighty God, Everlasting Father, Prince of Peace (Isaiah 9:6).

A lot of people today object to the idea of the virgin birth, but their problem isn't really with the virgin birth. Their problem is with their concept of God. For Gabriel told Mary, "With God nothing will be impossible" (Luke 1:37). Why should any believer have a problem with the virgin birth? If you can believe the first verse of Genesis, then you should have no problem with the rest of the Bible. If your God is great enough to create the heavens and the earth, then He's big enough to do anything, and that includes arranging a virgin birth.

Mary responded with simple surrender and submission. "Behold the maidservant of the Lord!" she said. "Let it be to me according to your word" (Luke 1:38). Mary initially may have felt "greatly troubled" at the angel's greeting and "considered what manner of greeting this was," (Luke 1:29), but she instantly decided to obey whatever the Lord might ask her to do.

Right after Mary received this news, she hurried to her elderly cousin, Elizabeth. As soon as Elizabeth heard Mary's voice, the Holy Spirit inspired her to say, "Blessed are you among women, and blessed is the fruit of your womb! ... Blessed is she who believed, for there will be a fulfillment of those things which were told her from the Lord" (Luke 1:42, 45).

Twice Elizabeth calls Mary "blessed." Why was she so blessed? Because no matter how staggering God's word might have seemed to her, she believed it—and thereby proved both her purity of character and her joyful willingness to obey the Lord, whatever He required of her.

THE MAGNIFICAT

The deeply spiritual character of Mary shines most brightly in what has come to be called *The Magnificat*. Nothing in Scripture equals it. Her joyful praise to the Lord overflows with insights and concepts of God from the Old Testament. This indicates that despite her young age, Mary was a devout woman and extremely well versed in the Scriptures. Listen to her glorious exultation to God:

> My soul magnifies the Lord, and my spirit has rejoiced in God my Savior. For He has regarded the lowly state of His maidservant; for behold, henceforth all generations will call me blessed.

For He who is mighty has done great things for me, and holy is His name. And His mercy is on those who fear Him from generation to generation. He has shown strength with His arm; He has scattered the proud in the imagination of their hearts. He has put down the mighty from their thrones, and exalted the lowly. He has filled the hungry with good things, and the rich He has sent away empty. He has helped His servant Israel, in remembrance of His mercy, as He spoke to our fathers, to Abraham and to his seed forever (Luke 1:46-55).

The Magnificat reveals Mary's understanding, her commitment and her devotion to the Lord. There is a good reason that God chose her to bear the Savior of the world.

IT'S NOT ALWAYS EASY

Obedience is not always easy. Mary made this discovery immediately upon her return home. The townspeople found her three months pregnant—without a husband. She and Joseph were still in the espousal stage.

In those days, engagements could be arranged for girls when they were as young as two or three. When family friends gave birth to children about the same time, they'd often say, "Hey, why don't we make arrangements right now for your little boy to marry our little girl when they grow up?"

A year before the engaged couple married, the pair got serious and entered into a second stage known as the espousal. An official ceremony marked the event, which began a chaste year of waiting and courting. This sacred espousal period was binding. You couldn't just decide you didn't want to be espoused. If that was the case, a divorce was required. Even though the pair did not consummate the marriage until after the wedding, if the groom-to-be died in that year of waiting, the wife-to-be would be considered a widow; hence the phrase, "a virgin who is a widow."

In light of all this, you can imagine what people thought when, during her espousal to Joseph, Mary showed up pregnant. You can be sure that rumors spread very quickly in Nazareth.

Joseph was devastated when he found out about Mary's pregnancy, for he knew he was not responsible. To feel betrayed by someone you love so deeply brings absolute desolation to the heart.

According to Jewish law, a woman found pregnant out of wedlock deserved death by stoning. If Joseph publicly exposed Mary's pregnancy, declaring, "Hey, it wasn't me," the people of Nazareth had a duty to stone her. Thus he weighed the merits of sending her away secretly, perhaps to relatives in some other town. While he contemplated his plan, the angel of the Lord came to him at night and said,

> Joseph, son of David, do not be afraid to take to you Mary your wife, for that which is conceived in her is of the Holy Spirit. And she will bring forth a Son, and you shall call His name JESUS, for He will save His people from their sins (Matthew 1:20-21).

Joseph proved himself to be a "just man," as the Bible calls him, when he obeyed the angel's instructions. Regardless of the rumors about the timing of Mary's pregnancy, and despite any damage to his reputation, he obeyed. And so Joseph took Mary to be his wife.

THE INFANT JESUS

Every year at Christmas we rehearse the story of Jesus' birth. Since all the inns at Bethlehem were full, He was born in a stable. His mother placed her newborn in a manger—a food trough for animals—and some befuddled shepherds soon wandered by to lay their eyes on the Savior of the world.

Eight days after His birth, His parents circumcised Him. And after Mary had fulfilled the days of her purification as specified in the law of Moses, they brought their newborn Son to Jerusalem to present Him to the Lord.

The couple approached the priests of the temple with two sacrificial turtledoves, indicating their poverty—they couldn't even afford a lamb. On the temple grounds they came into contact with an old man named Simeon, to whom God had made a promise: He would not die until he saw the Messiah. As soon as Simeon caught sight of Jesus, he knew God had fulfilled His promise. He took the Child in his arms and prophesied about Jesus,

> "Behold, this Child is destined for the fall and rising of many in Israel, and for a sign which will be spoken against." [Then he looked straight at Mary and said,] "Yes, a sword will pierce through your own soul also" (Luke 2:34-35).

Not long after this memorable encounter, the Lord once more spoke in a dream to Joseph and warned him to flee with Mary and the Child to Egypt, to keep Jesus away from the murderous Herod the Great (Matthew 2:13). About two years later, after the death of Herod, the Lord instructed Joseph again to return to Israel; and in yet another dream, God warned Joseph not to return to Judea. So Joseph, Mary and Jesus settled in Nazareth, the town where Jesus grew up.

Apparently the people of Nazareth never forgot the speculation about Mary and her pregnancy, because when Jesus returned to Nazareth as an adult, they said of Him, "Is this not the carpenter, the Son of Mary?" (Mark 6:3). These words could indicate that Joseph had died in the intervening years, but more likely it means that some of the early whispers and suspicions about Mary's pregnancy resurfaced. They called Jesus "the Son of Mary" rather than "the Son of Joseph."

These rumors eventually must have spread throughout Israel, for at one point the Pharisees in Jerusalem said to Jesus, "We were not born of fornication" (John 8:41)—as if to say, "but You were." The people had counted the months after Mary and Joseph got married—and they knew Jesus had arrived several months early. Thus, the people accused Jesus of being conceived out of wedlock; which indeed, He was ... but by the Holy Spirit, not as His enemies alleged.

While the Lord picked a godly virgin to bear His Son, that does not mean Mary remained a virgin her whole life. Contrary to one popular teaching, the idea of the perpetual virginity of Mary is an invention without biblical basis. The Scriptures speak plainly of Jesus' brothers and sisters: "Is this not [Jesus] ... the brother of James, Joses, Judas, and Simon? And are not His sisters here with us?" (Mark 6:3).

Matthew further tells us that Joseph did not have relations with Mary until after she had given birth to Jesus (Matthew 1:25).

This plainly implies that after the Savior's birth, Mary and Joseph consummated their marriage like any other married couple. Jesus no doubt grew up in a rather normal family.

JESUS IN THE TEMPLE

None of the Gospels tell us anything about the boyhood of Jesus, except for one incident recorded by Luke when Jesus was twelve years old. To celebrate the Feast of the Passover, Jesus and His parents traveled with a host of relatives and friends to Jerusalem.

No doubt Jesus had already celebrated His *bar mitzvah*, the ceremony that marked Him as an official "son of the covenant." Otherwise, the teachers in the temple would not have allowed Him to sit with them. For several days Jesus stayed in the temple, discussing the Law with these scholars—and His parents unknowingly left Him behind when they took off for home.

Some think how could Jesus stay in Jerusalem without His mother and father's knowledge? Pilgrims in those days traveled in large groups. And you know how twelve-year-old boys are. They have their own agendas. When I hiked with my grandsons of that age, they hiked five times farther. They're up the hills and down the hills. They're always taking these side excursions, while I just keep plodding along the path. I may see them on occasion, but I know they're keeping an eye on me.

Several hundred people probably came from Nazareth to attend the feast. And when this big company started to leave, Joseph and Mary just figured, *He's with some of His cousins playing around. Come evening, He'll find us.*

But when Mary and Joseph couldn't find Jesus anywhere in the company, they returned to Jerusalem—taking them three days to locate their Son. When your child disappears for a few hours, you want to call the police. And then when he shows up, unharmed and unconcerned, you want to spank him. You're so torn up emotionally that you become upset and angry.

Finally, Mary and Joseph found Jesus in the temple, sitting in the middle of the teachers of the Law. He asked them probing questions and listened intently to their answers. "And all who heard Him," says Luke, "were astonished at His understanding and answers."

His parents were amazed. "Son," Mary said, "why have You done this to us? Look, Your father and I have sought You anxiously." How could He have caused them such fear?

Jesus gave them a very matter-of-fact reply: "Why did you seek Me? Did you not know that I must be about My Father's business?" (Luke 2:46-49).

Scripture doesn't tell us when Mary told Jesus the facts of His birth, but He clearly knew them at this point. She had said, "Your father and I have been worried about you," and Jesus replied, "I've been about My Father's business." He didn't acknowledge Joseph as His father, but referred to God Almighty as His Father. Nevertheless, Jesus submitted Himself to their authority and returned with Mary and Joseph to Nazareth, where He lived in obscurity for the next eighteen years.

A MIRACLE IN CANA

Weddings in our day are usually joyous and colorful, but they're nothing in comparison to the wedding celebrations in that day.

The wedding party back then lasted much longer than just an hour or two; it could go on for days.

John chapter 2 records such a wedding, which occurred after Jesus had already chosen His twelve closest disciples. They were with Him when He accompanied His mother to the wedding. Either the host didn't anticipate the large number of guests, or those guests drank more than expected, because the gala celebration ran out of wine much too early. So Mary approached Jesus and said, "They have no wine" (John 2:3).

The Lord immediately replied, "Woman, what does your concern have to do with Me? My hour has not yet come" (John 2:4). The term translated "woman" does not imply emotional distance, but is actually a very endearing term. You might translate it, "Mother dear."

Jesus had a keen sense of timing. He took special care that no premature movement arose to acclaim Him as Messiah. So He told Mary, "Mom, it isn't the right time yet." Mary, however, found the servants and instructed them, "Whatever He says to you, do it" (John 2:5).

You probably know the rest of the story. Jesus turned gallons of water into wine—in fact, the best wine of the feast. For the first time publicly, He demonstrated His power over the elements. John comments, "This beginning of signs Jesus did in Cana of Galilee, and manifested His glory; and His disciples believed in Him" (John 2:11). Devout men and women had started following Christ and so the movement had begun—the movement that would ultimately bring Him to His hour of glory when He would give His life as a ransom for our sins.

A FAILED RESCUE ATTEMPT

One day, after Jesus' public ministry had begun to flourish, Mary and her other sons showed up to retrieve Him.

Perhaps Mary was concerned that as the crowds grew larger and Jesus ministered to their needs both day and night, He needed to eat. So she and her other sons sent a message to Jesus inside the packed house, asking Him to come out. But Jesus used this as an opportunity to teach the people and replied, "Who is My mother, or My brothers?" He looked at the crowd around Him and said, "Here are My mother and My brothers! For whoever does the will of God is My brother and My sister and mother" (Mark 3:33-35).

I would have great problems with this passage if I depended on Mary to intercede for me. I'm thankful that I don't need the intercession of Mary or any of the saints, because God has opened the door for me to come directly to Jesus. As Paul wrote, "There is one God, and one Mediator between God and man, the Man Christ Jesus" (1 Timothy 2:5). What a privilege, what a blessing!

AT THE CROSS

At Calvary, where Jesus died for your sins and mine, we see one final interaction between Jesus and Mary. She and several other women who had traveled with Jesus throughout Galilee stood by Him in His death, while all but one of His apostles had fled.

Mary stood near the cross along with Mary Magdalene and the apostle John. And when Mary saw her bloodied Son hanging there, a sword pierced through her own soul, just as Simeon had predicted. Oh, the suffering she must have felt, holding these secrets in her heart, and remembering what the angel had told her—and yet watching Him despised, rejected and ridiculed!

When Jesus saw His mother standing below Him, close by John, He said, "Woman, behold your son!" To John He said, "Behold your mother!" In other words, "Okay, John, take care of Mary. Watch over her." And the Bible tells us, "From that hour that disciple took her to his own home" (John 19:26-27).

The relationships we have in Christ are often far closer than the human relationships in our own families. At this point in His ministry, the brothers of Jesus did not believe in Him. In fact, they did not believe until after His resurrection. So because of their common belief in Jesus as the Messiah, a closer bond existed between John and Mary than that between Mary and her other sons.

A MARVELOUS EXAMPLE

The last time we see Mary in Scripture, she stands with the company of disciples in Acts 1, waiting upon the Holy Spirit. After that, she disappears from the text and we know nothing more about her.

While Mary certainly is not worthy of worship, she does provide us with a worthy example of a godly disciple of Christ. One trait in particular seems to stand out. See if you can identify it:

> Mary kept all of these things and pondered them in her heart ... His mother marveled at those things which were spoken of Him ... His mother kept all these things in her heart (Luke 2:19, 33, 51).

Mary thought long and hard about the things God had revealed to her about her Son. She pondered them. She turned them over in her mind. She meditated upon them. She embraced them deep within her heart and let those truths grow her faith. She believed God and His Word seriously—and that's what led to her godly, pure spirit.

I think it's both interesting and instructive that before Jesus died on the cross, He entrusted the care of His mother to John. Why John? For one thing, all of the other disciples had run away. But I think there may be something deeper here.

In his gospel, John never calls himself by name but always says the phrase, "the disciple whom Jesus loved." Only John uses it; none of the other gospel writers use that phrase to refer to him. No doubt John felt that Jesus loved him more than He did the others—and I believe that Peter probably felt that Jesus loved him more than the others, as did Matthew, Andrew and *all* the rest. Jesus has a way with people so that everyone feels special—just as you are special to Jesus.

It's important, though, that you know it. Can you refer to yourself as "the one whom Jesus loves"? As far as He is concerned, there's no one in the world like you. He loves you and He wants you to know how very special you are to Him.

Jesus loved His dear mother and made special arrangements to care for her after His death. But He doesn't love you any less than He loves her! "Who is My mother?" He asked. "The one who does the will of My Father, she is My mother."

Your name may not be Mary, but if by faith you obey the Father as Mary did, then you also have special arrangements waiting for you in heaven—guaranteed.

Paul: Apostle of Faith

Therefore, having been justified by faith, we have peace with God through our Lord Jesus Christ, through whom also we have access by faith into this grace in which we stand.

ROMANS 5:1-2

DURING MY FIRST PASTORATE in Prescott, Arizona, a desperate mother came by our house. Her son was a patient in the Whipple Veterans Hospital, dying of tuberculosis, and she wondered if I would visit him. I assured her I would.

"Oh," she replied, "don't go yet. He's very bitter against God and against the church. We'll have to wait until he's in a good mood. I'll give you a call when that happens."

"Okay," I replied, "you know best. But if he gets mad and curses me, it doesn't matter. I can handle it."

That very afternoon she called back, crying. "The doctors just told me that he's not going to live through the night," she said. "You'd better get out there right away."

I left immediately for the hospital, where I found him and began talking to him about the Lord. His father had been a minister and somehow he had become embittered and turned away from God. But since he knew the basics of the faith, I found it easy to share with him—and it just so happened that we hit it off well.

"Howard," I said, "things don't look so good. Maybe you ought to commit your life to Jesus Christ by faith and ask the Lord to forgive you and turn your life over to Him."

He looked at me and said, "Chuck, I know I should, and I intend to. But a year ago, I weighed 190 pounds. I was a member of a gang in Detroit, Michigan, and I cursed God with every breath. Now I weigh ninety pounds. I can hardly get a breath. To turn my life over to God in this condition would be cowardly. If the Lord should touch me and restore my health again, then I'll commit myself to Him."

"Well, Howard," I replied, "how do you know that God hasn't allowed this condition to come upon you because of His immense love for you? Maybe He knew that so long as you weighed 190 pounds and were the picture of health, you'd never come to Him. But He loves you so much that He allowed you to reach this weakened state, because He knew that the only way you'd ever turn your life over to Him is now, when it's all over."

For a bit he studied me and said, "Chuck, I think you're right." He saw the light and by faith he turned his life over to the Lord.

That is the gospel of grace as championed by the apostle Paul. Regardless of who you are or what you have done, when you come to Jesus Christ and through faith ask Him to be your Lord and forgive your sins, you receive the gift of eternal life.

Paul preached this message of grace through faith wherever he went—but not initially.

SAUL, THE PERSECUTOR

When you present yourself to an audience, you generally want to put your best foot forward. So it's interesting to see how Paul described himself to the Corinthians:

> I am the least of the apostles, who am not worthy to be called an apostle, because I persecuted the church of God (1 Corinthians 15:9).

Paul never got over the fact that at one time he tried to stamp out the church of Jesus Christ. The first time we see him in the book of Acts, he's standing guard as an angry mob of Jews stones Stephen to death for his faith in Christ. Saul (as he was then known) not only approves of their actions, he protects the robes of the men who took off their outer garments to hurl their rocks (Acts 7:58).

> Saul made havoc of the church, entering every house, and dragging off men and women, committing them to prison (Acts 8:3).

> Then Saul, still breathing threats and murder against the disciples of the Lord, went to the high priest and asked letters from him to the synagogues of Damascus, so that if he found any who were of the Way, whether men or women, he might bring them bound to Jerusalem (Acts 9:1-2).

Paul never tried to hide his violent and blasphemous past. He was pretty candid when he wrote in Galatians 1:13, "For you have heard of my former conduct in Judaism, how I persecuted the church of God beyond measure and tried to destroy it."

One day, everything changed for Saul. While traveling on his way to Damascus, a light "brighter than the sun" shone suddenly upon him, knocking him to the ground. A voice spoke to him in Hebrew: "Saul, Saul, why are you persecuting Me?"

Saul asked, "Who are You, Lord?"

The voice replied, "I am Jesus, whom you are persecuting. It is hard for you to kick against the goads."

Astonished and trembling, Saul asked, "Lord, what do You want me to do?" (Acts 9:4-6).

Jesus said to go into the city and wait for further instructions. Saul then picked himself up off the ground, opened his eyes— and found himself totally blind. His friends had to lead him by the hand into Damascus. There he sat for three days in the dark, refusing all food and drink as he reevaluated his entire life and mission.

I believe when Stephen preached that magnificent sermon before the angry mob, his words touched Saul, although he tried to close his ears to the truth. I think it raised questions in his mind. Because of Saul's thorough training in the Hebrew Scriptures, he recognized the truth of Stephen's argument. But he fought against it.

Many times the people who seem to be the hardest to reach for Christ are the very ones who are closest to receiving Him. They are fighting a fierce inner battle, so they react strongly against the truth. It is penetrating their hearts and they are hostile.

When Saul saw Stephen die and heard him say, "Lord, don't lay this sin to their charge," it had an effect upon him. God had begun a work by the Holy Spirit that Saul tried hard to fight.

This is why Jesus said, "It is hard for you to kick against the goads."

After three days, God sent a disciple named Ananias to Saul to help him receive his sight and, more importantly, to share the gospel of grace. Ananias didn't particularly want the job—he had heard how Saul had shattered the church in Jerusalem and probably knew that he himself was on Saul's hit list in Damascus—but he obeyed.

> Go, for he [Saul] is a chosen vessel of Mine to bear My name before Gentiles, kings, and the children of Israel. For I will show him how many things he must suffer for My name's sake (Acts 9:15-16).

Paul was to have a three-fold ministry: to preach the gospel to Gentiles, to kings, and to the children of Israel. Wherever he went, the apostle preached first in the Jewish synagogues, sometimes unsuccessfully. Paul ministered to King Agrippa and to the emperor, Nero, in addition to his great ministry among the Gentiles. God had uniquely prepared Paul for a ministry that would bridge the Jewish and the Gentile communities, between the Hellenists and the Hebrews.

PAUL'S UNIQUE BACKGROUND

Paul grew up in the city of Tarsus, a free Roman city strong in Grecian culture. That meant he was born a Roman citizen. For the first fourteen years of his life, his father schooled him in the Hebrew Scriptures as a Hebrew of the Hebrews, of the tribe of Benjamin. Yet his playmates were all of the Grecian culture, so he knew what it meant to be both a Jew and a Greek.

When he was fourteen, his father sent him to Jerusalem to further his Hebrew education under the tutelage of Gamaliel, a leading Jewish scholar. As a Pharisee, Paul became completely familiar with the Law and the Old Testament Scriptures, effectively talking with Hebrews and Hellenists. The apostle wrote in Galatians 1:15-16 that God had separated him from his mother's womb and called him that he might preach Jesus among the Gentiles.

Just as Paul speaks about being separated from his mother's womb, I can look back on my own life and see how God separated me at my birth and began preparing me for the work He had in mind for me, for His glory and for His kingdom. I can look back over each step and see God's hand at work. Many times I wandered off in the wrong direction, as Paul did, but God used even that to fulfill His purposes. God always brought me right back on track.

God has a purpose for each of us. He began early in our lives, working in us and preparing us for the work He had ordained for us to accomplish for Him. He loves to use our unique backgrounds for His glory.

Paul's background enabled him to one day declare, "To the weak I became weak, that I might win the weak. I have become all things to all men, that I might by all means save some" (1 Corinthians 9:22). God had chosen him and prepared him to cross cultural barriers to minister in a broad field of ministry.

A TIME OF SOLITUDE AND REVELATION

Immediately after his salvation, Paul began preaching that Jesus was the Messiah. Because of his vast knowledge of the Scriptures, his enemies felt both confused and confounded, because they could not resist his solid biblical preaching. So they decided to kill him.

When the local believers discovered this murder plot, they let Paul down in a basket over the city wall at night to avoid an ambush by the Jews at the city gate. Although Paul had a rather inglorious entry into the city, being led by the hand as a blind man, he had a more inglorious departure, escaping over the wall in a basket to elude death at the hands of his enemies.

Upon leaving Damascus Paul did not go immediately to Jerusalem, but instead traveled to the area of Mount Sinai in Arabia. He remained there for almost three years, during which time the Lord readjusted his entire understanding of the Scriptures. There God revealed His marvelous grace apart from the law, and the righteousness that comes through faith. This personal instruction by the Lord revolutionized Paul's ministry and he later wrote,

> The gospel which was preached by me is not according to man. For I neither received it from man, nor was I taught it, but it came through the revelation of Jesus Christ (Galatians 1:11-12).

Paul began to see the Old Testament in a new light. Looking back at Abraham, he realized Abraham's *faith* was accounted to him for righteousness. He understood that he didn't have to work to be righteous, but only believe in the sufficiency of Christ's work on his behalf. Faith in Christ was all he needed.

One day a group of men asked Jesus, "What work must we do in order to do the work of God?" Jesus responded, "This is the work of God: believe on Him whom He has sent" (John 6:29). God has made righteousness available to all of us through faith.

When Jesus took the cup, He said, "This is a new covenant, a covenant whereby you can become a child of God. This covenant is in My blood, shed for the remission of sins" (Luke 22:20). And so God has established through Jesus Christ a new way by which you and I can come to God. We approach Him through the righteousness of Jesus Christ, imputed to us by our faith in Christ. As Paul said, "To be found in Him, not having my own righteousness which is of the law, but that which is through faith in Christ, the righteousness which is from God by faith" (Philippians 3:9).

After three years with the Lord in the desert, Paul returned to Damascus and then to Jerusalem. But the believers there still feared him. Not believing his conversion to be true, they gave him the cold shoulder, and before long, Paul returned to his hometown of Tarsus.

Paul spent the next seven years making tents in Tarsus. So often, when a person comes to the knowledge of Jesus Christ, they think they need to immediately enter the ministry and begin to share the knowledge they've gained with others. But it interests me that although Paul had all those years of schooling in the Scriptures, his real ministry didn't begin until ten years after his conversion.

Paul had to relearn. It's always a slower process to relearn than it is to learn, because you have to first unlearn a lot of things you once believed.

CHURCH GROWTH

As Paul remained in Tarsus, a Gentile church in Antioch began growing by leaps and bounds. Barnabas, who was active in this move of God, left for Tarsus to find Paul, realizing that he had the ideal background to help the Gentiles coming to faith in Christ. So Barnabas brought Paul to Antioch, and this duo quickly became the spiritual leaders of this growing, Gentile church.

One day as the church of Antioch ministered to the Lord and fasted, "The Holy Spirit said, 'Now separate to Me Barnabas and Saul for the work to which I have called them.' Then, having fasted and prayed, and laid hands on them, they sent them away" (Acts 13:2-3).

How did the Spirit give these specific instructions? Here the church had gathered to pray, no doubt talking about the need to get the gospel out to the world. So how did the Spirit speak so pointedly about Saul and Barnabas?

I believe the message came through a word of prophecy. Someone in the group, anointed by the Holy Spirit, prophetically made this declaration. God made His divine will known through an obedient human servant. And so Paul and Barnabas set off on a missionary journey that would shake the world.

A CRUCIAL COUNCIL

Acts 15 describes how certain men, claiming to have apostolic authority, came down from Jerusalem to the church in Antioch and sought to put the Gentile believers under the law. They told those Gentile believers that they must be circumcised in order to be saved—an order which caused division in the church.

Paul and Barnabas, who vigorously opposed this view, made an important trip to Jerusalem to settle the matter before the whole church. They wanted the question answered: Exactly what relationship did Gentile believers have to the Mosaic law? They knew that many in the Jerusalem church were still following

Jewish customs and practices. Because Paul had received this glorious gospel of grace and realized that salvation is by faith through Jesus Christ and not by works, he wanted to settle the question once and for all. Did someone have to become a Jew in order to be a believer in Christ?

At this church council Paul and Barnabas reported how God had been working not only in Antioch, but also in many Gentile churches. They spoke of the miracles being wrought through the power of Jesus Christ. They described how these Gentile believers—who were not under the law or keeping the law—experienced the power of God and saw miracles from the Holy Spirit, exactly as Jewish believers in Christ.

The men who said a person had to be a Jew to be saved were really saying that individual had to be circumcised. Paul vehemently disagreed. "Look," Paul said. "Titus is with me. He is a Greek. And you haven't forced him to be circumcised. So, it isn't an issue."

How grateful we are for Paul's solid stand on the grace of God and salvation through faith! Had Paul not made such a strong stand and declared with such clarity this glorious gospel of grace, then Christianity would have become nothing more than a Jewish sect. Because Paul was willing to stand up for the truth, this magnificent gospel of grace is still preached among the Gentiles.

The church council officially recognized that, while the apostle Peter was sent primarily to the Jews, Paul had been sent primarily to the Gentiles. Thus, they recognized the individuality of callings within the church. In Christ there is neither Jew nor Greek, Barbarian, Scythian, bond or free. Christ is all and in all. "Paul," they said, "God has called you to those who are uncircumcised, to the Gentile world. And Peter has been called to the Jews, to those of the circumcision." The leaders of the Jerusalem church recognized no theological division, but merely that one man could minister effectively to one group, while the other man could effectively minister to a different group.

God's latitude exceeds that of man. Somehow we feel that everyone ought to be like us. And if they are not, well, they must be inferior. Take, for instance, the matter of worship. Some have worship teams, others have choirs. Some have guitars, others have organs, but one form isn't superior to another. Guitars aren't holier than organs, and robes aren't holier than jeans. What interests God is the heart. And God is in all.

Paul had an obvious ministry among the Gentiles. The Holy Spirit worked through him in his ministry to the Gentiles, just as He did through Peter to the Jews, with miracles, wonders and signs. The same God who used Peter to reach the circumcised also used Paul to reach the uncircumcised.

At the conclusion of the council, Peter, James and the other leaders of the church gave to Barnabas and Paul "the right hand of fellowship." In essence, "God bless you, guys. You go to the heathen. We'll go to the circumcision. We recognize that we have different ministries, different callings, and we will obey the call of God wherever He sends us."

The conclusion is that the church at Jerusalem completely endorsed Paul's ministry and theology of grace through faith. It declared the gospel to be one gospel whose content didn't change depending on the audience that heard it. So Paul would later write,

There is one body and one Spirit, just as you were called in one hope of your calling; one Lord, one faith, one baptism; one God and Father of all, who is above all, and through all, and in you all (Ephesians 4:4-6).

THE CONFRONTATION WITH PETER

Unfortunately, the council at Jerusalem didn't rid the church of this debate once and for all. Some false teachers showed up in Antioch and started to put Paul down. They said, "Paul is not really an apostle. He is inferior. Peter, James and John, they are the real deal."

In truth, of course, it was only the false teachers who were putting Paul down. Peter, James and John respected Paul and even gave him the right hand of fellowship. But these false teachers came in and troubled the people, telling them that faith in Jesus was insufficient. To be saved they had to keep the law and so become Jews.

In a visit to the Antioch church, Peter gladly ate with the Gentile converts—until these false teachers came along. Then he began to separate himself from the Gentile believers, fearing that the circumcision group would put him down as they had Paul. When Paul heard what was going on, he took immediate action.

When Peter had come to Antioch, I withstood him to his face, because he was to be blamed. I said to Peter before them all, "If you, being a Jew, live in the manner of Gentiles and not as the Jews, why do you compel Gentiles to live as Jews? We who are Jews by nature, and not sinners of the Gentiles, knowing that a man is not justified by the works of the law but by faith in Jesus Christ, even we have believed in Christ Jesus, that we might be justified by faith in Christ and not by the works of the law; for by the works of the law no flesh shall be justified" (Galatians 2:11, 14-16).

Paul could make such a strong statement because of his own background. When he wrote to the Philippians, he talked about the righteousness that, at one time, he sought to achieve through the law. And he said,

> If any man can boast in himself of his own righteousness, I can, more than all of you. I was a Hebrew of the Hebrews. I was a Pharisee. I had great zeal for God. And as far as the righteousness that can come by the law is concerned, I was blameless. But those things which were once important to me—the things I once looked at as positive—I now count as loss because of the excellency of knowing Jesus Christ, through faith (Philippians 3:4-9).

God sees you clothed in the righteousness of Jesus Christ. If you think you can improve upon that, you're sadly mistaken. God sees your righteousness as being complete. By your faith and trust in Jesus Christ, He sees you in Him and He accounts His righteousness to you.

READY TO GO

I grew up in a church which made me think I was righteous because I didn't smoke, I didn't drink, I didn't go to shows, I didn't dance, and I didn't do all the other things that the church declared to be unrighteous and unholy.

There was nothing wrong with avoiding the amusements the church condemned. In fact, it's healthy not to smoke. It's healthy not to get drunk. I'm glad that I obeyed, even though I did so under a false concept. I'm glad that I signed the pledge,

"I will not smoke and drink." The problem was, I thought that signing that covenant made me righteous. I thought it made me more righteous than the guys who snuck out to smoke their cigarettes.

In fact, making that covenant had nothing to do with my righteous standing before God. It had a lot to do with my physical health, but not my spiritual health. It's good that I didn't have my mind polluted by going to tasteless movies, yet that didn't make me righteous. The righteous standing that I enjoy before God is through faith in Jesus Christ alone, and not the works I have done for God or the things that I don't do. God declares me righteous because of my faith in the finished work of Jesus, who hung on the tree in order that He might redeem me from the curse of the law.

As Gentile believers, we are heavily indebted to the apostle Paul. So much of our church doctrine is based on the letters of Paul and on his clear and simple doctrine of salvation by grace through faith. The writings and teachings of Paul give us a tremendous foundation for our theology and for living.

Many years ago I pastored a little church where I was both the pastor and the janitor. On the side, I also repaired mobile homes. I was putting in seventy hours or so a week, just to keep everything going.

Late one Saturday night as I cleaned the church for Sunday services, I started feeling pain around my chest and numbness in my arm. I'd heard about heart attacks and I thought, *Hmm, this must be it.*

I sat down in the front row and said, "Okay, Lord, if I'm going, let's go. It's been a good life." I thought that perhaps I was leaving this earth, but after I sat down for a few moments, I felt better. So I got up and finished cleaning the church.

What gave me such comfort in that moment when I thought I might be taking my last breath? Paul's doctrine of salvation by grace through faith gave me the confidence that if I should die while cleaning the church, I'd instantly be in the presence of Jesus, where I would bask in His glory for eternity.

"Lord, my life is Yours. My life is in Your hands. You have saved me based on the finished work of Jesus, and by faith I stand on Your promises. I'm ready, Lord, if You want to call me home."

What peace we gain from knowing that God accepts us, not on the basis of our works or our talents or anything else we have done, but solely because of our faith in Jesus Christ. It's a beautiful thing—and I am so glad that God used Paul the apostle to declare this truth.

Faith

Peter: from Doubt to Faith

Peter answered Him, "Lord, if it is You, command me to come to You on the water." So He said, "Come." And when Peter had come down out of the boat, he walked on the water to go to Jesus.

MATTHEW 14:28-29

Have you ever had one of those days when everything went wrong and nothing worked? At the end of that frustrating, wasted day you looked back and said, "What in the world did I accomplish?" You wondered why you got out of bed in the first place.

That's the kind of experience Peter had one night—and yet what happened next set him on a totally new track.

AT YOUR WORD

It had been one of those futile, fruitless nights. All night long, up and down the shores of Galilee, they had cast their nets, pulled them back in, and found them empty. They knew these waters and chummed all the usual places, but still had no success. By morning all they had to show for their night's hard labor were weeds stuck in the nets.

As these fishermen cleaned their equipment, they saw a crowd along the shore, pressing against a Man and trying to get close enough to touch Him. And then they watched as this Man left the crowd and approached *them*. Before they realized what He was doing, the Man had stepped into Simon's boat. "Cast off from the shore a bit," He told Simon. The startled fisherman complied, and when he had pushed just slightly off shore, the stranger began to teach the people the things of God.

Simon listened with great interest as the Man gave words of hope, words of comfort, words of a God who loved people and was concerned for their salvation.

When the Man finished speaking—leaving a crowd enthralled by His words—He turned to Simon and said, "Now move out into deeper water and let out your net for a catch of fish."

The instruction probably annoyed Peter. He probably thought, *What? This teacher, who has probably never thrown a net in his life, is trying to tell me how to fish.* Peter's response was probably politely accommodating. "I really enjoyed the things You said about God. That was fascinating. You're a good teacher, but I'm a fisherman. You may know things about God, but I know fish. And I have to tell You, this really isn't the time of day to catch fish. We fished all last night and caught nothing. It was a futile, fruitless night." But then he stopped, shrugged his shoulders, and added, "Nevertheless, at Your word, I'll let down the net."

It was an obedience of blind faith—faith pitted against intelligence. "I'll do it because You said to do it. My mind tells me it's going to be a vain effort since there are no fish around right now." Peter looked upon the command as foolish, and yet he agreed, just to accommodate Jesus.

But note what happened: "And when they had done this, they caught a great number of fish, and their net was breaking" (Luke 5:6).

Peter had never seen so many fish. As a lifelong fisherman, this was his dream come true. He felt so excited that he did not immediately comprehend what had happened. It hadn't sunk in. He whistled and called for James and John, his partners, on the shore. They all came out and began to fill their little boats with fish until the boats got so full that they began to sink. And then suddenly Peter caught on: *This Man is no ordinary teacher.*

At that moment Peter got the first glimmer of light concerning the truth of Jesus, a glimmer that later burst forth in full revelation when the fisherman said of Jesus, "You are the Messiah, the Son of the living God" (Matthew 16:16). That grand revelation had its beginning the moment he saw the fruit of blind obedience to the command of Jesus.

SEEING THE TRUTH

The fishing experience startled Peter so much that he immediately fell down before Jesus. "Depart from me," he said, "for I am a sinful man, oh, Lord!" (Luke 5:8). In coming to recognize the real Jesus, Peter came to recognize his own true nature. This is always what happens when we see Jesus for who He is.

You never truly see yourself until you see yourself in the light of Jesus. We often have a higher opinion of ourselves than is warranted. "I'm not really as bad as I appear. You see, it's only circumstances that make me look bad. It's my wife; she is holding me back. It isn't me, it's the exterior influences that have kept me from real success." We have a false view of ourselves, an inflated sense of who we are.

But when you see yourself in the light of God's glory, everything changes. If you see a man proud and arrogant in his self-righteousness, then you can ascertain that he has not met the real Jesus. There's more hope for a prostitute and a drunkard to enter the kingdom of heaven than there is for him. It's not until you see the truth about yourself and recognize that you are a hopeless, helpless sinner, that you will call out to God for His mercy and grace.

Our problem is that we usually look at ourselves in the light of each other. When I look at myself by your light, I'm not too bad. If I step into a very dim bathroom and look in the mirror, I look pretty good—especially if I don't have my contacts in. But standing in the glare of the sun and looking in the mirror is devastating. It's bad news.

How you look all depends upon which light you're using to look at yourself. When you look at yourself in the light of Jesus Christ, every flaw is suddenly exposed and revealed. You see the real truth.

The sight of the real Jesus made Peter fearful and he cried out, "Depart from me, I'm a sinful man."

But notice Jesus' answer: "Fear not. From now on, you're going to catch men" (Luke 5:10). As soon as Peter acknowledged his sin, the Lord dealt with it, pardoned him, cleansed him, and then called him to a higher vocation.

SUCCESS BEYOND ALL EXPECTATION

It always amazes and blesses me to see the people God calls to catch men for His kingdom. They're not exactly the type most of us would pick. They're not always the cultured and the elite, the fashionable and the brilliant. No, quite often they are former street fighters, brawlers, drug addicts, and alcoholics.

In Acts 2 we see Peter fulfilling God's calling on his life. In his first message, some 3,000 men believe the message and are baptized. In Acts 4 he throws out the net again and some 5,000 more men are brought in. Peter truly did become a fisher of men.

Today at the Sea of Galilee, men are still earning their living by catching fish. You can watch them sail out in little dories and throw out their nets, even as Peter did. It's a beautiful body of water, abundant with fish, and thousands of men through the centuries have spent their entire lives fishing there. They go out every morning and return every evening to sell the day's catch. They live and die, just catching fish—and their lives don't amount to anything more than that. They just subsist.

That was Peter's life before he encountered Jesus. Yet because he responded to the call of Jesus Christ to catch men, Peter's name is known all over the world. Peter—an ordinary, plain, common fisherman—impacted the world and made a mark in history because of one simple act of obedience. When Peter saw the multitude of fish in his net, he knew it hadn't been his skill as a fisherman that brought his success. It was obedience to the command of the Lord.

Our best efforts can lead to empty nets. We can fish all night and catch nothing. But when God directs us and we obey Him by faith, we can have success beyond our highest dreams or fondest imaginations.

I think of my own years of ministry when I threw out the nets and caught nothing. And then suddenly, as I threw them out again they came back full, so full that I had difficulty drawing them in. I didn't perceive that I had thrown them out any differently than before. So I began to realize there was only one reason for it. The Lord purposed to fill the nets.

What a vast difference when the Spirit begins to direct our lives! We no longer rely upon our own experience, our own abilities, or our own understanding of human nature. Instead, by faith we obey the command of the Lord. And so we experience success beyond all our wildest hopes.

The result is that He gets the glory and the recognition for the success. All you can say is that He is the Master of the fish and the seas and the universe, and He has done what He has willed to do. "To God be the glory, great things He has done."

FAITH AND THE WORD

This story teaches us that faith acts upon the word of the Lord, even when that word seems contrary to our own personal experience and understanding. Faith acts upon the word, the command of the Lord, even though it may seem to conflict with our own understanding and knowledge of the circumstances.

Had Peter followed his own instincts, he would have returned home, gone to bed and hoped for better luck the next day. "But at Your word, I will do it."

God can use anyone in His service to catch men for Him—

common people like fishermen, mechanics, grocery clerks, and housewives. God uses people just like us. Plain, common, ordinary people can do extraordinary work for Him.

What is the Lord saying to you? It may not make sense to you. He may be saying, "Today I want you to witness to your mother once more."

"But Lord," you say, "I've witnessed to her many times, and the last time she got so upset she told me never to talk to her again about You, Lord."

"Lord, I've fished all night and caught nothing." But this may be the time!

What is the Lord directing you to do? He may be asking you to do the same thing you've tried already, and without success. It doesn't make any sense to try that again. *I've been fishing all night and caught nothing.* But if the Lord is directing you to let down the nets, then let them down. See what He might want to do.

The Lord's command always presents us with a choice: we can argue or we can obey. Peter fell somewhere in the middle. He argued, but then he obeyed. Call it reluctant obedience or incomplete faith. Sometimes we choose to argue. Many times I'll say, "Lord, I know it won't work. I've tried it. It won't work. I just know it." So I never get to that second part: "Nevertheless, at Your word I'll let down the net." And the result? I miss out on the success that God wants me to enjoy.

Go beyond the point of argument. Come to the area of obedience prompted by faith and discover what God wants to do in your life.

WALKING ON WATER

Like most of us, Peter had triumphs of faith and failures of doubt. Sometimes he had both within moments of each other.

Consider the time when he and the other disciples rowed across the Sea of Galilee at night against a strong headwind. Jesus had stayed behind and they had no idea how He would join them on the other side. But as morning dawned, they saw a solitary figure gliding toward them on the water. "A ghost!" they cried in fear.

But it was no ghost—it was Jesus. "Be of good cheer," He told them. "It is I; do not be afraid."

That was good enough for Peter. His fear left him and he suddenly felt full of faith. "Lord," he said, "if it is You, tell me to come to You on the water." That's quite a request. None of the other disciples even thought of asking such a thing. But Peter did—and the Lord replied to him, "Come."

Peter carefully lifted himself out of the boat and let his feet touch the water—and he didn't sink. He must have felt overjoyed as he began walking toward Jesus on the surface of the water. When he kept his eyes fixed on the Master, he continued to move over the waves. But once he began to notice the howling wind, his fears took over and the water sidewalk beneath his feet began to give way.

"Oh, Lord," he cried out, "save me!"

Instantly, Peter felt the strong hand of Jesus pulling him out of the deep. "O you of little faith," Jesus said to Peter, "why did you doubt?" (Matthew 14:25-31).

For a time, Peter exercised the faith to actually walk on water. So long as he kept his eyes on Jesus, cruising across the waves didn't seem like any big deal. But then he listened to the wind shriek and felt a spray of water on his face and realized he didn't have the sturdy planks of a boat under his feet. He started looking around and thought, *What am I doing out here?* At that moment his faith evaporated and he began plunging toward the bottom of the sea.

"Lord," he cried out, "help!"

I can almost hear Jesus chuckle as He said, "Oh, you of little faith. Why did you doubt? You started well—what made you lose your confidence?"

The difference between faith and doubt is where we fix our gaze. Each of us faces situations every day that have the potential to sink us. It is so easy for us to get our eyes on our circumstances. We look right and left and see the boisterous waves on all sides. As we focus on the problem, we begin to sink.

We need to keep our eyes on the Lord, who is Master over the sea, the wind and the waves. As long as Peter fixed his eyes on Jesus, he could walk over the surface of the raging water of Galilee. But when he took his eyes off Jesus and started concentrating on the wind and waves, he sank like a stone. It's no different for us.

I think it's great that when Peter started to sink, he knew whom to call. "Lord, save me!" I've been in the same boat. How many times I've cried, "Oh, Lord, save me!" And just like Peter, I've also experienced the gracious, saving hand of Jesus. "Oh, you of little faith, why did you doubt? You were doing all right, but here's My hand. Let Me help you out of this mess."

I DON'T KNOW HIM

It seems amazing that the same man who could at one moment proclaim Jesus to be the Christ, the Son of God, could, in practically the next breath, rebuke Jesus for declaring His intent to do the very thing He had come to earth to accomplish (Matthew 16:16, 22). Yet that was Peter—oscillating at times between faith and doubt, belief and unbelief.

Before Jesus' arrest, Peter boldly proclaimed that while all the other disciples might desert the Lord when things got tough, Peter would never do so. He couldn't imagine suffering such a lapse of faith. "Lord, I'm ready to go to prison. I'm ready to die with You." Don't think Peter was insincere. He meant exactly what he said. In his heart, he felt ready to go to prison and even die for Jesus. He is much like us when we make our bold, sincere promises to the Lord. Jesus, knowing better, told Peter that before the night had ended, he would in fact deny that he knew Him—not once, not twice, but three times. Peter couldn't believe it. "I would never do that!" he insisted.

But then came the arrest, the temple guards, the spears, the swords, the shouting, the torches and the fear. All of the disciples abandoned Jesus and fled—including Peter.

Peter didn't run away completely, however. He followed the Lord at a distance, trying to stay under cover. During the long night, three witnesses identified Peter, and each time he denied knowing the Lord. At the final denial, a rooster crowed, as Jesus had predicted. Luke tells us that at precisely that moment, the Lord looked at Peter—and Peter wept bitterly.

What sort of look did Jesus give Peter? Was it a look of rebuke? A look that said, "I told you so"? I doubt it. I think it was a look that said, "Peter, I understand. And I love you still." I believe He looked at him with eyes of love, perhaps the deepest love Peter had ever seen. And that's what broke Peter's heart.

The Bible says, "Don't you realize that it is the goodness of God that leads you to repentance?" (Romans 2:4). If someone comes down hard on you, your immediate tendency is to defend yourself, to stiffen, to justify your actions. But when a person puts his arm around you and says, "I understand and I'm praying for you. I love you, brother"—hey, that breaks you up. You have no defense. It melts your heart. And I think that's exactly how Jesus looked at Peter.

As soon as Peter saw Jesus' look of compassion and love, he ran out of the courtyard where he had been loitering and wept bitterly. *Utter failure!*

God, will I always be a failure? he must have wondered.

"No, Peter, not always," God could have replied. "In a few days you're going to receive power and you'll finally be the witness I want you to be." Peter felt so low at that moment that he probably wouldn't have believed such a promise. But after Pentecost, when the Holy Spirit arrived and filled him, he discovered just how much things had changed.

A LAME MAN WALKS

We can see how far Peter moved from doubt to faith through an encounter he had at the gate of the temple. As he and John entered the temple, they met a man who had been lame from birth. Each day friends carried this man from home and laid him at the Beautiful Gate so that he might beg for money from temple visitors.

Even to the present day in the Middle East you will find beggars such as this man. People with physical disabilities sit by the Damascus Gate or Saint Stephen's Gate, begging for money from those who enter the old city of Jerusalem.

When this man saw Peter and John about to enter the temple, he asked for money. Peter turned and said to him, "Look at us." The man did so, expecting some little gift, and Peter continued, "I don't have any silver or gold to give you, but what I do have I will gladly give: In the name of Jesus Christ of Nazareth, stand up and walk." Peter then stooped down, took the man by the right hand, and lifted him to his feet. Immediately the lame man's feet and ankle bones gained full health and strength (Acts 3:3-7).

Here was a man about forty years of age who had never taken a step in his life. All the people of Jerusalem knew him because every day they saw him begging in the same place. Peter spoke to this man a word of faith—and a healing miracle occurred on the spot.

Jesus had said to His disciples, "And whatever you ask in My name, that I will do, that the Father might be glorified in the Son" (John 14:13). And now these men, once so full of fear and doubt, were beginning to exercise real faith to tap into the power of Jesus Christ.

I believe it took a great deal of faith for Peter to take the man by the right hand and lift him to his feet. Can you imagine yourself doing it? What do you suppose went through Peter's mind? I know what would be going through my mind: *I hope this guy stands. I hope he doesn't collapse.* I wouldn't want to be accused of cruelty to the disabled if this guy should crumple.

Peter didn't have to worry. The formerly lame man began leaping and praising God as he entered the temple with the two disciples. Remember, that forty-year old man had never walked a day in his life. And suddenly he had the ability to not only walk, but also to jump and leap. How excited he must have felt over this miracle.

Of course, the people at the temple noticed, and they all came running to see for themselves what had happened. The buzz quickly spread, and hundreds, maybe thousands of men and women came crowding into Solomon's porch to see what God had done.

Peter and John saw that the people were looking at them as though they themselves were the source of the miracle. Peter couldn't allow such a huge misunderstanding to go unchallenged. So he immediately disassociated himself and John from the miracle.

"Why do you look at us as though through our own power or holiness we made this man walk?" he asked. "We didn't have anything to do with it. God healed this man. We have no more power than you do."

God uses men who never seek glory or fame for themselves. They have all come to the cross. They don't attract people to themselves nor do they desire to attract people. Their chief aim and preeminent desire is to bring glory to God's Son. And so Peter immediately pointed the crowd away from himself and to Jesus.

Peter declared boldly that it was through faith in the name of Jesus Christ that this formerly lame man received the ability to walk. But he didn't stop there. Peter didn't want anyone to say, "What a great man of faith you must be!" So Peter refused to take credit for his faith. He called it "the faith which comes through Him" (Acts 3:16). Jesus is the author and the finisher of our faith, according to Hebrews 12:2. The apostle Paul tells us that God has given to every believer a measure of faith (Romans 12:3). In 1 Corinthians 12:9, faith is listed among the gifts of the Spirit. Peter is saying that this miracle represented an exercise of the gift of God.

"The Lord gave me the faith. I don't go around raising lame people to their feet. It is the faith which is *by Him* that this man has received such perfect soundness in body, as you all can see for yourselves." He turned the attention away from himself and over to Jesus Christ—and then he used the incident to invite people into a personal relationship with the Lord. "Repent therefore," he said, "and be converted, that your sins may be blotted out, so that times of refreshing may come from the presence of the Lord" (Acts 3:19).

How I love that term, "blotted out," especially when it refers to my sins. You don't need to carry the guilt of your past. You don't need to mope around feeling condemned. God will blot out your sordid past, all of it, when you come to Jesus through simple faith in His name.

When you enter into a relationship with Jesus by faith, "times of refreshing" come to you from the presence of the Lord. Isn't it a glorious and refreshing thing to be in the Lord's presence? Even though at times I've come into services feeling physically weary, I always leave feeling strengthened and refreshed simply by being in God's presence. That's what faith in His name can do for all of us.

A NEW BOLDNESS

Not everyone was happy about the healing of the lame man. When Jerusalem's religious officials heard about Peter's emphasis on the name of Jesus, they summoned him to their assembly, hoping to intimidate him into remaining silent about the Nazarene.

By this time, Peter's doubts had disappeared. That's what happens when you're filled with the Holy Spirit. God's power had settled upon Peter and he would now bear clear witness to Jesus Christ, just as Jesus Himself had predicted.

Now, this wasn't natural for Peter. This assembly of high mucky-mucks had intimidated Peter before he was filled with the Holy Spirit. Outside this very council of religious leaders, Peter had denied his Lord three times. But now he's standing in the middle of them with his own life on the line, and he declares, "Let it be known to you all, and to all the people of Israel, that by the name of Jesus Christ of Nazareth, whom you crucified, whom God raised from the dead, by Him this man stands here before you whole" (Acts 4:10).

What a transformation! What a difference when the Holy Spirit fills a man.

The religious leaders warned Peter and John not to speak in Jesus' name again, but of course their threats fell on deaf ears. You can't quiet men filled with the Spirit. There's simply no way to silence them.

"You've told us not to speak," Peter said. "God has told us *to speak*. Now whether it is right for us to listen to you or to God, you be the judge. But as for us, we have no intention of listening to you more than to God. We cannot help but speak the things we have seen and heard. And we will not be quiet about them."

True to their word, Peter and the rest of the disciples continued to testify about Jesus Christ. And true to their word, the religious leaders hauled them in again and had them beaten. How did the disciples respond?

They rejoiced.

Now, if you were beaten because of your witness for Jesus Christ, what do you suppose you would do? It would be very tempting to just say, "Well, that's the end of that. I'll never do that again." But the disciples rejoiced. They said, "Oh, Lord, how good You are to count us worthy to suffer shame for You!"

How do you stop people like that? You don't, because you can't—not with threats, beatings, or even martyrdom. Such people are simply unstoppable.

Peter had come a long way since the days when he expressed doubt rather than faith. What made the difference in him was the filling of the Holy Spirit. On our own, we can do nothing. But with God, all things are possible. Peter discovered this over time, but once he did, everything changed. He had made the journey from doubt to faith.

The Soldier & the Mother: Great Faith

I have not found such great faith, not even in Israel!

MATTHEW 8:10

O woman, great is your faith! Let it be done to you as you desire.

MATTHEW 15:28

ONLY TWICE IN THE FOUR GOSPELS did Jesus commend anyone for having great faith—both times His praise went to a non-Israelite. He never commended His own disciples for great faith. He never lauded a priest or Levite or a member of the Sanhedrin for great faith. The only individuals He ever singled out for expressing great faith were a Roman soldier and a Syro-Phoenician woman from Canaan.

Faith, you see, isn't something conferred through position, title or bloodline.

MEN OF AUTHORITY

Several times the New Testament mentions elite Roman soldiers called centurions, and every time they are described in a positive light. Each Roman legion had 6,000 soldiers, divided into sixty squadrons of 100 men, with each squadron commanded by a centurion. Even today, the word "century" refers to 100. Centurions were equal in rank to a master sergeant and represented the elite of the Roman army. They were specially chosen men—select, honorable and well-qualified.

One day Jesus entered the city of Capernaum and found a group of elders from the local synagogue waiting for Him. They had come on an urgent mission from a Roman centurion whom they highly respected.

The elders told Jesus that the centurion had a favorite servant who had fallen seriously ill with palsy. Palsy is a disease that attacks the joints of the body causing excruciating pain, paralyzing the individual and leaving him an invalid. It is a torturous, painful condition. In this case, the servant had grown so ill that he was near death.

When the centurion heard reports of the widespread healing ministry of Jesus, he asked the elders of the synagogue to approach Jesus to heal his servant. A special relationship had grown between this Roman centurion and the Jewish leaders, for he had paid for the construction of their synagogue. The elders "begged Him earnestly" to grant the centurion's request, for they said he loved Israel and was worthy of Jesus' favor.

It is possible that one of the Jewish officials who came to Jesus was Jairus, a ruler of the Capernaum synagogue (Luke 8:40-56). The religious officials described this centurion as an unusual man, graced with many worthy spiritual characteristics.

Jesus granted the soldier's request and started toward his home, accompanied by the synagogue leaders. When He approached the house, however, the centurion sent other friends to Jesus with a message:

> Lord, do not trouble Yourself, for I am not worthy that You should enter under my roof. Therefore I did not even think myself worthy to come to You. But say the word, and my servant will be healed. For I also am a man placed under authority, having soldiers under me. And I say to one, "Go," and he goes; and to another, "Come," and he comes; and to my servant, "Do this," and he does it (Luke 7:6-8).

While the Jewish elders had described the centurion as a "worthy" man, the centurion himself says, "I am not worthy that You should enter under my roof." The words translated "worthy" in this passage are actually two different terms in the original Greek. The centurion is saying, in essence, "I'm not capable of entertaining You." By custom, a Jew was forbidden from entering the house of a Gentile. While I'm certain that Jesus would have entered his house had the soldier not sent these second messengers, the centurion probably realized that such an incident would inflame further controversy between Jesus and the Jews. Therefore he said, "I'm not worthy that You should come into my house."

However, when the soldier says, "I did not even think myself worthy to come to You," he uses a different term. There he employs the same word the Jewish elders used to describe him as a worthy man. So we have their opinion of him and his opinion of himself. They called him a worthy man; yet, he said, "I'm not worthy to come to You."

Humility always gets the attention of God. But so does faith, and this Roman soldier had both in great amounts.

In essence the centurion told Jesus, "I know all about authority. I am also a man under authority"—recognizing that Jesus ministered under the authority of God the Father.

The man who rules well is the man who understands that he also is ruled—that he functions under the authority of someone else or that he labors subservient to a set of laws. Yes, he has authority, but he's not the final authority. He serves under a greater authority.

As a military man, this centurion understood the chain of command. And in Jesus, he recognized a Man of both authority and power. "I understand Your authority in the spiritual realm," he was saying. "I also recognize Your authority over the physical realm. Therefore, I know that You have the authority to merely speak the word and my servant will be healed. There's no need for You to come to my house. I know that all You have to do is give the command, and my servant will be made well. Just as I can tell a servant to come and he comes, so can You command this disease to go and it will go."

Jesus could hardly believe His ears. To think that He would find such great faith in the heart of a Roman centurion. Luke says that Jesus marveled at the man, turned around and said to those accompanying Him, "I say to you, I have not found such great faith, not even in Israel!" (Luke 7:9).

Jesus had spent considerable time with His disciples—and yet He hadn't found such faith in them. He had several encounters with the Jewish religious leaders, but He didn't find any great faith in them. He had interacted with all kinds of people, but never had He found the kind of faith that this Roman soldier demonstrated.

Matthew tells us that Jesus said to the centurion's represen-tatives, "Go your way; and as you have believed, so let it be done for you" (Matthew 8:13). When the centurion's friends returned to his house, they found the sick man completely well. Matthew adds a postscript to this story. He reports that Jesus said,

> And I say to you that many will come from east and west, and sit down with Abraham, Isaac, and Jacob in the kingdom of heaven. But the sons of the kingdom will be cast out into outer darkness. There will be weeping and gnashing of teeth (Matthew 8:11-12).

Death is not the end of our existence—life continues. "It is appointed unto man once to die, and after that the judgment" (Hebrews 9:27). A believer in Christ can look forward to enjoying the kingdom of God and sitting down with Abraham, Isaac, and Jacob and enjoying marvelous conversations with them about the faithfulness and glory of God. What an experience that will be.

Not everyone will see or enjoy that kingdom of God. It is interesting that Matthew, and not Luke, writes that, "The sons of the kingdom will be cast out into outer darkness. There will be weeping and gnashing of teeth." Matthew wrote his gospel to the Jews, while Luke wrote his gospel to the Gentiles. Matthew, therefore, gives a serious warning to his own people: There is the eternal kingdom of God and the eternal kingdom of darkness, and every man and woman has a destiny in one of those two places. That's a given—and you are the only one who will determine where you will spend eternity. Just because you were born a Jew doesn't give you a reservation in heaven. Just because you keep the Sabbath and go to synagogue means nothing in terms of your eternal destiny. What is your relationship to

Jesus Christ? Have you placed your faith in Him? Have you asked Him to forgive your sins? Only those who have a saving relationship with Jesus Christ, by grace through faith, will ever see the kingdom of God.

Jesus marveled at the faith of the centurion and said He had found nothing like it anywhere in Israel. He did find it one other time—but again, not in the heart of an Israelite.

AN OVERCOMING FAITH

Jesus often rebuked people for their lack of faith—even His own disciples.

It is interesting that He didn't chide the non-Jewish mother who came to Him in desperation, seeking to have her daughter released from severe demonic possession. By the end of the encounter Jesus proclaimed that she had great faith—but she had to overcome a great deal to earn that description.

First, she came to Jesus against her *prejudice*. Second, she persevered against the *silence* of Jesus. Third, she proceeded against *exclusion*. And finally, she won against a *rebuff*.

PREJUDICE

The Jews were a clannish people. They would not mix with people of other races. John 4 tells how Jesus asked a Samaritan woman to give Him a drink from the well of her town, and she marveled that He would talk to her: "How is it that You're asking me for a drink? You're a Jew, I'm a Samaritan. We don't deal with each other." A Jew would not enter a Gentile house. When the Lord called Peter to take the gospel to the Gentiles, he received an invitation to the house of Cornelius, a Roman centurion. Peter told the man, "God told me to come here, or else I wouldn't be here. It is not lawful for me to come into the house of a Gentile" (Acts 10:28).

This Gentile woman came to Jesus against sharp, racial distinction. She was so driven to find relief for her daughter that she came against severe prejudice. No doubt she had tried everything, perhaps visiting wizards and shamans and subjecting her daughter to incantations and exorcisms. But nothing had worked. When she heard Jesus had arrived in her area, she saw hope. Most likely she had heard of His reputation, which, according to Mark's gospel, had spread throughout all of Syria by this time. She figured He was the last hope for her daughter. If He didn't come through, she would lose her.

SILENCE

A second obstacle proved even more difficult. When this woman cried out to Jesus and said, "Lord, Son of David, have mercy on me," Jesus did not answer her a word (Matthew 15:22-23).

His silence must have been excruciating for her. Yet she wasn't about to give up because of a little silence. She addressed Jesus with a Messianic title—Son of David. Somehow she had heard enough about Jesus that she believed He was the promised Messiah. So she called for mercy and for help.

The silence of God can be a tough obstacle. When we land in trouble and pray, but it seems as though God remains silent, we can grow discouraged. Why doesn't He respond? It seems like heaven's door has slammed shut on us, even as things grow worse. Many people fail at this testing. When God remains silent, they despair and turn away.

Not this woman—she saw hope in the silence of Jesus, which only pushed her further. He didn't say yes, but neither did He say no. It is interesting that she had more hope in the silence of Jesus than we often have in the promises of Jesus. We have glorious promises about prayer, yet so many times we get discouraged. "Well, I don't know if that applies to my situation," or "Well, I know it's there, but this is really tough."

EXCLUSION

As she continued to pursue His disciples, they approached Jesus saying, "Lord, she's irritating. Give her what she wants and send her away." They had little concern for the woman's daughter. They simply wanted relief from this woman's pestering.

Within earshot of the woman, Jesus responded to His disciples, "I have been sent only to the lost sheep of the house of Israel," meaning this woman—a Syro-Phoenician from Canaan—was outside of the covenant. It must have hurt to hear those words, which Jesus addressed to His disciples and not directly to her. But she still wasn't deterred. Persevering, she came and worshiped Him. "Lord," she said, "help me" (Matthew 15:25).

When we pray over a need and it seems we get no response from God, often Satan uses this delay as an opportunity to condemn us. He'll say, "How can you ask God to help you out of this mess you made yourself? You have no right praying. You've failed Him miserably."

A lot of people listen to Satan's lies and accusations and become discouraged in prayer because they look at themselves and say, "I know I don't deserve it. I know I'm not worthy. Maybe I should just forget it. I really shouldn't ask God for anything."

This woman didn't come to Jesus because she felt qualified. She didn't come saying, "Lord, I want justice." Only a fool would say that! She came saying, "Lord, I need mercy." Her appeal was not based on her own merit—it was based on the mercy of Jesus, and so she continued to press Him.

Like this woman, we don't come to the Lord because we deserve His blessings or goodness. We come because God is gracious and merciful. And despite the fact that she had no right to come to the table, you do have a right to come—if you have placed your faith in Jesus. The door is open and the Lord invites you to come in. Jesus made the way for us to become His children, sit at His table, and to partake of the fullness of God's blessings and grace.

Mark's gospel tells us that at this point Jesus entered a house, but the woman followed Him and fell at His feet and began to worship Him. And once more she had to overcome a formidable obstacle, even as she pleaded, "Lord, help me."

REBUFF

When this woman again asked Jesus for His help, He turned to her and said, "It isn't right to take the children's bread and give it to the dogs" (Mark 7:27).

If we had no understanding of the Greek language, we might get upset with Jesus at that comment. But the word He used there was a Greek term that could better be translated, "little puppies." Every household had a little puppy that would wait around the table for the children to toss scraps of bread to them. In those days, they didn't use utensils for eating. They ate as God intended man to eat, with his hands. That's why it was so important to wash your hands before the meal.

At that time, however, they just pulled off a piece of bread, dipped it in one of the various sauces on the table and ate it. Want a piece of meat? Just grab the roast, pull off a chunk and chew on it. At the end of the meal, of course, your hands would be pretty juicy and greasy, so you'd reach for the loaf of bread, pull off a piece and wipe your hands. And then you'd toss that piece of bread to the little puppy that waited expectantly for table scraps.

In Jesus' softened response, this woman saw an open door. "That's right, Lord, I agree," she said. "But even the little puppies eat the crumbs that fall from the master's table."

That's when Jesus said, "O woman, great is your faith! Let it be to you as you desire" (Matthew 15:28). She had broken through and overcome. Her daughter was healed from that very hour.

A SAVIOR IN THE KNOW

We must look a little closer in order to understand this story and Jesus' actions. As the Son of God, Jesus knew all things. John tells us that He didn't need for anybody to report to Him about people, because He knew what was in them.

The moment the woman came to Him, Jesus knew He was going to heal her daughter. The truth is, He acted as He did in order to draw her faith out to its fullest expression. His method tested her faith, to be sure, but it also gave her the opportunity to express her faith to its greatest measure.

Every time He took a step back, she took a step forward. He intended to draw her into the closest, most intimate relationship of faith possible—for her, yes, but also to encourage the people around her. As we soon read, after He healed her daughter,

"Then great multitudes came to Him, having with them the lame, blind, mute, maimed, and many others. And they laid them down at Jesus' feet, and He healed them" (Matthew 15:30). Her faith opened the door for her daughter's healing and also for the work of the Lord in that region.

Oh, the power of prevailing prayer! It not only meets your needs, but it also opens the door for others to enter in and to receive the mercy and the grace of God.

SHE WOULDN'T STOP

Why did this woman remain persistent in the face of so many obstacles? She had such a great love and concern for her daughter that she refused to be turned away. She would not take no for an answer. She didn't let discouragement stop her. She persisted until she received from the Lord the answer she needed.

We can learn several lessons from this story. First, the silence of Jesus doesn't necessarily indicate no. I think of the preacher who stood before his congregation and said, "There have been some disgruntled people here, so I'd like to invite all of you who want me to leave the church and no longer pastor here to speak up." When no one said anything, he declared, "Well, then. Silence is consent. I'm staying on."

Sometimes God's silence is just a matter of timing. It isn't that He has no intention of answering your prayer. Perhaps He wants to work a few things out in your heart and mind first. Maybe He is seeking to draw you out, just as He drew out this woman's expression of faith to bring her from the place of asking to the place of worshiping.

Maybe you have a child who has become a real problem. She has become openly defiant, or he is rebelling against your authority. You may be to the place where, along with this woman, you would say, "He's severely demon-possessed." You're at your wit's end and don't know what to do.

Don't give up. Press in. Fall at His feet. Worship Him. Before long, you'll see God's work in the life of your children.

Or it could be that you're on the other side of the coin. It may be you're the object of prayer. Maybe you're the one for whom your mother has been praying for years. What a glorious thing it would be if this were the day that the Lord should say, "Oh, woman! Great is your faith ... be it done unto you even as you desire."

I encourage you to surrender your life to God. Quit running. The Bible says, "Woe to him who fights with his Maker!" (Isaiah 45:9). Don't fight with God anymore. Get down on your knees and turn your life over to Him, and then find a phone and call your mom. Share with her the good news of what God has done in you.

Whatever is troubling your heart, I encourage you to bring it to God. Bring it in humility. Don't come on the basis of what He ought to do for you, but on the basis of His grace and mercy. Present your request to Him, worship Him, and ask Him to perform His perfect work in you. Let the Spirit of God mold you, shape you, and bring you into full conformity with that which God has in mind for you. And then rejoice as you hear His words, "Let it be done to you as you desire."

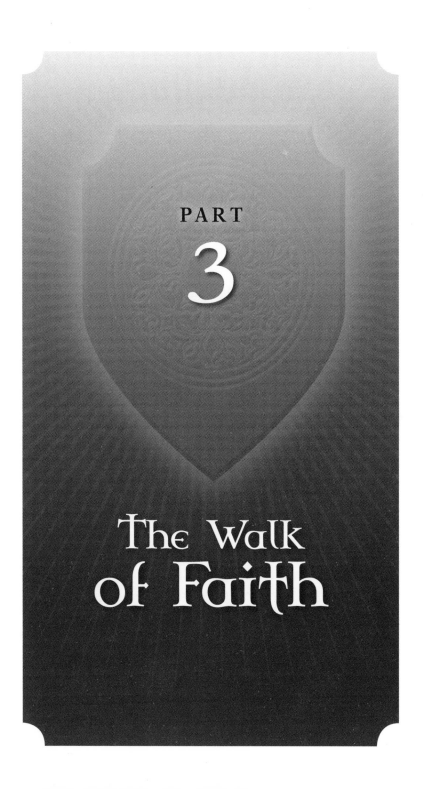

PART

3

The Walk
of Faith

Faith

15

Living by Faith in a Faithful God

Not a word failed of any good thing which the LORD
had spoken to the house of Israel. All came to pass.

JOSHUA 21:45

THROUGHOUT THE BIBLE, GOD DISPLAYS Himself as being faithful and worthy of our trust. We find one of the best examples of His faithfulness when Israel, under the leadership of Joshua, conquered the Promised Land.

At one point Joshua stood at almost the same spot where Abraham had stood at Bethel some 476 years earlier. Abraham had come to a parting of ways with his nephew, Lot, and he probably felt a little dejected. Lot had chosen to take the area of the Jordan valley, leaving Abraham alone with his cattle and his servants. As Abraham stood there, perhaps with his head down, the Lord said,

> Abram, lift up your head, and look to the north, and the south, and the east, and the west. As far as your eye can

217

see, I am going to give to you and to your descendants this
territory for their inheritance (Genesis 13:14-15).

Abraham looked to the north toward Mount Hermon, to the
east toward Mount Gilead and Moab, to the south toward
the wilderness area of Beersheba, and to the west to the
Mediterranean Sea. And Abraham believed God and the promise
that God had given him.

Centuries later, Joshua stood in the same area. And as he looked
to the north, the south, the east, and the west, he realized that
as far as his eye could see, the children of Israel were dwelling
in that land. Up toward Mount Hermon, the tribes of Asher,
Zebulun, Naphtali, Issachar, and Manasseh had established
themselves. He looked toward Gilead and Moab, where the
tribes of Reuben, Gad, and half the tribe of Manasseh lived. To
the west he viewed where Ephraim had settled. Looking south
toward the Jerusalem range of mountains, through Hebron to
Beersheba, he knew that the tribes of Simeon, Dan, Benjamin,
and Judah had made their homes there. Everything he could
see belonged to God's people. And he knew that God had kept
His covenant with Abraham—to the letter.

Some seven years earlier, as Joshua stood on the other side of
the Jordan River, the conquest of the land still lay before him.
He had certain apprehensions. The Israelites had heard about
this land inhabited by gigantic men. Their cities had high walls
that reached to heaven, with fierce and strong inhabitants that
surely outnumbered Joshua's forces. As Joshua prepared to
enter the land, God had told him,

> Every place that the sole of your foot shall tread, I have
> given to you. There shall not be any man able to stand
> before you. Fear not: for you shall divide this land for an
> inheritance for these people (Joshua 1:3-6).

God kept His word. The Israelites took all of the cities, despite their high walls and giants. Even when several kings united in a strong federation, God delivered their huge pagan armies into the hands of Joshua. Not a king or an alliance of kingdoms could stand against Joshua. And every place that Joshua put down his foot now belonged to the people of God.

In seven years they conquered the whole land. God destroyed the enemy kings, even as He promised. The word of God had proven faithful. And so Joshua gives this testimony: "Not a word failed of any good thing which the LORD had spoken to the house of Israel. All came to pass" (Joshua 21:45).

God remained faithful to His word, even though His people did not always remain faithful. The Israelites had broken covenant with God many times. At one point they even tried to get someone to lead them back to Egypt. But God remained faithful to His promise. You can rely on God's absolute faithfulness to keep His word.

A GENOCIDE FOILED

Although God had promised Abraham that his descendants would remain forever, a time came when the Hebrew people faced extinction. Haman, the right-hand man of the Persian king, Ahasuerus, deceived the king into signing a decree that sounded the death knell for the people of God. According to the decree, on a particular day throughout all of Persia, non-Jews were to kill every Jew in the community. To sweeten the deal, whoever killed a Jew could have his possessions.

One of God's people, Mordecai, sent a message to his cousin, Esther, who had married King Ahasuerus. The king did not know she was a Jewess. "Do you think that you will escape if all of the people perish?" Mordecai asked. "Go in and talk to your husband and somehow have him recant this order."

"Mordecai," she said, "you don't know the protocol of the Persian court. You don't just talk to the king anytime you wish, even if he is your husband. If I go in without being called and the king doesn't raise his golden scepter, the guards will immediately take off my head. You are asking me to risk my life."

Mordecai sent another message: "Don't think that you can escape. If this decree goes through, you also will perish. And how do you know that God has not brought you to the kingdom for such a time as this?" Then he added, "If you fail God at this point, He will deliver His people from another corner. God will save His people, one way or another. God's word is going to come to pass. He will deliver them through another channel; but you will have lost everything" (Esther 4:13-14).

Esther agreed with his assessment and said, "Pray for me. I will go to the king—and if I perish, I perish." Through Esther, God not only saved the nation, but actually increased its stature.

Mordecai was absolutely confident that God would work. "You may fail, Esther, but God won't fail." In the same way, you may fail, but God's Word will never fail. "Not a word failed of any good thing which the LORD had spoken to the house of Israel. All came to pass."

THE PROMISE OF THE SON

What was true of God then is true of God now. Throughout history—and to the present day—God has remained faithful to keep His word.

God promised He would send His Son to be born of a virgin, to die for the sins of the world that He might bring eternal life and redemption to all who would believe. In the book of Isaiah God promised that a Child would be born, a Son would be given—His own Son, Jesus. The government would be upon His shoulders and He would be called Wonderful, Counselor, Mighty God, Everlasting Father, and Prince of Peace (Isaiah 9:6).

Two chapters earlier God had said, "A virgin shall conceive, and bring forth a Son; you shall call His name Immanuel," which means "God with us" (Isaiah 7:14). And later Isaiah prophesied, "He was wounded for our transgressions and bruised for our iniquities. All we like sheep have gone astray; we turned every one of us to our own ways; and God laid on Him all of our iniquities. For the transgression of My people He was smitten. And He was numbered with the transgressors in His death" (Isaiah 53). Not one word of God failed.

God promised that the Messiah would be despised, rejected of men, a man of sorrows, acquainted with grief—and He was. God had promised that His enemies would pluck out His beard and spit on His face—and they did. God had declared that Christ would be betrayed by a friend for thirty pieces of silver and that the silver would be thrown down in the house of the Lord and used to buy a potter's field. And it all happened just as He said.

When Judas came back to the temple with the money he had received for betraying Jesus, he said to the religious officials, "Take back this money. I have betrayed innocent blood."

"That's your problem," they replied. In a rage Judas threw the money on the floor of the temple and left.

"What shall we do with this money?" they asked. "We can't put it back in the treasury; it is blood money." Someone suggested, "Let's buy a potter's field" (Matthew 27:3-10). So what God had declared hundreds of years before came to pass, right down to the last detail. God kept His word precisely.

A MIRACLE DAY

As we look around today, we see that God continues to keep His word. God had said to Ezekiel, "In the last days I will gather again My people from all over the world where they have been scattered. And once more I am going to establish them in the land. At that time the world will see a miracle: for they will see a nation born in a day" (Ezekiel 28:25).

The world saw that miracle on May 14, 1948, when Israel became a nation once more. No nation in history has ever come together again after its people had been ejected from their land for more than a few years—and God gathered His people from all over the world and established them in their land after more than *seventeen centuries* of exile! God kept His promise.

God spoke to the mountains of Israel and said, "You shall be inhabited" (Ezekiel 36:8, 10). Today they are inhabited. You can put your faith in a God who always keeps His promises.

When churches gather for worship around the world, it is a witness to the faithfulness of God to keep His word. God declared that when His own people rejected Him, He would stretch out His hands to the Gentiles and they would receive the eternal life offered them (Isaiah 49:6). Today we are the fulfillment of God's promise to bring salvation to the Gentiles. What God declared would happen, has happened.

What great hope and assurance this brings to us as children of

God. His Word cannot fail. Jesus said, "Heaven and earth shall pass away, but My Word shall never pass away" (Matthew 24:35). Again we are told that, "God is not a man that He should lie, nor the son of man that He should repent; hath He not spoken, and shall He not make it good?" (Numbers 23:19).

You can stand today in faith on the Word of God assured that God loves you. You can feel confident that all things are working together for good because you love Him and have been called according to His purpose (Romans 8:28).

A HOPE OR A TERROR

To the child of God, the faithfulness of God brings glorious assurance and a blessed hope. But to those who are not children of God, it brings fear and terror, because you can be sure that God will keep *all* of His Word.

God has said that there is only one God and one Mediator between God and man, the Man Christ Jesus (1 Timothy 2:5). And Jesus said, "I am the way, the truth, and the life. No one comes to the Father except through Me" (John 14:6). Jesus said, "I am the door of the sheep. All who ever came before Me are thieves and robbers" (John 10:7-8).

Whoever seeks eternal life through a progression of reincarnation, or through their own good efforts, or through any religious system—if they trust in anything other than the shed blood of Jesus Christ for the remission of their sins—then one day they will find that God will keep His word and will look upon their righteousness as filthy rags. They will be rejected from His presence, because they have rejected His only way, through Jesus Christ.

The Bible tells us, "Do not be deceived, God is not mocked; for whatever a man sows, that he will also reap. For he who sows to his flesh will of the flesh reap corruption" (Galatians 6:7-8). You can count on that. If you are living after the flesh and sowing to your flesh, then you can expect to reap corruption. He will keep His word.

The Word of God tells us that a man who despised Moses' law was put to death on the testimony of two or three witnesses.

> Of how much worse punishment, do you suppose, will he be thought worthy who has trampled the Son of God underfoot, counted the blood of the covenant by which he was sanctified a common thing, and insulted the Spirit of grace? For we know Him who said, "Vengeance is Mine, I will repay," says the Lord. And again, "The LORD will judge His people." It is a fearful thing to fall into the hands of the living God (Hebrews 10:29-31).

> This is the testimony: that God has given us eternal life, and this life is in His Son. He who has the Son has life; he who does not have the Son of God does not have life (1 John 5:11-12).

That is God's Word—and God is faithful to keep His word. Does this terrify you? If it does, I urge you to ask Jesus Christ to wash you and cleanse you from your sin. For Jesus has said, "The one who comes to Me I will by no means cast out" (John 6:37). He will receive you today. He will pardon your sins. And then you can rejoice in the faithfulness of God to keep His promise of eternal life through faith in Jesus Christ.

If you will trust in Jesus Christ, God is faithful to account you righteous in Christ Jesus. God is faithful to give you eternal life and you will live and reign with Him forever and ever. But if you reject Jesus Christ, then God is also faithful to His word and you will be shut out from the presence of God forever. *God keeps His word. Always.*

BET YOUR LIFE ON IT

The proof of the Bible can be found any time you want to look around. Not a single word of God has failed to this point. And if God has been faithful to this point, you can be sure He will continue to be faithful to the end. Though heaven and earth pass away, His Word shall stand forever. You can count on that.

God keeps His word to all generations. From the beginning to the end, the Word of God is true, faithful and reliable. All His promises are yes and amen (2 Corinthians 1:20). In Him there is neither shadow nor variableness of turning (James 1:17). What He has said, He will do. What great assurance that brings to our hearts, for we know that the glorious future He has promised to us is based upon nothing less than His Word!

It is interesting that from the beginning of the revelation of God to its end—through 4,000 years of inspiring various human authors—there are no glaring contradictions between the facts of science and the Word of God. These men touched on many fields in their writings: biology, history, literature, and so forth. Through the years, supposed men of science have pointed out "errors" in the Word of God. The Bible has often come under the critical eye of unbelievers. They pick out some Scripture and use it to try to show that the Bible couldn't possibly be the Word of God, since it contradicts the current scientific understanding of our universe.

The Bible declares that the stars are innumerable. As Abraham looked up at the heavens, God promised that his descendants would be like the stars—so innumerable that no one could count them. For years, unbelieving men of science scoffed at the Word of God, because although the Bible says you can't count the stars, they thought they could. Some ancient scholars sat outside all year long, counting every star they could see. One of them counted 6,016; another fellow counted 6,064. For many years, experts thought the 6,000 mark was fairly accurate—until the telescope came along. The bigger the telescopes, the more they revealed the truth of the Bible. Today everyone accepts the fact that the stars can't be numbered. They had to revise their science textbooks, but they didn't have to revise the Bible.

Centuries ago men said that the world was flat, although the Bible said it was round. The experts thought that Columbus would topple over the edge of the world. The Bible said that God hung the world on nothing, but the people scoffed. Today, of course, we realize that it really does hang in space, with nothing holding it from above and nothing supporting it from below.

After all of these years we don't have to go back and change the Scriptures to conform to the "true facts" of science. Have you noticed that the earth is no longer considered to be four billion years old? The latest articles say five billion to maybe twelve billion. Think how fast the earth is aging! It was only one billion when I was in high school. Why the constant revision? They find they need more and more time for evolution to reach its present state of complexity. That's why I'm not worried that any new discovery of science will discredit the Bible.

When I pastored in Tucson years ago, a very learned professor started attending our church. Dr. Albro had been a professor at the University of Minnesota. He took a great interest in me as a young man, for which I am thankful. He tutored me in several fields of knowledge and we would sit together for hours in the evening discussing ancient history and archaeology.

At that time an archaeology class from the University of Arizona had just discovered some Indian bones that it claimed were the oldest ever discovered in the Western United States. They estimated the bones to be about 10,000 years old.

I asked Dr. Albro, "Tell me, they say 10,000 years, but how do they know 10,000 years versus 1,000 years or 5,000?"

"Well, Chuck," he said, "let's say that you and I are out on an archaeological expedition and are digging up some remains. If we find some Indian bones and we say, 'These are at least 1,000 years old,' no paper is going to write about it, because they've found a lot of 1,000-year-old bones. If we say we've discovered bones 5,000 years old, nobody will write about it, because someone else already said they found bones that old. So your bones have to be the oldest bones ever found. We have to make them older than any bones yet discovered so that we can get the publicity and get more money for our expedition."

My mouth dropped open and I said, "You mean *that's* how scientific it is?"

"Exactly!" he answered.

So it's always the most distant star ever discovered or the biggest galaxy ever found. It has to be farther or bigger or older than the last one or it doesn't make the news.

Undeniably, God's Word needs no revision; it remains true forever. Man's word changes, but you can put your whole trust in the Word of God. It's been true from the beginning and it will be true forever.

HE IS ABLE

A little saint of God whom we knew for many years gave me one of the greatest exhortations I ever received. Whenever I would bring up a problem or a difficult situation, she'd say, "But Charles, God is on the throne."

How right she was. Doubting God's promises leads to depression, but believing God's promises helps you go on your way singing and rejoicing. "The Lord is so great! He is beautiful. I thank the Lord and praise Him for His greatness and His power and His provision." You can have that victory of praise and a confident life because you know God will perform His word.

Of course, God will perform His word whether you worry about it or not, so you might as well be happy. You might as well rejoice and praise the Lord, because He is going to do it anyhow. "Rejoice in the Lord always," Paul said, "again I say rejoice" (Philippians 4:4). God is able!

I think those are three of the most victorious words in the whole Scripture. He is able! It's so glorious when I feel my own weakness, see my own limitations, know that I have gone my limit and have done as much as I can—though my work is failing, I know that He is faithful and able.

God is faithful. He who has promised will perform His word, despite our shortcomings or fears or lapses in faith. God will do His work and take care of you. His word will come to pass.

From generation to generation He remains faithful—and He cannot deny Himself.

How Can I Pray in Faith?

The effective, fervent prayer of a righteous man avails much.

JAMES 5:16

MY MOTHER WAS A GREAT WOMAN of prayer. Whenever my sister, brothers or I got hurt, we'd run to Mom and she would pray for us. We never went to doctors—Mom just prayed.

We lived on the edge of town, with a lot of bean fields around us, and in September the farmers would thresh their beans and make tall bales of bean straw. Sometimes we kids would have clod fights using the bales for cover. One day I peeked around a bean straw haystack—and a clod flew straight into my eye, knocking my eye out of the socket.

I ran home as quickly as I could. "Mom," I shouted, "I need prayer!" She pushed my eyeball back into the socket and prayed for me—and that was it. We looked to the Lord for His help in all kinds of situations. I just grew up that way.

Another time I hurt myself and came running to Mom for prayer. She laid her hands on me and said, "Jesus, heal little Charles now." I still hurt, so I said, "Momma, pray again; and this time pray like you really mean it."

I think that's probably a good definition of effective, fervent prayer—where you're praying like you really mean it. It's more than just a casual, "We thank You, Jesus, please ... and if not, give us the grace to bear it." There's something about being desperate in prayer that makes us effective.

I fear that we offer too many sleepy prayers. We don't feel deeply stirred by the situation, so our prayers never rise above the level of a yawn.

ALWAYS A LOCAL CALL

David never did much yawning, because his problems always brought him to his knees. We have so many psalms because David had so many problems. One of my favorites is Psalm 61.

> From the end of the earth I will cry to You, when my heart is overwhelmed; lead me to the rock that is higher than I (Psalm 61:2).

David teaches us that we can call out to God at any time and from any place. What a beautiful thing! The Jews consider prayer a local call from Jerusalem. Americans, they say, have to call long distance. But David insists that from the ends of the earth—no matter where we are—we're near to God.

An old song used to declare, "You can be a million miles from the gates of peace but you're only one little step from God." No matter how far you may have roamed, regardless of how far you've wandered away from God, it only takes one step to get back to Him. And that's a good thing too when your heart feels overwhelmed.

Many things overwhelm our hearts. When a friend or a loved one is dying and medical science can do nothing about it, your heart becomes overwhelmed. When your husband or your wife gets interested in someone else and leaves you, it's overwhelming. When your children are in open rebellion and friction rules the home, it's overwhelming. Or when you've lost your job and have no way to pay the rent. No one stands with you—and you feel overwhelmed.

What should you do in cases like these? David says, "Lead me to the rock that is higher than I."

It's wonderful to know there is a place of strength, salvation and refuge that is higher than I. When I've come to the limit of my ability, I take great comfort in knowing that I have One who can take things up for me. When I've hit the wall and feel crushed, how wonderful it is to flee to the rock that is higher than I. Who is that rock? In the very next psalm, David declares,

> Truly my soul silently waits for God; from Him comes my salvation. He alone is my rock and my salvation; He is my defense; I shall not be greatly moved (Psalm 62:1-2).

As David pondered this thought, his faith grew. The longer he meditated on his Rock, the more his faith expanded until he could write, "He only is my rock and my salvation; He is my defense; I shall not be moved" (Psalm 62:6). Did you notice how his perspective changed? The second time around, David took out the "greatly." He went from "I might be moved a little bit, but not much" to "When God is my rock and my strength and my defense, I shall not be moved at all."

When I face a desperate situation, my heart is heavy. And so I take it to the Lord in prayer. I lay my problem before the Lord, and as I do, the Spirit of God ministers to me—even while I'm praying. By the time I finish my prayer, I have victory. I know God will take care of it. I have the assurance that the Lord will work everything out. My fears blow away and my anxiety dissolves, and most of the time I end up rejoicing.

Christians who suffer through overwhelming situations frequently become the most spiritual people you'll ever meet, precisely because their troubles have driven them to prayer. I heard a friend once talk about his mother, a deeply spiritual woman and a great prayer warrior. "I want you to know I'm responsible for her deep spirituality," he said. "During my teenage years, I kept her on her knees."

David said, "When my heart is overwhelmed, then lead me to the rock." Notice that we need to be led to the Rock. That is the work of the Holy Spirit. He leads us to Jesus Christ, our Rock, our strength, our defense.

Every evening the men of our church pray for those who no longer know where to turn. They've hit the wall. They don't know what to do. Sometimes when a person reaches that place, he will turn to the bottle to forget his troubles, trying to drink his mind into oblivion. Many times people turn to drugs. Some get so desperate they jump off bridges. Beat by the circumstances of life they think, *I can't face another day. I can't go any further.*

We pray for those people every night: "Lord, lead them somehow where they might learn of Your help and Your strength. Help them to know that You're so ready to rescue them, if they'll just call upon You."

Maybe you're reading this book in answer to those prayers. Perhaps you feel overwhelmed by the circumstances of life. You don't know where to turn. You don't know where to go. If your difficult circumstances are more than you can bear—then come to the Rock that is higher than you. Jesus Christ will deliver and strengthen you. He will lead you to a place of strength and victory. Then you will be able to say with David,

> He also brought me up out of a horrible pit, out of the miry clay, and set my feet upon the rock, and established my steps. He has put a new song in my mouth—praise to our God; many will see it and fear, and will trust in the LORD (Psalm 40:2-3).

That's what God wants to do for you. He'll take you out of that miry clay and lift you out of that horrible pit—if you'll just turn things over to Him and give Him a chance to work.

DON'T BOX GOD IN

When we pray by the Spirit, we don't insist that God answer our prayers in only one way. Just because He answered prayer in one manner at one time doesn't mean He's locked into that method forever. David understood this. In answer to a specific prayer regarding a crucial battle, God's Spirit led him to victory over the Philistines. But his enemies didn't stay down for long:

> Then the Philistines once again made a raid on the valley. Therefore David inquired again of God, and God said to him, "You shall not go up after them; circle around them, and come upon them in front of the mulberry trees. And it shall be, when you hear a sound of marching in the tops of the mulberry trees, then you shall go out to battle, for God has gone out before you to strike the camp of the Philistines" (1 Chronicles 14:13-15).

This is where we often make a mistake. We think we have God's methods down pat, so we don't bother to pray for His direction. David had enough wisdom to know that although he would soon face the same enemy in circumstances similar to what he had seen before, he needed to inquire of the Lord. Instead of saying, "Come on, guys. Let's go!" he once more sought the counsel of the Lord.

"Shall we go out against them again?" he asks. God replies, "No, not this time around. I've got a different plan." God is not confined to one method. We should never follow patterns simply because they worked in the past. We need to continually seek God's wisdom and guidance for *every* new situation. Spirit-led prayer seeks God's way of accomplishing His will.

While the church is often guilty of ritualism, it's also guilty of rut-ualism—we keep trying to do things in the same way. We forget that the only difference between a rut and a grave is the length and depth. You can get buried in a rut if you stay in it long enough.

So, keep yourself open in prayer to the leading of God's Spirit. Continue to seek God's mind and His ways, and realize that God may want to lead you in a totally new way this time around.

I have told my church that should the Lord see fit to take me home before He comes again for His church, and new leadership is raised up to lead this flock, please do not say, "But when Chuck was here, this is the way he did it." Times change and it's important that you do not automatically go into battle with the same methods that brought you victory the last time. God may have a new way of fighting this battle—and the only way to keep open to God's new leading is to stay on your knees in prayer.

DON'T GET IN A HURRY

David was a sinner, just like the rest of us, so he didn't always listen to the counsel of God. Sometimes he didn't even ask for it.

When King Saul chased him around Israel, seeking to take his life, David reached a point of despair where he said in his heart, "There is nothing better for me than that I should speedily escape to the land of the Philistines" (1 Samuel 27:1). In other words, "I don't believe God can preserve me here. So I'm going to run away. There is nothing better for me to do."

Oh, what a false conclusion! There is nothing better for you than to submit yourself totally to the will of God in prayer. David allowed his fear to fight off his faith.

The word "speedily" gives you the key to David's mindset. Whenever Satan begins to pressure you into action, he usually suggests you take the quick way. "Hurry. Don't think. Don't ponder the consequences. Move! Quick!" How many times has this tactic landed you in trouble? You act before you have the opportunity to pray or think things through. And you move out on your own without seeking the counsel of God.

This was David's problem. He had the priest with him, who had brought along the ephod to consult God for him. God had warned David that Saul was indeed coming. As David sought God through the priest, God delivered him. But in this case, we read nothing about David seeking the Lord or asking for the will of God. Instead, he acts out of his own analysis of the situation—and he does it quickly. "I'd better speedily get down there!"

Watch out when Satan begins to push you. "You don't have time to pray about this; you'd better act now. If you don't get it now, it's going to be gone forever. You're going to miss this opportunity." Satan often pressures us into actions that we spend years regretting, because we hurried into a situation without waiting upon God. If God wants it for you, then it'll be there tomorrow. Spend a week in prayer; it'll still be around next week.

Years ago I saw a beautiful black Oldsmobile that I wanted, but it was out of my price range. A salesman had me drive it around and pointed out that the car had only 12,000 miles on it, but I simply couldn't afford the thing.

A month later the salesman called me: "We still have this car down here, Chuck—and it's sure a nice car."

"Yeah," I said, "but it's out of my range."

Two months later the guy called again: "The boss told me to tell you to name your price. He can't get rid of this car. It's such a nice car that he can't understand why it won't sell. He figures you must be praying. So tell us what you can pay for it."

Boy, did I enjoy that car!

If God wants you to have it, then you're going to get it. You don't have to sign on the dotted line right now. You don't have to cave in to the old sales pitch, "It's going to be gone tomorrow. We have five guys waiting in line to get this." If God doesn't want you to have it, then let them take it. But if He wants you to have it, He'll give it to you in His own time and in His own way. Commit the issue to Him in Spirit-soaked prayer.

A REVOLUTIONARY DISCOVERY

An Old Testament prophet named Hanani gave me an insight into God that revolutionized my own prayer life. The prophet said to King Asa,

> For the eyes of the LORD run to and fro throughout the whole earth, to show Himself strong on behalf of those whose heart is loyal to Him. In this you have done foolishly; therefore from now on you shall have wars (2 Chronicles 16:9).

With man there are probably three basic kinds of givers.

First is the man who gives in when someone sells him on an idea. He might not be too interested at first, but show him a fancy brochure and tell him what a great program you have—and let it drop that a businessman down the street just gave a thousand dollars—and pretty soon he's sold on the idea. "Well, that's great," he says. "I'd like to have a part in it."

Second is the fellow who responds to a need once someone informs him of it. "This neighborhood needs a gymnasium," you say. "Kids are running wild on the streets. They need supervised play, and here's our plan." He thinks it's a great idea and he writes out a check. You don't have to sell him on the idea; you simply have to inform him of the need.

The third type of giver grew up on the streets and got into a lot of trouble as a kid. He had no access to a recreation center to keep himself occupied. Thus he began to devise his own means of entertainment ... sometimes in destructive ways. Perhaps he spent a few years in juvenile hall. But now that he's matured and has become successful in business, he sees kids suffering from the same plagues that hurt him. And he thinks, *It would be wonderful if we had some kind of planned recreational program for these young people, some place where they could be supervised and get character built into them.*

So he starts looking around to see what might be done. He hears of your plans and gets excited. What you want to do is exactly what he wanted to do! Soon you get a big check in the mail, totally unsolicited. He's been looking for such a place to invest his funds and your work fits the bill.

To listen to our prayers, it would seem that a lot of us think God is most like the first kind of giver. We believe the best way to motivate Him to action is to give Him a good sales pitch.

My early life of prayer was just that: sales pitches. "Now Lord, You can't lose on this one. Because if You'll do this for me, this is what I'm going to do for You. Just help me get this little '36 Ford black coupe with the twin spots, the twin antennas, and Lord, every Sunday I'll go around and pick up my friends to take them to church. How can You lose?" Of course, I also envisioned myself driving past Santa Ana High and letting those Smitty mufflers bark five days a week. Evidently, my sales pitch didn't impress Him. I never did get the car.

Others think God is like the second kind of giver. For this person, prayer time is information time. That person thinks, *Surely once God knows all of my needs, He'll come through.* But what did Jesus say? "Your Father knows what you need before you ever ask Him" (Matthew 6:8). God doesn't need to be informed of our needs.

God is most like the third giver. "For the eyes of the LORD go to and fro throughout the entire earth, to show Himself strong on behalf of him whose heart is loyal to Him." That tells me that

God is looking for a place to invest His resources. God wants to do a work. He is simply searching for people in harmony with His will so that He can channel His resources through them.

We usually make the mistake of trying to direct the flow of the Spirit. We build the channels and then say, "Okay, Lord, now flow through this channel." I think it would be to our advantage—and far wiser—to find out where the Spirit is flowing and get in that flow. God is looking for people who do what He wants done, people in harmony with His purposes and His will. When God finds them, He channels His resources through them and their lives become rich and blessed.

So often during prayer, the Spirit of God ministers to your heart. He brings assurance and comfort. That's what prayer is really about. It's meeting together with God, laying out your complaints, laying out your burdens, telling Him your feelings—and then letting Him minister the strength and comfort of His Spirit to you. Through prayer you receive the assurance that God is going to take care of it. Praying in the flow of the Spirit ends in confidence and in victory. It's glorious!

Believers who pray like this don't trust in the flesh. They trust in the eternal God. They get in the flow of what the Spirit wants done. The key is getting your heart in harmony with God's heart. When you get in sync with God's will, your life will become blessed and enriched in a way you've never known.

So long as you try to work things out on your own, however, you'll be like King Asa: "Therefore from now on you shall have trouble." So long as you trust in the flesh, you will have problems. Find God's channels and get yourself in them, rather than trying to create your own. Train your heart to follow God with a pure loyalty and then watch Him pour His resources through you.

THE POWER AND MYSTERY OF PRAYER

The walk of faith is a difficult walk. We would like it much better if we could get some specific indications along the way. Yes or no? This way or that way?

Walking by faith is not only difficult; it can also be confusing. If we keep getting blocked in something we're praying about, is God saying no, or is Satan trying to hinder us from doing the work of God? It can be difficult to know when to persevere in prayer and when to realize, *I'm trying to buck God. The Lord doesn't want me to do this.* It encourages me so much to know that God does not leave me alone in my praying. In fact, His Spirit prays for me when I'm not even sure how to pray.

> Likewise the Spirit also helps in our weaknesses. For we do not know what we should pray for as we ought, but the Spirit Himself makes intercession for us with groanings which cannot be uttered (Romans 8:26).

Suppose you have a friend who repeatedly gets in trouble with the law. He gets arrested again and calls you to post bail. You love the guy and you want to help him, but you question yourself. Are you really helping him by bailing him out repeatedly? Or are you just enabling him to continue his rebelliousness because he never has to face the full consequences of his behavior? How do you pray for such a man?

I'd suggest something like the following: "God, what do I do about this guy? I bring him before You. He's in a mess again, Lord. God, I don't know how to pray for him, but I ask that You interpret my prayer according to Your will." Sometimes that's the very best way, to pray in the Spirit. You simply give it all over to Him.

I wish I had a more definitive way of ascertaining when God wants me to move and when He doesn't. I don't. I'm just like you. I pray in faith, trusting God. And then I move and hope I've done the right thing. I trust that God is great enough that if I've made a mistake, He'll help me to correct it.

Years ago at a pastors' conference, a request for prayer came in for a pastor's wife scheduled for cancer surgery. The note got passed to the leader of the conference. "Lord," he prayed, "when they open her up, let them find no cancer."

A phone call soon came. The surgeons had opened her up—and found cancer in her lymph nodes. In fact, it had spread throughout her body. So they just closed her up again.

The pastor who brought this request to the conference said, "Chuck, I don't understand it. Here he prayed, 'Lord, when they open her up, help them to find no cancer;' and when they opened her up, they found her so cancerous they didn't even operate. They just closed her up again. I'm devastated."

I asked him, "When is it too late? Is it too late now? Are you saying that God can't do anything right now? Even now," I continued, "the Lord can touch and heal. Why should our faith be predicated upon a time factor? Let's pray for her." We prayed and agreed together that God would touch her body. Then we placed her in the Lord's hands for His work.

Not long afterward this pastor showed up at our church, all smiles. After further examination and lab tests, the doctor had informed the woman, "This has never happened before—we're awfully sorry—but there's nothing wrong with you. You don't have cancer. We don't know what to say … we can't explain it."

We can explain it, of course. God—who is in the business of healing and can make a diseased body whole and healthy anytime He wants to—healed this woman in response to Spirit-led prayer. That doesn't mean He chooses to heal anytime we ask Him to, but it does mean that He is fully able to do so.

We can never go wrong by putting our whole trust in the Lord, who always answers our prayers according to His gracious, loving nature. "The effective, fervent prayer of a righteous man avails much," James tells us—but not even that kind of prayer forces God to do our bidding. So let us continue to pray in faith, believing wholeheartedly in our trustworthy God—and then leave the outcome to Him.

How Can I Step Out in Faith?

Now therefore, give me this mountain of which the LORD *spoke in that day; for you heard in that day how the Anakim were there and that the cities were great and fortified. It may be that the* LORD *will be with me, and I shall be able to drive them out as the* LORD *said.*

JOSHUA 14:12

SEVERAL YEARS AGO AFTER A Sunday morning worship service, some kids wheeled their grandfather up to me at the front of the sanctuary. "Chuck," they said, "would you pray for our granddad?"

"Sure," I said, and I laid hands on him. I had just read Acts 3, where Peter lifted the lame man to his feet. So as I prayed for this man I thought, *Well, why don't I lift him to his feet? I mean, Peter did it*. So I lifted the guy out of his wheelchair and onto his feet. "In the name of Jesus," I said, "walk." And the guy started walking.

"Grandpa is walking!" the kids cheered, as the elderly man strode up and down the aisle.

Then they informed me of their real request: "He has a cold. We wanted you to pray for his cold."

"Why didn't you tell me that?" I said, astonished.

Now, I don't know where I got that faith. I don't make a practice of lifting people out of wheelchairs. But at that instant I had the faith for this man to be healed. I only had to step out in faith to see the miracle.

The following Wednesday night I spoke in a church in Tucson, Arizona. After the service a man brought his wife up to me in a wheelchair. "Chuck," he said, "my wife has suffered a stroke. Would you pray that God would heal her?"

So I laid hands on her and prayed. Then I patted her on the shoulder and said, "God bless you, sister. We'll continue to pray for you."

As the man wheeled her out, my son, Chuck Jr., said, "Dad, why didn't you lift her up like you did that guy last Sunday?"

"The Lord didn't give me the faith for that," I said. "I didn't feel impressed to do it. I had no impulse to lift her up." Stepping out in that kind of faith is one of those great intangibles. Sometimes you have the faith, other times you don't. It's a gift, not a reservoir. You need God's wisdom to know when He opens the door and beckons for you to take a great step of faith.

ASK FOR WISDOM

A lot of people do crazy things in the name of faith, when it's really nothing more than spiritual foolishness. James writes,

> If any of you lacks wisdom, let him ask of God, who gives to all liberally and without reproach, and it will be given

to him. But let him ask in faith, with no doubting, for he who doubts is like a wave of the sea driven and tossed by the wind (James 1:5-6).

If you ask the Lord for wisdom to help you make the right decision about a special step of faith you're contemplating, then believe that He will give you that wisdom. Ask in faith, trusting the Lord. The Bible repeatedly instructs us to trust in the Lord with all our heart—to believe His promise that He will direct our paths. An indecisive person rarely accomplishes anything worthwhile for God. You probably know wishy-washy believers who waver back and forth. "I wonder if I should try it? Maybe I should just forget it. But if I don't try I'll miss my chance ... maybe I should give it a try. But what if it fails?"

If you're genuine in your desire to be led of the Lord, then I believe He'll hinder your plans if they're not His will. That has happened many times to me. When the Lord puts a roadblock in my way, I don't try to push it out of the way.

Do we believe God when He says, "The steps of a good man are ordered by the LORD, and He delights in his way" (Psalm 37:23)? If we do, then taking a step of faith becomes easier. And every once in a while the Lord lets His people see how He uses that faith to accomplish His will.

Years ago I attended a Saturday brunch after speaking at a weekend retreat. A pastor friend of mine, Steve, accompanied me. At one point the conversation turned to the terrorist bombing of the U.S. Marine outpost in Beirut. "There's an interesting story about that bombing," I told the group.

"A young Christian soldier had a tremendous witness for Christ at that outpost. He often stepped out in faith to speak of his love for the Lord. His sergeant hated his witness, however, and gave him every rotten duty he could think of. This young man would just smile and do the job. When the sergeant insulted this young man for his faith—which happened often—the Marine would respond, 'Sarge, the Lord loves you. He wants you.' His bold witness just galled this sergeant.

"The Marines in Beirut got one ration of beer a day. One day this sergeant decided he wanted to get drunk, so he told his men, 'No beer rations today for any of you!' He hoarded everyone's beer so he could get totally soused, even though he was scheduled to guard the gate that day.

"'Would you mind taking my duty at the gate today?' he asked the young Marine. 'I'm going to get drunk.'

"'Sure, Sarge, be glad to do anything for you,' the young man replied. That was the day the terrorists came with a car bomb and blew the place apart, killing this outstanding Christian while he stood guard. The government sent the young man's Bible and personal effects back home to his parents after his death.

"The blast left the sergeant handicapped with serious life-threatening wounds. The Marines sent him back to the States for hospitalization and when he finally got out, he made a visit to the parents of the young man.

"'I was the sergeant over your son,' he confessed, 'and I feel responsible for his death. I should have been standing guard duty that day, but he was there in my place. I'm so sorry.'

"'No,' they replied, 'you're wrong. You shouldn't be dead. It's right that he was there because you weren't ready to die and he was. It's all a part of God's plan.' They handed the sergeant a Bible and continued, 'He wrote us about you. We'd like you to take our son's Bible.'

"The sergeant took the Bible out of courtesy, but he just put it on a shelf at home and decided to drink himself to death. Life had become too painful and he really didn't want to go on living any longer.

"One day while cleaning his room, he accidentally knocked the Bible off the shelf. It fell open and out popped a letter this young man had written to the sergeant. In that letter the deceased Marine told of the love of Jesus Christ for the sergeant and of his own love for him and of his desire to see him saved.

"'Sarge,' he had written, 'I would gladly give my life if it could bring you salvation.'

"This was more than the sergeant could handle. He accepted the Lord and eventually ministered at Calvary Chapel of Capistrano Beach. He did a fantastic work with handicapped children and God used him in a mighty way."

After I told this story to the group over brunch, we all departed and went our separate ways. The very next day, my pastor friend, Steve, decided to tell this same story to his church. As he described the sergeant's conversion, a lady in the congregation began to weep uncontrollably. She stood up and announced, "I was the wife of that sergeant. I divorced him a long time ago because he was such a miserable person." That very morning she accepted the Lord.

What are the chances that I would tell the story, that Steve would repeat it the next day, and that the ex-wife of the sergeant would be in that service to hear about a man she hadn't seen or heard from in years? How wonderful are the ways of the Lord! You never know how God might choose to use our efforts when we step out in faith.

CALEB STEPS OUT

When Israel reached the borders of the Promised Land for the first time, Moses sent twelve spies to check out the territory. The men took forty days to look everything over.

On their way back to the camp, Joshua and Caleb stopped by the Valley of Eshcol to cut a huge bunch of grapes. They were so big they had to tie the grapes to a big stick and carry it upon their shoulders. They wanted to show the people the staggering fertility of the Promised Land.

As soon as Joshua and Caleb displayed the amazing produce, however, the other ten spies began explaining the obstacles the people would face in trying to take the land. They described giants and high-walled cities and fierce inhabitants. The people heard these fearful stories and began to murmur. That's when Caleb stepped in. He "quieted the people before Moses, and said, 'Let us go up at once and take possession, for we are well able to overcome it'" (Numbers 13:30). In other words, "Come on, people, let's go for it! It's a great land. Are there problems there? Sure, but God is with us!"

The other ten spies vehemently disagreed. "They'll eat us up," they insisted. "We looked like grasshoppers in their sight—and that's how we felt too." At that moment, the people made a huge mistake. They listened to the unbelieving ten rather than to Joshua and Caleb, who were filled with faith. All that night, the Israelites wept aloud. They spoke of finding a leader to take them back to Egypt. And when Joshua and Caleb tore their clothes in a sign of public protest and pleaded with the people to have faith in God and to march into the Promised Land as directed, they spoke of stoning them to death.

That was too much for God. He broke into the meeting and decreed that only Joshua and Caleb would enter the Promised Land. Everyone else in the nation would die in the desert as they wandered in circles for forty long years.

Four decades later, after the last of the rebels had been buried, God once again brought His people to the border of the Promised Land. This time, with Joshua in command, the nation entered the land and won battle after battle. Eventually Caleb came to his old friend and said, "Joshua, after we spied out the land, remember that Moses promised me I could have the territory I explored. Now look—I'm eighty-five years old, but I'm just as strong today as when we spied out the land. So I want your permission to go and take the land promised to me."

I love the grit of this old fellow. At eighty-five years of age he says, "I'm ready to go to battle. I'm ready to take the land God promised me." Joshua gladly gave Caleb the go-ahead to invade the territory of Hebron, where Caleb promptly seized all the land promised to him. The Bible summarizes his exploits like this:

> Hebron therefore became the inheritance of Caleb the son of Jephunneh the Kenizzite to this day, because he wholly followed the LORD God of Israel (Joshua 14:14).

Caleb stepped out in faith when an entire nation voted against him. He followed the Lord when everyone around him, except for Joshua, said, "We can't do it!" God preserved Caleb in soul and body for over four decades so that he could step out in faith once more and take what God had given him. While the corpses of his contemporaries rotted in the desert, Caleb made the Hebron land his own—all because he stepped out in faith.

Age doesn't matter when someone steps out in faith. If God is behind it, then God will see it through.

DON'T MISREAD GOD

Some people feel absolutely terrified of taking a step of faith and surrendering themselves completely to the will of God. Why? Because they've misread God—and badly. They don't trust Him. They think if they take a step of faith and surrender fully to God, the next thing they know, they'll end up under mosquito nets in Africa with huge bugs covering the ceiling, spiders dropping down in platoons, and dozens of snakes coiled up on the floor.

If God leads and empowers you to take a step of faith, He will also plant a divine desire for that thing on the fleshly tablet of your heart.

If God wanted you to go to New Guinea, He would probably first give you a tremendous fascination with biology. Kay and I happened to go to New Guinea once, and some lady missionaries had invited us over for lunch. As soon as we arrived, they started showing off their mounted bug collection. They lived in the jungles along wild rivers and had a board with beautifully colored beetles, butterflies and giant moths. These were women who squealed with delight, not fear, if a bug ran across the floor. "I don't have that one yet!" they'd say, just before grabbing it, chloroforming it to death and pinning it to a board.

Doing the will of God is a delight and a treasure. You will never be disappointed if you step out in faith to wholeheartedly do His will.

One hundred and twenty-five miles into the jungles of Irian Jaya—with no roads to get there—we once met a handsome young American with two beautiful young children. The only way to reach his place was by plane. It would take a month or more to go cross-country, which was a horribly difficult way to go. This young family lived among the natives so that this Christian father could translate the New Testament into the villagers' own language. As he walked me around the village, he said, "Tell me that when you follow the will of the Lord, God doesn't lead you to the most beautiful, glorious spot in the world to raise your children!"

And it was beautiful. Streams flowed down both sides of the village, so pure that you could drink the water right out of them. He was so in love with the place. Now, I could handle it for a week or so, but he loved everything about it. Why? Because God wrote His law on the fleshly tablet of his heart. When we step out in faith, God does not condemn us to a life of drudgery or misery. He gives us His very best.

GOD USES UNLIKELY PEOPLE

God loves to use unlikely people to do His work. He has chosen the simple things of the world to confound the wise (1 Corinthians 1:27). And what do all of these people have in common? They display a willingness to step out in faith.

Some people look at the men and women whom God has used to do great things and say, "But they don't even have their doctorates!

Who gave them the authority?" They can't understand how God could use men and women without pedigree, status, social or political clout. It's shocking to them that God can use such unlikely people to do His work. The truth is that God can take the most improbable person in the world—the individual voted most apt to fail, most likely to end up in the penitentiary—and use him or her to touch thousands of lives for Jesus Christ. You know what this means, don't you? If God can use them, then God can use you.

When we lived in Tucson, we had a wonderful, outgoing neighbor named Jan. The Lord used us to kick-start Jan's spiritual walk. Back then, many people living in Tucson struggled with asthma. And time and again, we saw Jan step out in faith to point her asthmatic neighbors to Christ.

Jan often talked over her back fence to one particular neighbor. "Look," she said one day, "you don't have to keep using that atomizer. This guy next door is a preacher. He prays for people and they are healed. Come over to my house. I'll call him up and he'll pray for you."

Jan called me. After hearing about their conversation, I walked over to her house and prayed for her neighbor—and God healed her. Consequently, Jan started bringing me all her asthmatic neighbors—and God healed them too. One day Jan told me, "Chuck, I just got a call from my friend. She's on the way to the hospital to have an operation. I told her, 'Don't go to the hospital; come to my house. Let my neighbor pray for you.'"

So the gal came by and we prayed for her—and the Lord healed her too. The doctors examined her and said, "Hey, you're all right. You don't need the operation."

I'm certain it was not my faith. It was Jan's faith. Having seen the work of God, she took a step of faith that said, "If Chuck prays for you, then you're going to be healed." How exciting that God would choose to honor the faith of this ordinary woman.

FAITH OR FEAR?

If you want to step out in faith, you have to get over your fear. Fear and faith cannot co-exist. Fear will dispel your faith and faith will dispel your fear.

Satan is an expert at using fear and anxiety to stop people from doing the work of God. Fear happens when we fix our eyes upon the enemy and his threats—faith happens when we fix our eyes on the Lord and His promises.

Remember the Lord! "Those who are with us are more than those who are with them" (2 Kings 6:16).

Remember the Lord! "Yea, though I walk through the valley of the shadow of death, I will fear no evil; for You are with me" (Psalm 23:4).

Remember the Lord! "The fear of man brings a snare, but whoever trusts in the LORD shall be safe" (Proverbs 29:25).

When you remember that the Lord is with you and that He is wholeheartedly for you, then you can say along with David, "The LORD is on my side; I will not fear. What can man do to me?" (Psalm 118:6).

WHAT WOULD YOU DO?

Toward the beginning of human history, an ordinary man had a crucial choice to make. Would he obey God's direction, or would he cave in to the mockery of those around him?

I'm glad Noah stepped out in faith and obeyed God, because otherwise you and I would not be here. Noah lived in a wicked era so debased and sinful that the Lord decided to wipe humankind off the face of the planet. "But Noah found grace in the eyes of the LORD," we read. "Noah was a just man, perfect in his generations. Noah walked with God" (Genesis 6:8, 9). What a testimony and what a witness for us.

God told Noah of His plan to eradicate from the earth the violent human beings that had ruined His beautiful creation. He instructed Noah to build an ark that would save not only him and his family from a worldwide flood, but also preserve representatives of all the creatures God had made.

The Bible calls Noah a preacher of righteousness (2 Peter 2:5). Apparently he preached to his neighbors throughout the time it took him to build the ark, warning them of God's impending judgment. No doubt the people laughed at Noah's warnings and mocked him as he spent day after day building a big boat in an area without any bodies of water. Surely, Noah knew how outlandish his work must have seemed to everyone who came by to jeer. But he believed God, and so he took a huge step of faith and complied with God's unusual set of instructions.

And here's what makes his story so unique: He built the ark for a hundred years, the whole time suffering the verbal abuse of those who mocked him and his work. Would you have stayed with such a peculiar task for a century?

Noah did. By faith he built an ark that saved his family. That boat brought salvation because he obeyed God. When God shut him inside the ark, now filled with animals, the die was cast. Noah and his family stayed safe inside, but for everyone else on the outside, it was too late. The flood came and took them all away. As Peter wrote, "For if God ... did not spare the ancient world, but saved Noah, one of eight people, a preacher of righteousness, bringing in the flood on the world of the ungodly ... then the Lord knows how to deliver the godly out of temptations and to reserve the unjust under punishment for the day of judgment" (2 Peter 2:4, 5, 9).

Stepping out in faith may seem like foolishness to a host of skeptical observers, but if God is the One who has inspired your step of faith, and you obeyed, you too will find grace in the eyes of the Lord.

THE PEACE OF TOTAL COMMITMENT

Some time back a pastor came to me in a panic. He wanted to buy a new facility for his growing congregation but he needed to borrow money to get it. He came to our church, practically on his hands and knees, begging us to loan him the money.

He wailed, "I don't know what I'm going to do if I don't get the funds for a new building. I don't know what will happen if we can't buy it." And so, the board voted to loan him the money.

A short while later I heard him on the radio, talking about the new building. "We believed God to buy us this property," he declared, "and the Lord came through. We just trusted God for the provision. Praise the Lord!"

As soon as I heard his words, I said to myself, *No, you were down here in a panic, begging on your hands and knees. You weren't trusting God. You were trusting Calvary Chapel to loan you the money.*

Stepping out in faith is not begging someone else to help you out of a jam. Stepping out in faith means trusting God to honor His promises in regard to some endeavor He's leading you to undertake. It doesn't mean taking things into your own hands and then talking afterwards about how God honored your faith.

One of the best ways to draw near to God is to make a full commitment to His will. This is a commitment that says, "Lord, if You want me to step out in faith in this way, then I'll do it. I'll do my little part, and then You take over." When God does take over, then all the glory and praise belongs to Him. You can't brag because you stepped out in faith—but you can certainly enjoy the fruit of seeing what God can do in response to your faith.

How Can I Stand Firm in Faith?

For as the heavens are higher than the earth, so are My ways higher than your ways, and My thoughts than your thoughts.

Isaiah 55:9

A FEW YEARS AGO, A MAN ABOUT MY AGE approached me at a men's retreat, looking very distressed.

"Chuck," he said, "I'm having a real hard time. I have loved serving God for years. I've been a very successful builder and we've donated much of our profits to the Lord's work. We've never bought property or built on it without seeking the guidance of the Lord. When we're finished with the houses, we lay hands on them and pray God will bless the occupants of the homes. We've really taken God into a partnership with us in this business and have always sought to do the will of the Lord."

He choked up a bit before continuing. "I got caught in a recession and lost my fortune. The houses didn't sell and we had to go into bankruptcy. Now I have lost my health. I'm no longer able to build. And I can't understand why God would strip me of money that I've been saving for retirement at a time in life when I am too ill and too old to recover."

That man believed that God is good and wise, and that He blesses His children. He simply could not reconcile the difficult circumstances he faced with what he knew of God.

Many people find themselves in the same condition as this man, distressed in spirit because they cannot understand the ways of God. How can we stand firm in our faith in Christ, when circumstances seem poised to crush us?

HE DOES THINGS DIFFERENTLY

If I were God and I had the power and the ability to control the affairs of the world, I would certainly change a few things. For one, I would not allow the wicked to prosper. I'd strip them bare, but I would cause the righteous to prosper. I would pour out heaven's blessings and prosperity on those who love me.

But then I suppose I would face a real dilemma, wouldn't I? Because when men declared that they loved me, how would I know they *really* loved me? Maybe they just loved the perks. Maybe they served me only because of the blessings I gave.

I think God often asks us a tough question: "Will you trust Me when you don't understand? When you don't know why you face such difficult circumstances—can you trust Me then?"

Is it real trust when I can see the answers, or when it's obvious what God is doing? Or is it real trust when I can't see and when I don't know?

How many times has your spouse asked you, "Do you love me, Honey?" In the early years of our marriage, my wife used to push up her nose like a pug and ask me, "If I looked like this, would you love me? Do you love me because of my looks or do you love me because of my cooking—do you *really* love me?"

How deep is your love for God? How committed are you to Him?

Job remained committed to God despite his horrible circumstances. Satan had suggested to God that Job loved the Lord only for the perks. Satan said, "Hey, You've given that fellow so much. He has more than anybody could ever desire. And You've put a hedge around him; You won't let me get to him. If You allow me to take away all of those perks, he won't love You anymore. He will curse You to Your face."

God allowed Satan to strip Job of his wealth, his family, his friends ... even his health. In the midst of his loss, Job cried out, "Though He slay me, still I will trust Him" (Job 13:15). You might think that by this point the whole story would immediately come to a happy ending. God would say triumphantly, "See, Satan? You've stripped Job of everything, and yet he still loves Me."

But that's not what happened. Job made this amazing statement in chapter 13, but the happy ending didn't arrive until chapter 42. In between, Job continued to agonize over his personal catastrophes—and God didn't appear to him in a vision or a dream or even in a still, quiet voice to explain what happened. Job had to sit in the dust, listening to his friends accuse him of sins he never committed. How do you explain why God would allow that?

AN INFINITE GOD

God has the advantage of foreknowledge. He knows the future—all of it—and the consequence of every action. What may look to me like a tremendous blessing, therefore, may in reality be a curse. And what looks to me like a curse can turn out, in God's hands, to be a tremendous blessing.

So many things have come into my life that I thought were a curse, so I asked God to remove them. I *begged* God to remove them. Finally, I accused God of not listening or caring about me. But more often than not I found out that the things I wanted removed actually turned out to be great blessings.

The only way to account for this is to realize that God knew the end result before the problem ever appeared. In love, He let a difficulty stand until He had finished the work He intended to do in me.

I don't know how many times I've had to go back to God and say, "Lord, I'm so sorry. I didn't understand. Forgive me for the thoughts I've had toward You! If only I had known." The Lord said through the prophet Isaiah,

> For as the heavens are higher than the earth, so are My ways higher than your ways, and My thoughts than your thoughts (Isaiah 55:9).

God's ways are *infinitely* higher than our ways. We measure the earth by using linear measurement. But we measure the heavens by light-years. God's thoughts and ways are billions of light-years higher than our thoughts and ways. No wonder we can't understand what He's doing much of the time. We are infants trying to understand the complexities of quantum physics.

Do you think it would be loving to give your children everything they wanted? "Daddy, I want a lollipop. No—I want a whole box of lollipops. I want a lollipop in my mouth all day long." Would you give in to the request?

I'm amazed at how quickly kids learn the psychology of manipulation. "If you really love me, Daddy, then you'll give me a box of lollipops and you'll let me lick them all day. If you don't, I'll know you really don't love me."

It's because you *do* love them and you don't want them to decay their little teeth that you limit their consumption of lollipops. You know that if you indulge their desire, they could destroy their health. They would get so full of sugar that they wouldn't want to eat nourishing food.

Children, of course, don't understand tooth decay and nutrition. I had a two-year-old granddaughter who had strong opinions about the word "no." If you told her no, she'd say you were mean—no matter what the reason. *Any* "no" constituted meanness. What she wanted, however, wasn't always good for her. And she just didn't understand that sometimes love is behind the "no."

Now magnify that situation a trillion times and you have a slight idea of the conditions that exist between God and man. We think certain things would make us very happy, and if God really loved us, He would comply with our wishes. He would give me that little red sports car so I could cruise around the neighborhood. But as I make the request, the Lord can see that vehicle smashed up against a telephone pole with me shattered inside it. And so God says no. Does that "no" indicate a lack of love? Of course not. Because He loves us, He sometimes disappoints us in the very things we think are so vital. Other times, in order to teach us to trust Him fully, God takes from us the things we rely upon.

When we are disappointed with God's "no," we must remember that God's ways are not our ways and God's thoughts are not our thoughts. The Word tells us that God's ways are "beyond finding out" (Romans 11:33). We may not understand, and we may not like the answer we've been given, but we can always trust that God is working out His better plan.

THE ETERNAL PERSPECTIVE

While our thoughts are usually focused on our present comfort, God is always thinking of our eternal welfare. This often creates a problem because we are very shortsighted.

Peter says that we have enormous difficulty seeing things afar off (2 Peter 1:9). We see only what's here and what's near—what's temporal. But God sees the eternal and understands the eternal plan He's working out in our lives.

Many saints of old whose lives are recorded in the Bible had a rough journey. They endured great hardships and God tested their faith to the limit. As they went through hard times, the Word of God says they endured as seeing the invisible (Hebrews 11:27). You read of the things they suffered and you wonder, *How could they ever endure that?* They did so because they had caught the eternal perspective.

Thus Moses chose to suffer affliction with the people of God rather than to enjoy the pleasures of sin for a season, because he had enough sense to look at the eternal consequences. Moses could have been known as the son of the Pharaoh's daughter.

He could have enjoyed all the luxuries and excesses of the royal court of Egypt. He chose rather to identify with the people of God because he realized that all earthly pleasures had an end.

Serving God, on the other hand, has eternal value. Moses knew that God had a reward waiting for him (Hebrews 11:25-26). He could look down the corridors of time and see the limitless benefits of living as one of God's people.

Paul the apostle suffered through tremendous hardships—beatings, a stoning, a shipwreck, flogging, unjust imprisonments—and yet he said, "For our light affliction, which is but for a moment, is working for us a far more exceeding and eternal weight of glory" (2 Corinthians 4:17). Do you see a contrast? This affliction is light when you compare it with the weight of glory. This affliction is for a season, but it brings an eternal reward.

As you keep your eyes on the eternal, you find the ability to endure "as one seeing the invisible." Paul wrote, "We do not look at the things which are seen, but at the things which are not seen. For the things which are seen are temporary, but the things which are not seen are eternal" (2 Corinthians 4:18). Thus the apostle could say, "The sufferings of this present time are not worthy to be compared with the glory which shall be revealed in us" (Romans 8:18).

Often I don't understand God's ways. Yet I know He is working out His eternal purposes in my life through these disappointments and hardships. Realizing that God does love me and deals with me from an eternal perspective has helped me to commit my ways to Him. As the psalmist tells us,

Commit your way to the LORD, trust also in Him, and He shall bring it to pass. He shall bring forth your righteousness as the light, and your justice as the noonday (Psalm 37:5-6).

One day you'll see the value of your situation. It may look dark today. You may not be able to see what God is doing. It may seem like living a righteous life doesn't pay. While you're telling your customers the truth, the guy down the street is lying to them—and they're leaving you to buy from him. You know they're going to be disappointed. You know he can't keep his promises. Meanwhile, you're honest ... and losing business to him.

One day, however, in the light of God's eternity, you'll see that righteousness does pay. So how do you stand firm in your faith in the meantime? Commit your ways to the Lord and He will bring it to pass.

DON'T ACCUSE GOD

The Bible tells us, "Let those who suffer according to the will of God commit their souls to Him in doing good, as to a faithful Creator" (1 Peter 4:19). You may be suffering right now. You may not be able to reconcile your difficult situation with God's love. You may have reasons from a logical standpoint to challenge the Lord's work, because you see no sense in it. I've heard people say, "God really let me down. He didn't show up. He must not care what happens to me." People sometimes make rash accusations against God simply because they don't understand the eternal plan He's working out.

Instead of making rash accusations against God, commit your way to Him. Consider the possibility that your suffering is according to the will of God. In the midst of your pain, remember that He is still your faithful Creator. The suffering will end, but He will always remain faithful. And when you continue to stand strong in the faith despite your hardships, God sees—and one day soon He will reward you.

WHEN YOU FACE DEATH

We may not understand what God is doing in our lives, but as death approaches, we can know a peace and an assurance that defies the world's comprehension. David wrote, "Yea, though I walk through the valley of the shadow of death, I will fear no evil: for You are with me" (Psalm 23:4).

The presence of the Lord gives such comfort and strength in the hour of death. Someone has said that if you want to see the real proof of Christianity, note how the Christian dies in contrast with how the atheist dies.

Voltaire, the French atheist, loved to say about Christ, "Crush the wretch." But as he died, he screamed, "More light! More light! More light!" His nurse rushed out of the room, pale and shaken, and vowed to never again attend the death of an atheist. She thought he was living the miseries of hell even before he lost consciousness.

Goethe, the German philosopher, said, "I am about to take my last journey, a great leap into the dark." Contrast that with Paul the apostle, who said,

> I have fought the good fight, I have finished the race, I have kept the faith. Finally, there is laid up for me the crown of righteousness, which the Lord, the righteous Judge, will give to me on that Day, and not to me only but also to all who have loved His appearing (2 Timothy 4:7-8).

Years earlier Paul wrote, "For to me to live is Christ, and to die is gain" (Philippians 1:21). Many people live by the philosophy, "Eat, drink, and be merry. Party it up." They may want to live by that philosophy—but is it a philosophy they want to die by? Have you ever wondered how you would respond as you faced death?

When we lived in Huntington Beach, a mentally-imbalanced veteran of the Korean War came by our house. His family attended our church, and we knew about him and his mental problems. As he walked up to the door, Kay saw him through the window and said, "Chuck, it's him. Don't answer the door."

"We have to answer the door," I replied. "He knows we're here."

"Well, be careful," she warned. "He's crazy. He's apt to pull a gun on you."

When I opened the door, he said, "Chuck, I want you to come out to the car."

Kay stood behind the door whispering, "Don't go! He's nuts! He'll shoot you!"

But I have a philosophy about humoring the feeble-minded. You don't want them to get into a rage. If you go along with them, many times they'll stay calm. They usually only turn on you if you cross them.

So we walked to the car together and he opened the passenger's side door. "Get in and sit down," he said. So I did. He then walked around to the driver's side, got in, sat down and pulled out a .45. I could see the shells in the chamber. Pointing it at my stomach, he pulled the trigger twice.

I instantly thought, *You're looking at eternity. And you're married to a prophetess.* But I had no fear of death.

He began to laugh. "You talk a lot about death and being with the Lord," he said, "and I just wanted to see how you would react if you were really facing death." He laughed some more and then explained, "I filed off the firing pins so it wouldn't go off. You passed my test."

Every believer's life is in God's hands. That's why David's poem is quoted so often at Christian funerals: "Though I walk through the valley of the shadow of death, I will fear no evil: for You are with me."

HE FINISHES WHAT HE STARTS

You may worry that some unpleasant reality in your life means that God has forgotten about you. Not so. The Bible insists, "The LORD will perfect [or complete] that which concerns me" (Psalm 138:8). God never starts something that He doesn't intend to finish. "Being confident of this very thing, that He who has begun a good work in you will complete it until the day of Christ Jesus" (Philippians 1:6).

If you have come to a saving faith in Jesus Christ, it is because the Lord has planted that faith in your heart. He has called you. You are one of His chosen. "For by grace you have been saved through faith, and that not of yourselves; it is the gift of God" (Ephesians 2:8). God gave you the gift of faith to believe in Jesus Christ. He is the One who, by His Spirit, drew you to Himself. Salvation is of the Lord! Therefore the Bible calls Jesus Christ, "the author and finisher of our faith" (Hebrews 12:2).

Some people get confused at this point. They say, "Pray that the Lord will help me to hold on until the end." They compare their life of faith to enduring a marathon. Have you ever seen the Boston Marathon? Each year thousands of eager entrants begin the race. Some of them run two blocks and then give up—but they still wear the T-shirt that proclaims, "I ran in the Boston Marathon." Thousands of people start that race but far fewer finish.

In a similar way, many people jump into this race of eternal life with no intention of finishing. So long as exciting things are happening, they stick around. They're like the seed planted on stony ground; it may sprout quickly, but it has no root (Matthew 13:20-21). When troubles come, they depart. They build a religious house on the sand and when a heavy storm hits, their house collapses.

If you have sincerely placed your faith in Jesus Christ, you don't have to worry about hanging on to the end. The Lord will get you to the finish line. He will finish what He started.

KEEP UNDER THE SPOUT

Years ago when I first began in the ministry, I knew I wasn't qualified to pastor a church, so I went out as an evangelist. I traveled into the Ozarks and held some meetings in churches that still used the old *Stamps-Baxter* hymnal, and I liked to thumb through the hymnal and read the song titles.

I still remember a couple of them. One was, "Tell Her Now; She Can't Read Her Tombstone When She's Dead." Another read, "He Won't Compel You to Go Against Your Will, He'll Just Make You Willing to Go." Yet another title read, "Under the Spout Where the Glory Comes Out."

I like that one, because that's essentially what Jude meant when he wrote, "Keep yourself in the love of God" (Jude 1:21).

We're to keep ourselves under the spout where the glory comes out. Keep yourself in the kind of growing, loving relationship with God in which He can do all the things for you that He so desires to do. God wants to bless you. God wants to lavish His love upon you—even when it seems like He's left the building.

So how can you stand firm in your faith? The old hymnal still has the answer: Stay under the spout where the glory comes out.

Faith

19

How Can I Pass Tests of Faith?

Examine yourselves as to whether you are in the faith.
Test yourselves.

2 CORINTHIANS 13:5

WHAT IS THE LEAST FAVORITE DAY IN SCHOOL? Friday, because that's usually test day. Oh, how we hate tests!

Did you know that God also puts us to the test? And we don't always feel pleased when He does so.

"Just trust Me," God says.

"Well, Lord, show me what You're doing. Show me why I'm going through this. Let me understand, Lord." We don't like having our faith tested—but it needs to be.

TESTS FOR REALITY

Why does God test our faith? It's so easy for us to casually say, "I believe God and I believe His promises. I trust God." But our words do not always match reality. We make great assertions about our faith, but in actuality, our faith is weak and we don't even know it. So God puts us to the test to reveal what's in our hearts.

God doesn't test us to see whether our faith is genuine. He knows the truth about our faith. We don't know, because our hearts are "deceitful above all things and desperately wicked." But He also said, "I, the LORD, search the heart" (Jeremiah 17:9-10). God puts me through tests to show me the truth about myself. It's important that I know, lest I believe that I'm stronger than I really am.

When we declare our faith in God, He will put our faith to the test. Would I trust Him if He should strip me of my possessions—or of my family? Do I *really* trust Him? God allows our trust to be proved. While these testings take many forms, the purpose of the test is not to destroy you but to allow you to know the truth about yourself, and to discover the strength you can have when you put your trust completely in the Lord.

When they built the space shuttle, they knew the nose of the shuttle would be exposed to extreme pressure and heat as it re-entered the earth's atmosphere. Thus, they designed tiles for the shuttle's nose that could withstand tremendous heat and pressure, and they put them through all kinds of tests. The purpose wasn't to destroy the tiles; it was to prove whether they could withstand the heat and the pressure of re-entry.

If you feel like you're in the fire, then know that your faith is being tested to the limit. God is going to prove some things to you. You're going to discover just how great (or little) your faith is. Peter said,

> Don't count it strange concerning the fiery trial which is
> to try you, as though some strange thing has happened to
> you (1 Peter 4:12).

God allows us to go through the fire, but He gives us the
promise,

> When you pass through the waters, I will be with you;
> and through the rivers, they shall not overflow you. When
> you walk through the fire, you shall not be burned (Isaiah
> 43:2).

We used to sing, "Jesus, Jesus, how I trust Him! How I've proved
Him o'er and o'er. Jesus, Jesus, precious Jesus! O for grace to
trust Him more!" [4] He'll give you that grace, but He'll also put
you to the test that you might discover how genuine your faith
is that you profess.

TESTS FOR GROWTH

God allows testings not only to show us our own hearts, but
also to grow our faith. We learn from a small test that He is
faithful, and then when the next test comes along—maybe a
bigger test—we remember how faithfully He has come through
for us the last time. In this way our faith grows. Eventually
we grow to the point where even the big issues don't worry us.
Instead, we say, "God has been faithful all the way along. He
will take care of this too."

In the early years of our ministry, Kay and I went through
several tests. The first church we pastored paid us a salary of
fifteen dollars a week, while we had to pay forty-five dollars a
month for our apartment. We never knew where the evening

---

[4] "'Tis So Sweet to Trust in Jesus," words by Louisa M.R. Stead, 1882.

meal would come from. Sometimes we'd find groceries left on the front porch. Sometimes people would call and say, "Would you guys like to come over for dinner tonight?"

Usually, God provided for the evening meal from that afternoon's mail. We'd go to our post office box and find a five-dollar bill or a check for ten dollars ... enough to get food for dinner. It became so consistent, so regular, that we almost began to trust in the post office. One afternoon, we went over to the post office to get our money for dinner—and to our chagrin, the box was empty. We returned to our little apartment, dumped out Kay's purses, went through all my pants and coat pockets, searched all the dresser drawers ... and found thirty-seven cents. We headed for the market to find out how nutritious a meal we could buy. We felt quite proud of ourselves and amazed at what you can get for thirty-seven cents when you're really hungry.

At the register, the fellow totaled it up and said, "Thirty-seven cents." I dumped out all the pennies and every other coin that we had. As we started for the door, he called after us. "Hey, kids, come back here a minute."

We returned and he said, "You kids have that little church down the street. My boys go to Sunday school down there and I've been intending to do this for a long time, I just kept forgetting." Then he reached under the counter and gave us a ten-dollar grocery certificate.

"Honey," I said, "go over to the meat case and pick out a couple of steaks." It was obvious that God was treating us for dinner that night, so why not eat steak? He can afford it!

As I look back upon my life and the development of my spiritual walk, I believe those six months that Kay and I spent in

Prescott, Arizona, were probably the most valuable six months in our ministry. There we learned basic lessons of faith and we discovered the faithfulness of God. We learned to trust God for our daily bread.

Through tests in little things, we discover over and over that God is faithful. Then we begin to realize, *God can provide $100 just as easily as five dollars.* Next we realize, *He can provide $1,000 just as easily as He can provide $100.* Testings help us discover the faithfulness of God ... and our faith grows.

EVERYONE GETS TESTED

The Lord tries the faith of His children, even the "heroes of faith." God tested Abraham's faith many times and in many ways—and Abraham didn't pass all of them. Each time he failed, God required him to take the test again.

Abraham did not have a perfect faith. Yet God accounted his faith for righteousness. After God had promised him, "Your seed is going to be like the stars," his wife said to him, "Take Hagar, and raise up a seed through her." Abraham followed her counsel and in so doing had a lapse of faith.

In a way, I'm comforted by that thought. My faith isn't perfect either. There are times when, like Abraham, I know what God wants to do, but somehow I feel that He can't quite pull it off without my help. I find myself trying to bring to pass the desire and the purpose of God by my own genius, as though He is not capable of doing it Himself.

Like Abraham, I sometimes get impatient with God. "He didn't work within my timeframe. He had two weeks to do it, and when He didn't come through, I guess it's all up to me. I'll take over from here, God. I'll finish the job."

I also have lapses of faith where I fear. I'm afraid of what the enemy might do. I don't fully trust in God's preserving power and His keeping grace. So it comforts me to read that God accounted Abraham's faith for righteousness—though it was far from a perfect faith.

THE SUPREME TEST

Abraham eventually faced the supreme test of faith. For when his son, Isaac, had grown—perhaps he was somewhere around thirty years of age, still unmarried and with no children—God asked Abraham to do the unthinkable.

> Abraham, I want you to take your son, your only son, Isaac, the one whom you love. I want you to offer him as a burnt offering to Me on a mountain that I will show you (Genesis 22:2).

Remember, God had promised Abraham that "through Isaac shall thy seed be called" (Hebrews 11:18), but now God is saying, "Offer Isaac as a burnt offering to Me on a mountain that I will show you." That is the supreme test of faith!

What would you do? What would you think? Abraham figures, *God, You've promised me that through Isaac my seed will be called. He's not married and he doesn't have any children. I know You're going to keep Your promise—but now, Lord, You're asking me to offer him as a sacrifice. You have a big problem, Lord.*

Nevertheless, faithful to God's instruction, Abraham traveled with his servants and Isaac for three days from Hebron until they reached Mount Moriah. There Abraham told his servants, "You remain here. The lad and I will go and worship God and will come again" (Genesis 22:5). As Abraham journeyed up the hillside with his son, Isaac said, "Dad, we've forgotten the sacrifice." Abraham answered, "Son, God will provide Himself a sacrifice. In the mount of the LORD it shall be seen."

When father and son reached the top of that hill, Abraham bound Isaac and placed him on the altar. The book of Hebrews tells us that Abraham believed that if it became necessary, God would raise Isaac from the dead in order to fulfill His promise (Hebrews 11:19).

God was painting a beautiful picture. When He said, "Take now thy son, thine only son, Isaac, and offer him as a sacrifice on a mountain which I will show you" (Genesis 22:2). He was foreshadowing what John would write centuries later: "For God so loved the world that He gave His only begotten Son" (John 3:16). God sacrificed Jesus, whom He loved, for the sins of the whole world—very near the spot where Abraham had built his altar some 2,000 years before. Abraham called the place *Jehovah Jireh*, which means, "The Lord will provide Himself a sacrifice"—which, indeed, He did through Jesus Christ.

Did you realize that God allowed His only begotten Son, Jesus Christ, to be tested? We read that the Holy Spirit led Jesus into the wilderness to be tempted by the Devil. Jesus passed the tests, but not before facing the same kinds of temptations we experience—the temptation of trying to gain glory and fame in the world, to draw attention to ourselves; to use the powers which God might give us for our own selfish ends. We are told that Jesus was tempted in all things just like we are, yet without sin (Hebrews 4:15). Because He suffered temptations, He is able to help us when we are tempted.

Job's faith was severely tested when Satan was allowed to strip him of everything. Having lost his fortune, his family, and his friends, Job fell on his face and said, "The LORD has given, and the LORD has taken away. Blessed be the name of the LORD" (Job 1:21). Job passed the test.

Joseph's commitment to purity was tested when he was in Egypt serving Potiphar. His wife became infatuated with Joseph, sought to seduce him, and daily put him under pressure to enter into an illicit relationship. His purity was severely tested, but Joseph passed the test.

Your faith will also be tested. And by grace as you trust in God and His promises, you too can pass the test.

JOY IN TESTING

What kind of attitude should we display in times of testing? Scripture tells us to "Count it all joy when you experience divers temptations" (James 1:2).

When I am going through a test, oftentimes I find myself complaining. I find it difficult to say, "Oh, praise the Lord that I'm going through this most difficult test. I'm so happy I'm being tested so severely." That's not easy for me, and yet it is something the Bible exhorts me to do.

If we rejoiced only when we won the lottery, how would we be different from anyone else? Watch what happens on television when they say, "You've won!" You see people scream and squeal and jump up and down with joy. So what? Anybody can rejoice when they're a winner. Having joy in the time of victory, in the time of prosperity, in the time of blessing, is no witness at all. Jesus said it's no big deal to love those who love you; the heathen do that. Jesus suggests that you should do more because of what He has done for you. So Peter wrote,

> Beloved, don't think it strange concerning the fiery trial which is to try you, as though some strange thing has happened to you: but rejoice, to the extent that you partake of Christ's sufferings; that when His glory is revealed, you may also be glad with exceeding joy (1 Peter 4:12-13).

Again we are told to rejoice as we look at the effect of God's tests. Peter lived it, he didn't merely write it.

When Peter and some of the apostles were arrested for preaching Jesus, the Jewish magistrates did not know how to handle them. They had threatened the apostles earlier with severe consequences if they didn't quit preaching Christ, but they went right back to it.

Next the council commanded the apostles not to speak in the name of Jesus, and then had them beaten. How did the apostles respond? "They departed from the council, rejoicing that they were accounted worthy to suffer shame for the name of Jesus Christ" (Acts 5:41). Jesus said to His disciples,

> Blessed are you when men shall hate you, and when they exclude you and revile you, and cast out your name as evil, for the Son of Man's sake. Rejoice in that day, leap for joy! For indeed your reward is great in heaven (Luke 6:22-23).

He tells us to rejoice and to leap for joy when we find ourselves hated or reproached because of our witness for Jesus Christ. Rejoice, because you have a great reward in heaven. The joy comes from looking beyond the testing to the fruit and the result it will bring.

Some people say that you should rejoice for everything. That's idiocy. Many things in this world are heartbreaking. I can't rejoice over all the corruption and sin in our world. I'm sad for the calamity that it's bringing upon itself. When Jesus foresaw disaster coming upon Jerusalem, He wept over it, knowing the children would be dashed in the streets. Likewise, the perversion we see in our twisted society, which is completely out of alignment with God's order, causes me to grieve.

God does not deny us our natural emotions, nor does He intend for us to be unfeeling stoics. Sorrow is natural, and we need not feel guilty if we cry over the loss of a loved one or weep over a hardship. But we do not sorrow as those who have no hope, and we do not sorrow indefinitely. We grieve for a season. Peter wrote, "Though now for a season, if need be, you are in heaviness through manifold temptations" (1 Peter 1:6 KJV).

This "season" contrasts with our inheritance that is incorruptible, undefiled, fades not away and is reserved in heaven for us. That's the eternal joy promised to us through Christ Jesus. For the time being, as Paul said in 2 Corinthians 5,

> We who are in these bodies so often groan, earnestly desiring to be delivered from this body: not to be an unembodied spirit but to be clothed upon with the body which is from heaven (2 Corinthians 5:1-4).

Because of the hope that is in us, we can look beyond the great heaviness we may be feeling and say, "Oh, bless God! One of these days I'm going to be free from the limitations of this old, corrupt body and dwell with God forever."

THE RESULT OF TESTING

Testing, we are told, results in patience. "Knowing this, that the trying [or the testing] of your faith produces patience"

(James 1:3). Paul wrote, "We glory in tribulations, knowing that tribulation produces perseverance" (Romans 5:3).

I am not always patient. I want to see things done right away, preferably before noon. Yet we are exhorted in the Scriptures to wait patiently on the Lord.

John the Baptist got a little impatient with Jesus as he sat in prison. He sent his disciples to the Lord with a question: "Are You the One we are looking for or shall we start looking for someone else?" (Luke 7:20). Like John, we can get impatient when it seems like God is in no hurry to accomplish His purposes. James says,

> Be patient, therefore, brethren, unto the coming of the Lord. Behold, the husbandman is waiting for the precious fruit of the earth, and has long patience for it, until he receive the early and the latter rain. So be ye also patient; establish your hearts: for the coming of the Lord is drawing near (James 5:7-8).

I find myself impatient for the Lord's return. I look at the world thinking of my grandchildren growing up in such decadence and I say, "Oh, Jesus, come quickly." But James said, "Have patience, establish your soul."

In the book of Revelation, Jesus said, "Behold, I come quickly." John responded, "Even so, come quickly, Lord Jesus" (Revelation 22:20). I am with John: "Come quickly, Lord Jesus." David said, "Wait on the LORD; be of good courage, and He will strengthen your heart; wait, I say, on the Lord!" (Psalm 27:14). I find that difficult but necessary, because whenever I don't wait, whenever I decide to take things into my own hands, I always make a bigger mess. So James wrote,

> Let patience have her perfect work, that you might be perfect and complete, and lacking nothing (James 1:4).

God's ultimate purpose for these testings is to bring you into spiritual maturity and into a relationship with Him where you discover His faithfulness in all your circumstances.

If you're going through heavy testing and you've been calling your friends and pouring out your woes to them, the Lord says, "Count it all joy." With His help, you can take your eyes off the trial and focus instead on the maturity God will work out in you. Rejoice in the hope you have in Christ Jesus!

TESTING AS "PRECIOUS"

Peter—the rough, tough fisherman who was ready to fight at the drop of a hat—showed a real fondness for the word "precious" in his writings. In 1 Peter 1:19, he uses that word to describe the blood of Christ, and the cornerstone—which is Jesus—in 1 Peter 2:6. In 1 Peter 3:4 he tells us that a gentle and quiet spirit is precious in God's sight.

> In this you greatly rejoice, though now for a little while, if need be, you have been grieved by various trials, that the genuineness of your faith, being much more precious than gold that perishes, though it is tested by fire, may be found to praise, honor, and glory at the revelation of Jesus Christ (1 Peter 1:6-7).

Gold is known as a precious metal because of its rarity and tremendous value. But the testing of your faith is "more precious than gold which perishes." Gold will perish; but the inheritance you have is incorruptible, undefiled and does not fade away. The trial of your faith now is important for your growth and for your development.

An athlete puts his body through tremendous rigor and exercise, especially if he is training for the Olympics. He runs until it hurts, and then he keeps on running. He pushes his body, not to destroy it, but to develop muscle and endurance.

When testings and trials come, train yourself to see them as tools in God's hand to strengthen your faith, increase your stamina, and bring you to maturity. Learn to see those times of testing as the precious instruments they are.

TESTING PURIFIES US

In order to be rid of the dross within, gold must endure a trial of fire. As gold is liquefied by heat, the dross rises to the molten surface and is skimmed off by the goldsmith. Only when he can see his reflection on the surface of the gold will he remove it from the heat. At that point, he knows the gold is pure.

See the spiritual parallel? God wants to see His face reflected in you. This only happens when you're purified. And so He puts fire under your faith so that dross in you—the old junk embedded in the sin nature—can break loose and rise to the surface.

Why is it so important that the dross be removed from your life? Because God created you to bring Him praise, glory and honor (1 Peter 1:7). When I look at my children and I see them committed to the Lord Jesus Christ, loving and serving Him, I feel so good inside. I think, *All right!* God wants to be able to look at you and say, "All right!"

When the Lord sees your love, your devotion and your commitment to Him, He receives glory from your life and obedience. As Paul said, you become a trophy "to the praise of the glory of His grace" (Ephesians 1:6). That's your ultimate purpose.

We are living in one of the most exciting ages in the history of man. But it is also one of the most difficult periods of history in which to live a truly dedicated, committed Christian life. I doubt that worldly influences have ever been stronger. I believe it is harder to live for Jesus Christ now than it was in the days when they were feeding Christians to the lions. A lot of us have the kind of commitment and tenacity to die for Jesus Christ—but are we able to live for Jesus in a degenerate, corrupt age?

Jesus questioned this. "When the Son of Man comes, will He really find faith on the earth?" (Luke 18:8). Living in an age of materialism and opulence does not help anyone to live a dedicated, committed Christian life.

In speaking of the last days, Jesus said, "Because lawlessness will abound, the love of many will grow cold" (Matthew 24:12). We see men going deeper and deeper into the moral quagmire, sinking lower in depravity than we could have imagined. In this decadent age when so many pressures come upon us to lower our standard, it isn't easy to hold the high standard required by the Word of God.

That is why God tests your faith. But oh, thank God for the testing, lest we should "be ashamed at His coming" (1 John 2:28). He's coming when we think He won't. He may come in the very moment that you finally give in to the weakness of your flesh and decide to do that which you know is wrong. And what shame you will have at His appearing. You need to remain strong in these days if you're going to "be found to praise, honor, and glory at the revelation of Jesus Christ" (1 Peter 1:7).

How Can I Grow in Faith?

And the apostles said to the Lord, "Increase our faith."

LUKE 17:5

I SPENT TWO MISERABLE YEARS of my life in Corona, California, trying to pastor a church full of disgruntled, wary people who had been convinced that the Lord could never bless that church. Back then I was young, strong, and ambitious—and I had curly hair. But they weren't impressed. I gave that congregation my best energies and my best years.

We started in that little church with fifty-seven people—and after two years of my best efforts, we ended up with twenty-five. I consider that my wilderness experience, a time when I began to question whether God had ever called me into the ministry.

While in Corona, however, I met an interesting couple at the Alpha Beta market where I worked. Whenever the wife would walk up to the checkout stand, she always seemed so happy and pleasant. One day I said, "You must be a Christian."

She lit up and said, "Yes, I am. Are you a Christian?"

"I am. I pastor a little church up the block."

"Oh, we go to a church out in Mira Loma," she said. In time I also met her husband, whose mother started coming to our church. Yet this couple never visited our church because they didn't want to break their ties in Mira Loma.

After two years, Kay and I got so discouraged at that little church that we left Corona. We just couldn't handle it anymore. It was so disheartening that I actually left the ministry for a time before I pastored another church in Huntington Beach.

I served for fifteen years under a denomination, but again, I was brought to a crossroad. I was tired of the politics and ready to quit the ministry once more. At this time, the couple we had met in Corona invited us to start a Tuesday night Bible class in their home. God blessed the class and it grew.

The husband said, "Hey, we're getting fat in the Word. God is blessing tremendously. We need to reach out. Let's form a corporation and put you on the radio for fifteen minutes each morning on KREL in Corona." So we went on the radio and started advertising our Bible class on Tuesday nights, giving out the address.

The following Tuesday night I couldn't find any place to park in the neighborhood. I thought, *I hope people aren't discouraged from coming to the class when they have to park a couple of blocks away.* When I walked up to the house, I found people standing outside, trying to get in.

"What is going on?" I asked, thinking maybe there had been an accident or something.

"There's going to be a Bible study here tonight," they replied.

We'd better move to the American Legion Hall, I thought. So eventually we moved. We continued to grow and soon we had to move again, this time to the Women's Club—at last I found myself doing what I had always wanted to do, pastor an independent church. In one beautiful year God made up for the two bad years I had experienced earlier in Corona, as God brought together a dedicated, committed body of believers.

While all this was going on, some people I had met years earlier approached me, "Chuck, we need a pastor at our church, Calvary Chapel in Costa Mesa. Would you be interested?"

"Yes, I would," I answered.

When I went home and told my wife, she said, "Why would you leave a growing church? Why would you leave these people who love you? For the first time in your life God is really blessing your ministry. Why would you leave these people to go down to Costa Mesa? It is so much smaller and there are factions there. Why do you want to go down there?"

Kay decided to speak with a psychiatrist in our church. "Take Chuck out to lunch and find out what is wrong. He's been working too hard." Besides pastoring the church, I was teaching at a high school. And we'd just bought a brand new home, which brought with it a lot of extra projects.

The psychiatrist took me to lunch and said, "Tell me about your mother. Did you love her? How was your relationship with her?" He then went on to ask a bunch of questions about my childhood.

My wife and I couldn't discuss the subject. I felt the call of God to go to Costa Mesa and she equally felt certain God wouldn't call me to do something like that.

One evening, after talking again with the friend who had contacted me about Costa Mesa, I started praying on the drive home. "God, help me. I don't know what to do. I feel that I should go to this new church, but I don't want to buck Kay...."

When I arrived home, Kay met me at the door—and she never met me at the door. I could tell she had been crying. I figured something had happened to one of the kids. "Which one?" I asked. "What happened?"

"The kids are okay," she said. "They're all asleep."

"So what's wrong?"

"I've been praying and God's been speaking to me," she answered.

"And what did He say?"

"Chuck, God said I have to submit to you, even if I think you are crazy. God told me that you're the pastor. It's your ministry and I've got to submit to you."

"Ah, Sweetheart, that's so great, because I was talking with Floyd again tonight and …"

"Shhh!" she said. "Don't say anything. I don't want to talk about it. I don't want to hear about it. At this point, I'm only ready to submit. I'm not ready to move."

That's how we wound up at Calvary Chapel Costa Mesa. And God has blessed. He allowed me to give two of the best years of my life to an agonizing little congregation that dwindled under my ministry, just to show me that it has nothing to do with me. It isn't my genius, my capacities, or my personality. It isn't my anything. It's God who does the work, when He is ready and when He wants.

As I look at the marvelous growth we've experienced at Calvary Chapel, I have to say, "It's all the work of God. I can take no credit for it. I found out at the height of my abilities and my energy that the best I could do was to dwindle a congregation of fifty-seven down to twenty-five. God causes growth, whether in a church or in a believer's life of faith. He expects us to cooperate with Him, of course, but any growth that occurs comes only from the Lord.

THE MANY FACES OF INADEQUATE FAITH

God gives to each believer a measure of faith, but He wants to help us develop unwavering faith. Before we explore that, perhaps it would help to see what immature faith looks like.

If you observe how some believers live, you can tell that something is lacking in their faith. If they truly believed the Bible, they could not engage in the life of the flesh as they do. Their behavior reveals their lack of faith in several ways.

First, while the Bible says the fear of the Lord is the beginning of wisdom, it also declares that the fear of the Lord is to hate evil (Proverbs 9:10; 8:13). Some men and women profess a faith in Christ but have no hatred of evil. They coddle evil in their lives and even exhibit an attraction toward it.

Second, their lack of faith shows up in their halfhearted commitment to the things of the Lord. If it's convenient and if it doesn't interfere with their other plans, then they serve God. The Lord is not at the top of their list of priorities.

Third, if such believers had a complete faith in the Word of God, they would be bolder in their witness for Jesus Christ, for they would realize that those without Christ are destined to an eternity without God. Their concern for seeing lost people brought to Jesus Christ would overpower their feelings of self-consciousness or inadequacy.

Fourth, their lack of faith manifests itself in the way they handle their problems. The despair they often display reveals a significant lack of faith. Some people come to us almost in hysterics. They do not trust that God is in control. They live in constant fear and anxiety instead of the full confidence that comes through a mature, robust faith.

All of these immature believers need to have their faith perfected and made mature. How, exactly, does God make this happen?

PERFECTING YOUR FAITH

The apostle Paul had a tremendous concern for the faith of the young believers in Thessalonica. He had preached that Jesus was the Messiah, and many had come to believe because of his testimony.

Paul had been in Thessalonica only a short time when such severe and relentless persecution arose against the Christian faith, causing him to leave suddenly. His friends helped him to get out of town under cover, even though his job in that church remained far from finished. Although many Thessalonians had come to a saving faith in Jesus, Paul had little time to establish them in a growing walk with Christ.

Because of this, not long after he left their city, Paul wrote the Thessalonians that he had been praying fervently, day and night, that he might see their faces and so "perfect" what was lacking in their faith (1 Thessalonians 3:10). He couldn't stop thinking about the young believers he had suddenly left behind. He felt such a deep concern about their spiritual welfare that Paul instructed his protégé, Timothy, "Go back to Thessalonica and encourage them. Comfort them and establish them in the faith. And then, please, return to me and report what you have seen."

Remember, these men and women were just babes in Christ. Paul feared that the severe persecution might discourage them and prompt them to leave the way of Jesus. So in his letter the apostle reminded his friends that his life had been appointed to tribulation. "I told you that persecution seems to be the lot of my ministry," he said. "Everywhere I go and minister, problems arise."

Paul had known this about his ministry career from the very beginning of his life in Jesus. After his conversion on the Damascus Road, he remained blinded for several days. His friends had to lead him into the city, where he stayed in seclusion. Finally the Lord spoke to a disciple in Damascus by the name of Ananias. "Ananias," He said, "go to the street called Straight and inquire at the house of Judas for Saul. He's praying."

Ananias could hardly believe the Lord's instructions. "Lord," he replied, "are You sure? I've heard about this fellow, Saul, raising havoc with the church in Jerusalem—and now he's come here to Damascus to arrest all those who call upon Your name!"

The Lord replied, "He is a chosen vessel of Mine, and I shall show him how many things he must suffer for My sake" (Acts 9:11-16). The Lord didn't say, "Saul, I want you to follow Me—and it's all going to be a bed of roses." Instead He said, "I want you to follow Me. You're going to be beaten; you're going to be stoned; you're going to be shipwrecked; you're going to go through all kinds of hardships. But the present sufferings will not be worthy to be compared with the glory you shall have when you come to be with Me."

In this way Paul reminded his Thessalonian friends God had appointed him to tribulation—and now that promised tribulation had come. They had experienced it for themselves. Paul knew he could handle the persecution, but he didn't know if these new believers could.

When Timothy returned to Paul after his visit to Thessalonica, the young man reported that the members of the young church were still growing in their faith and increasing in their love for Christ. What comfort Paul felt after hearing that positive report! This confirmed that his labor had not been in vain.

Oh, how pastors and missionaries love to hear such positive reports! The apostle John once wrote, "I have no greater joy than to know that my children walk in truth" (3 John 1:4). A pastor's greatest joy is to know that those to whom he has been ministering, those to whom he has given his life, are walking in truth. Conversely, when those to whom he has ministered and prayed with, cried over and felt great concern for, turn from the truth and follow after error, there's no greater sorrow. I know personally what a difficult, agonizing experience it can be.

So what great encouragement Paul must have felt to know that those to whom he had been ministering in Thessalonica were going forward in the faith. Paul gave thanks to God for this. Yet he still had a burning desire to return to them so that he might "perfect" their faith.

PRAYING FOR GROWTH

How does faith grow? One route is through prayer.

Paul wanted the Thessalonians to know that he prayed constantly for them. He prayed first that he might see their faces. "I want to see you again." He had left them so abruptly that he probably didn't have time to say goodbye. Paul worried that they might feel like deserted children, and he longed to see them again.

Men and women grow in faith when their lives continually interact with one another. "As iron sharpens iron, so a man sharpens the countenance of his friend" (Proverbs 27:17). Faith grows best in the soil of loving, committed friendships. Paul wanted his friends to know that he hadn't forgotten about them, that in fact he cared for them very deeply.

Second, Paul told his friends he wanted to be with them in order to perfect what was lacking in their faith. Essentially, he said, "I wasn't there long enough to get you really grounded in the faith— to fully establish you in your walk." When the Thessalonians realized how much Paul, their "father in the faith," was willing to risk by returning to a city that had proven so antagonistic toward him and his gospel message, it encouraged them to get serious about their faith.

HOW IS FAITH PERFECTED?

If someone you've never seen before asked you to loan them $100 and said, "Just trust me," you'd be skeptical and with good reason. But if a good friend said that, you wouldn't hesitate. It's easy to trust someone who has proven to be faithful.

Paul told us in Romans 10:17 that, "Faith comes by hearing, and hearing by the Word of God." The Bible demonstrates the faithfulness of God to stand by those who put their trust wholly in Him. In the book of Hebrews we read of those who, by putting their faith in God, subdued kingdoms, built a track record of righteousness, obtained the promises, stopped the mouths of lions, quenched the violence of fire, escaped the edge of the sword, were made strong out of their weaknesses, showed courage in battle, and routed foreign armies. Women of faith saw their dead loved ones raised to life again (Hebrews 11:33-35). Many epic stories from the Old Testament declare the faithfulness of God in delivering His people from the most adverse circumstances—all because they put their trust in God. And when we read and meditate on these examples, our own faith grows.

Jesus once spoke a parable about a sower. He described the four kinds of soil where the seed fell. Within each seed lies the encoded DNA, the design by which the original plant might reproduce. All of the information necessary for sending down roots, for causing the plant to sprout up, for developing the type of leaves that are to nourish it—whether the plant is deciduous or evergreen—all of that pertinent information is encoded in the DNA. How amazing that all of this information lies in that tiny bit of DNA! So think of the implications when Jesus told His disciples, "The seed is the Word of God" (Luke 8:11).

Encoded in the Word of God is everything you need to reproduce Christ in you. It's all there in the Bible as you read it. Empowered by God's Spirit, through faith, it has the ability to transform you. God said, "My Word shall not return unto Me void, it shall accomplish the purposes for which I have sent it" (Isaiah 55:11). As you read the Word of God in faith, it will work in you to reproduce Christ in you.

Peter wrote, "We have been born again, not with corruptible seed, but of incorruptible seed, by the Word of God which lives and abides forever" (1 Peter 1:23). We are born again and receive new life when the Word of God gets firmly planted in our hearts. As we grow in a living knowledge of God's Word—and as we put that Word into practice daily—our faith grows.

In a similar way, Paul told his friends in Thessalonica, "For this cause also, we thank God without ceasing, because when you received the Word of God, which you heard of us, you welcomed it not as the word of men, but as it is in truth, the Word of God which also effectually works in you who believe" (1 Thessalonians 2:13).

God's Word will work effectually in all who believe. By the Word of God your faith is perfected, increased, and completed. That's why I devote myself to teaching God's Word, as I know that faith comes by hearing and hearing by the Word of God.

As you spend time with the Lord in His Word, He blesses you and increases your faith. And as your faith grows, you acquire a greater trust and confidence in Him, which helps to dispel anxieties and fears. If you want your faith to grow, then you must spend extended time in God's Word, the Bible. While you can do several other things to help your faith grow, there is simply no substitute for the Word of God. Remember, it is always God who causes spiritual growth—and His primary tool is His Word.

ASK FOR HELP

One day Jesus talked to His disciples about forgiveness. "If a brother trespasses against you," He said, "rebuke him. And if he repents, forgive him. And if he trespasses against you seven times in one day, and he repents, forgive him" (Luke 17:3-4).

The disciples found Jesus' instruction very hard to receive: "Do You mean that seven times in one day I'm to forgive the same person for the same offense?" They shook their heads and said, "Lord, increase our faith" (Luke 17:5). They realized, "I can't do that! It's not within my capacity."

It's not within mine, either. When someone injures me, I'm more likely to say, "Hey, that's not right!"

And if the person says, "Sorry, brother," I will readily forgive him.

But if the person then turns around and does the same thing again, I say, "Hey, wait a minute here!" And when it happens the third, fourth and fifth time? By the time the seventh trespass rolls around, I'm ready to punch that guy. I don't want to forgive.

The disciples realized they didn't have the kind of forgiveness that Jesus required. At least they were honest about it. "Help us, Lord," they said. "We can't do that on our own. Please, increase our faith." Feeling an acute lack of faith, they had the sense to ask Jesus for more.

Do you sense your own need for a stronger faith? If so, follow the example of the disciples and ask Him for an increase. Thank Him that He has given to every man and woman a measure of faith—and then ask Him to increase the measure He gives to you. Ask Him to perfect whatever is lacking in your faith.

ORDINARY PEOPLE

Whenever we read of men like the prophet Elijah, we have a tendency to attribute to them as being special. We look at them as being different from us. We think, *Those are men of real faith ... special instruments of God.* But James tells us Elijah was a man just like we are. He was a common, ordinary man (James 5:17).

It is true that Elijah had tremendous victories, but he also had great fears. He became discouraged, just as we do. He sometimes ran from his problems, such as the time he ran from Jezebel because he feared for his life. Elijah didn't have a perfect track record. He was just a man who believed and trusted God—and God used him. You have the same potential as Elijah, or any of the other greats of the Bible. If you cooperate with God to grow your faith, you'll be amazed at what He'll do through you.

Several years ago in Goroka, Papua New Guinea, I met a young native girl who had established a school for about 700 children. In her very soft, quiet way, she shared how the Lord had led her to open the school. She shared about a time when a village chieftain had died and the villagers asked her to pray for him—and God raised him from the dead. She told me too that many blind people for whom she had prayed had regained their sight through the power of God. Her testimony moved me so much that I wanted to come home, grab our TV man, and take him back over there to film her story. I thought, *These are some of the most powerful things I've ever heard.* How the power of God has worked through this quiet, gentle girl!

But why should that surprise us? God loves to use ordinary people and build into them people of extraordinary faith. God chooses ordinary people because they have little interest in gaining glory for themselves. They simply recognize that God is doing the work and they give Him all the glory.

A FAITHFUL GOD

When we put our hope and trust in God, and when we depend upon the promises in His Word, we can face any adversity with confidence and courage. We can do this because we've learned to trust in the God who always shows up. We know He will see us through.

God is going to work things out in your life for His glory. His purposes shall stand! May you be buoyed and strengthened in that confidence as your faith in Him continues to mature and be perfected.

Jesus,
the Chief Cornerstone

I ONCE HEARD AN INTERESTING STORY concerning the building of Solomon's temple. The stones of the temple were all quarried off-site and brought to the Temple Mount, with each stone labeled to show where it fit. Quarry workers had carved them in such a way that the blocks interlocked, meaning the builders didn't have to use mortar. As the temple rose on Mount Moriah, observers heard no sound of hammer or trowel.

The story goes that one stone arrived without any markings on it. The builders didn't know where it went. And so they thought, *They've made a mistake at the quarry. They've sent us this stone that doesn't seem to fit anywhere.* So they cast it aside. Over time, weeds grew and covered the discarded stone.

Finally, the time came when the only piece lacking was the chief cornerstone. So the builders sent a message to the quarry: "Hey, you guys haven't sent us the chief cornerstone."

The quarry workers replied, "Yes, we did. It is on our records that it left here some time ago." A big dispute arose over the issue until someone finally stumbled across a stone hidden in the weeds—and they realized that the stone the builders rejected was in fact the chief cornerstone.

The Bible speaks of Jesus Christ as the stone that the builders rejected—and yet He is the Chief Cornerstone of God's entire plan of redemption. In Him alone can you and I find salvation. Only by faith in Him can we enter or see the kingdom of God.

Once we place our faith in Jesus, our adventure of faith begins. We learn to trust Him for our needs, for guidance, for everything that matters. But we always have a choice: Will we believe His promises and exercise our faith? Or will we doubt and reject His Word and choose unbelief?

Consider the following contrasts between faith and unbelief. On which side do you fit?

> Faith believes the promises of God. Unbelief doubts God's promises.

> Faith believes the Word of God because it is true. Unbelief doubts the truth of the Word.

> Faith sees that God's help is greater than any force that can come against you. Unbelief looks at the problems and declares it just can't be done.

> Faith sees Christ's love when He is reproving you. Unbelief imagines anger in Christ's loving words.

Faith helps the soul to wait when God delays. Unbelief gives up if there is any tarrying at all.

Faith gives you comfort in the midst of fear. Unbelief brings you fear in the midst of comfort.

Faith makes heavy burdens light. Unbelief makes light burdens heavy.

Faith helps us when we are down. Unbelief brings us down when we are up.

Faith brings us near to God when we are far from Him. Unbelief puts us far from God when He is near.

Faith sets men and women free. Unbelief holds them in bondage.

Faith purifies our hearts. Unbelief pollutes our hearts.

Faith makes our most feeble works acceptable to God through Christ. Unbelief makes even our greatest works unacceptable, for whatsoever is not of faith is sin, and without faith it is impossible to please God.

Faith brings peace to our soul. Unbelief brings strife and trouble, like the tossing waves of the sea.

Faith causes us to see the preciousness of Christ. Unbelief sees no beauty that we should desire Him.

Faith helps us experience fullness in Christ. Unbelief leads to leanness of soul.

Faith gives us victory. Unbelief leads to defeat.

Faith causes us to see glory in the things of the unseen world. Unbelief sees only the misery and the things of the present, material world.

By faith Abraham was given the Land of Promise. By unbelief Moses was not allowed to enter the land.

By faith the children of Israel passed through the Red Sea. By unbelief they perished in the wilderness.

By faith Peter walked on the water. By unbelief he began to sink.

Through faith our cup runs over. Through unbelief the cup is always empty. [5]

Jesus Christ, the Chief Cornerstone, invites you to walk in faith with Him each day. His love for you is sure. His plan for you is precious. He opens wide His arms and offers you an invitation. "Come to Me, you who are burdened and heavy laden, and I will give you rest" (Matthew 11:28).

Don't cast Him aside! Don't reject Him, as the builders of Solomon's temple discarded the chief cornerstone so many centuries ago. Follow Him joyfully in full assurance of faith—and learn for yourself the truth of these stunning words:

Behold, I lay in Zion a chief cornerstone, elect, precious, and he who believes on Him will by no means be put to shame (1 Peter 2:6).

---

[5] *Come and Welcome to Jesus Christ* by John Bunyan, 1894. (Excerpt paraphrased.)